BACK IN THE
BIG TIME

BACK IN THE BIG TIME

Sheffield Wednesday's Return To Division One 1984–1986

John Dyson

Foreword by Alan Smith

pitch

First published by Pitch Publishing, 2022

Pitch Publishing
9 Donnington Park,
85 Birdham Road,
Chichester,
West Sussex,
PO20 7AJ
www.pitchpublishing.co.uk
info@pitchpublishing.co.uk

A CIP catalogue record is available for this book from the British Library.

ISBN 978-1-80150 170 5

Typesetting and origination by Pitch Publishing

Printed and bound in Great Britain by TJ Books, Padstow

Contents

Foreword by Alan Smith	9
Introduction	13
The Cast	18
1. Context	19
2. 1984: August to December	23
3. An Interview with Mike Lyons	44
4. The Players	49
5. An Interview with John Pearson	77
6. 1985: January to May	83
7. An Interview with Lawrie Madden	97
8. The Reserves and Youth Team	101
9. An Interview with Mark Smith	117
10. Cup Runs	122
11. An Interview with Andy Blair	152
12. 1985: August to December	158
13. An Interview with Peter Shirtliff	179
14. The Boardroom and Finances	183
15. An Interview with Gary Shelton	194
16. 1986: January to May	199
17. An Interview with Tony Gregory	213
18. Behind the Scenes	220
19. An Interview with Ian Knight	240
20. Management and Tactics	247
21. An Interview with Garry Thompson	262
22. The Fans' Perspective	268
23. Snippets	291
24. Conclusions	293
Acknowledgements	296
Bibliography	298
Appendix One: Player Statistics	301
Appendix Two: League Tables	303

For Shelana, Joe and Sam.

Thanks for everything.

Foreword by Alan Smith

I LAUGH sometimes when I tell people that I was Howard Wilkinson's first signing at Hillsborough! I was delighted when he asked me to join him and the Owls in the summer of 1983. I knew him well from our time together working with the England semi-professional team. I understood that it was a fantastic opportunity to work with him in Sheffield.

And what great times we had! You'll read in this book of a period when the whole club was together. There were superb professional relationships between the management, the players and the staff. And it came together on the field, from promotion in our first season to winning at Anfield, Old Trafford and elsewhere when back in Division One.

These were wonderful times for me and, more importantly, the club and its supporters.

Howard Wilkinson was the ultimate professional. He was methodical, thorough, dedicated to being the best that he could be and to improving the club at every level. We got on very well, both career-wise and personally. I knew that on joining the Owls I'd be able to pursue a role as physiotherapist for the club. Many clubs historically had what I called 'the men in white coats' in the background, club doctors effectively, and a trainer or similar working with the players on a day-to-day basis.

In my mind, a physiotherapist combined the two roles and that was something that motivated and interested me. I wasn't the first person to hold such a role in professional football, but I believe I was the first to do so at Hillsborough. Working with Howard and absorbing his ideas around training, diet, fitness and much else meant that these were exciting times. I worked directly with the players on all those areas and much more.

You'll hear tales in the book of all the running we did. I loved it. It also helped ensure that the players reached and stayed in peak physical condition. Times were a little different back then. Modern players have their own training programmes over the summer and for the most part arrive back fit and in decent shape. In the 1980s, pre-season training was needed in some cases to get players back into condition. The running helped with that. Howard, Peter Eustace and I led from the front, so there could be no complaints. To be fair, though, we did sometimes have a breather after 45 minutes! The players continued and their fitness improved with it. The number of goals we scored late in games is unmistakable evidence of that.

Of course, we also had to trust the players. We'd give them advice on diet, for example, but they didn't come into the club for breakfast as they might nowadays. We expected that they would make sensible choices. We were fortunate that the squad of players we had were so professional. They were good at following the advice and were all in together for the benefit of the club.

The club also had a good record with injuries and recovery from any that were suffered. In the 1980s clubs had smaller squads than today, and only 12 were named on a matchday. One substitute! I was reminded by reading the book that Howard only used 20 players in 1984/85 and 22 the following season. In that first season, 11 players appeared more than 40 times, three more than 50. Remarkable statistics.

No player ever wants to be injured. Those I worked with in that period were professional and dedicated to getting fit and back on the pitch. One of the roles of the physiotherapist is working out the best way of achieving that. Some players benefited more from the proverbial arm round the shoulder, others wanted to get on with whatever needed to be done. The players overall deserve major credit for their fitness record.

I'll mention one – Nigel Worthington. His efforts in recovering from a cartilage injury and subsequent operation suffered on the first day of pre-season training to return for the first game of the 1985/86 season were outstanding. It was also symbolic of how the squad were dedicated to the cause of Sheffield Wednesday.

I felt it important that supporters and others gained knowledge of what went on behind the scenes. *The Owl* magazine would publish an update of those who were injured, along with how their rehabilitation was progressing. I don't think that today's managers would like that so much, preferring to keep players' fitness levels behind closed doors. I hoped to educate those who were interested in what goes on in the physio's room. I even authored my own book in the 1980s (*Soccer Injuries: Prevention and First Aid*) with the aim of helping those in the game, from the grassroots upwards, prevent and treat injuries.

It was a busy time for me. Alongside my role at Hillsborough, I continued working with the England set-up. By the years covered in this book I had not yet graduated to the full England team, but I did work with the younger age groups including the under-21s. The longer periods away coincided with the close season as the under-21s took part in summer tournaments. I am grateful for the support of the club and Professor Frank O'Gorman, who kept things running smoothly at Hillsborough when I was away.

I'd also like to pay credit to the chairman, Mr McGee, and the board of directors at the time. They were special people who always held the cause of Sheffield Wednesday close to their hearts. They helped create a wonderful family atmosphere at the club. Everyone felt valued. I was so pleased to read in the book the memories of others who worked behind the scenes. It made clear to me that Hillsborough was a great place to work.

I've been asked if I remember individual games from my career. The answer is yes, but not always for the same reasons as supporters or players. Unfortunately, as physio, I recall times where I was called into action or where players suffered an injury. That's not to say there weren't memorable games in this period. I remember the FA Cup semi-final at Villa Park and the 4-4 draw in the League Cup against Chelsea for example.

There's a picture of the squad sat in a circle approaching extra time in the Chelsea game. Stood around offering guidance and support are Howard, Peter Eustace, Mick Hennigan and myself. It illustrates to me the closeness of the management team and how we all chipped in to help the players and the squad.

You'll read in the book of great successes of the team. We travelled to Anfield early in the 1984/85 season and defeated the European champions! Add in cup runs, huge attendances home and away and my professional success, I hope you'll agree that these were fantastic times for me and for the club.

I'll add finally that my son Paul, who Owls supporters will remember stepping into my shoes at Hillsborough, also remembers these times with great fondness. He reminds me that his first game as a fan was a 2-0 win vs Carlisle in the 1983/84 promotion season, and that as a promising youngster he trained with Mick Lyons and Clive Baker. Great memories for the Smith family!

I am delighted, therefore, to write these opening words. For readers who remember these times, I hope the book brings back great memories. For those who were too young, I hope it gives a flavour of what was a fantastic period to be involved with the club.

Enjoy the book, and up the Owls!

Alan Smith, May 2022

Introduction

SATURDAY, 5 April 1986 was an exciting day in Liverpool. Thousands of people made their way to one of the biggest sporting occasions of the year. Some celebrities, including Anne Diamond, Russell Grant and Brookside actor Simon O'Brien, even jetted in on Concorde before taking their place among the crowd. Thieves took advantage of the carnival atmosphere, raiding the hotel that was hosting the chief sponsor, Seagram, and stealing £300,000 worth of jewellery belonging to the chief executive's wife. The crowd was the biggest in recent years and anticipation was high.

We are, of course, discussing the Grand National horse race, won by West Tip, the 15/2 second favourite, and ridden by Richard Dunwoody. The crowd at the Aintree Racecourse, just north of Liverpool, was 75,637, with millions more watching live on BBC's *Grandstand.*

For Liverpool's football fans, though, the excitement was elsewhere. It was also FA Cup semi-final day. Liverpool were playing Southampton at White Hart Lane in London. Everton, meanwhile, were to face Sheffield Wednesday at Villa Park in Birmingham.

As the bookies counted their winnings – and one punter licked his wounds, having placed £50,000 on the favourite Mr Snugfit – the football fans of Liverpool also celebrated. The game at White Hart Lane was goalless before two extra-time strikes by goal machine Ian Rush brought victory for the Reds.

At Villa Park the other semi-final also went to extra time. After a goalless first half, the game sprung to life in four second-half minutes. Everton took the lead just after half-time with a lob by future Owl Alan Harper. Carl Shutt soon headed the equaliser. Despite the best efforts of both sides, that was the end of the scoring in the regulation 90 minutes. Eight minutes into the first half of extra time, Owls hearts were broken by Graeme Sharp's winner. Everton held on and the city of Liverpool could look forward to a cup final between its two biggest teams.

Like Liverpool, the city of Sheffield had been struggling economically in the years leading up to the semi-final. The city suffered significant job losses during the late 1970s and the 1980s in traditional industries such as clothing, metal engineering and coal. Steel remained the dominant industry of the city until the late 1970s, when world steel demand collapsed, resulting in a series of plant closures in the city.

The collapse of the Sheffield steel industry and the restructuring that followed led to massive redundancies, and unemployment reached record levels in the 1980s. Prior to 1979, the city of Sheffield had been used to having an unemployment level below the national average, but within eight years of the Thatcher government coming to power, the official rate of unemployment reached 16.2 per cent. The city was also reeling from the after-effects of the 1984/85 miners' strike.

Economic and social issues were not limited to Sheffield; they directly affected the national game. Around the country, football was struggling to keep attendances up in a time of high unemployment. Everton won the FA Cup in 1984, but the average attendance at Goodison Park that season was below 20,000. Gates at Liverpool, Arsenal and Aston Villa had dropped between 20 and 38 per cent from their 1970s peaks.

Astonishingly, despite the team finishing third in the league and reaching the semi-finals of the UEFA Cup, Nottingham Forest's attendances in 1984 were down 45 per cent on their earlier highs. Overall attendances at Football League matches reached a post-war low of 16.5 million in 1985/86.

Football also had an image problem. Hooliganism had existed for decades, but the mid-1980s marked a high – or rather low – point. The blackest year for the game was 1985. In March, there was extended rioting at an FA Cup game between Luton Town and Millwall at Kenilworth Road – 81 people were injured. On 11 May, at Birmingham City's St Andrew's stadium, a 14-year-old boy died after a wall collapsed following pitched battles between Leeds United and Birmingham followers. On 29 May, another collapsed wall at Heysel stadium in Brussels after disturbances between Liverpool and Juventus followers led to the deaths of 39 people – 32 of whom were Italian, including two children.

Earlier in May, on the same day as the death at St Andrew's, another tragedy took place, but this time it was not as a result of hooliganism. At Bradford City's Valley Parade stadium, 56 people were killed and 265 injured when the main stand caught fire during a match against Lincoln City. The old wooden structure became an inferno within minutes of a small fire starting beneath the seats, probably as a result of a discarded cigarette. The fire was fuelled by a build-up of litter under the ageing structure.

The government acted after the fire and the later inquiry by banning new wooden grandstands, closing other stands that were deemed unsafe and banning smoking in wooden stands. Meanwhile, the prime minister Margaret Thatcher called for stiff prison sentences for football hooligans, and the sports minister Colin Moynihan began to make plans for an identity card scheme for football fans.

Following the Heysel disaster, English club sides were banned indefinitely from European competition. The ban stayed in effect for five seasons (six for Liverpool) – directly affecting Sheffield Wednesday the following year. The *Sunday Times* summed up football as a 'slum sport played in slum stadiums increasingly watched by slum people'. An image problem indeed.

The football fans of Sheffield looked to their teams to supply some escapism from these economic and social difficulties. Although Wednesday were not immune to problems of hooliganism, the previous manager Jack Charlton worked hard at improving the behaviour and reputation of Owls followers around the country. In his 1996 autobiography, Charlton states: 'I think I am right in saying to this day, Sheffield Wednesday supporters enjoy the reputation of being some of the best behaved in Britain.'

This positivity was reflected in attendances at Hillsborough. Rather than falling dramatically, the average attendance grew from a low of 10,643 in 1978/79 to 27,780 in 1984/85. The blue-and-white side of the city at least had good reason to be positive about their team. Around the time of the Owls' promotion back to Division One in 1984, Charlton told local reporters, 'The people of Sheffield are in for a treat.'

The club had been promoted under the management of Howard Wilkinson, who took on the role in time for the 1983/84 season. Many of the team that won promotion remained in place in the seasons following as Wilkinson launched his assault on the top league. Wilkinson was clear about his aims for Wednesday, telling the club's official monthly publication *The Owl* in October 1985: 'It is my ambition to make Sheffield Wednesday one of the most successful clubs in Europe.'

The tactics adopted by Wilkinson and the team became somewhat notorious. One London newspaper described the Owls' style of play as 'bruising, Northern, long-ball, kick and rush'. How that was different to a southern or Midland version of the same was not made clear. Whatever the style, it was successful. The team finished in eighth position in 1984/85, having spent much of the season in the top six. By the time of the FA Cup semi-final defeat against Everton in 1986, the Owls had dropped to ninth place, despite spending extended periods earlier in the campaign in the top six again.

Maybe the semi-final defeat marked the end of something. Maybe. As Liverpool partied, Owls supporters made their way back from Birmingham dejected by defeat. Fights broke out in the pubs of Derby as fans stopped off for a drink to ease the pain of the loss.

The image of Owls' full-back Mel Sterland flattened in the penalty area as Graeme Sharp wheeled away celebrating the winning goal featured heavily in the evening newspapers. Sterland and other members of the Wednesday team left the field in tears after the final whistle. Defeat in a game which the Owls dominated for lengthy periods was a hard one to take for players and fans alike.

Wednesday still had seven league games to play. A dejected team, with nothing to play for, it might have been argued. Wilkinson's Owls proved to be nothing of the sort. They won five of those games and drew the other two to end the season in fifth place. It was the club's highest league placing since 1960/61. The city of Liverpool may have celebrated long into the night on Grand National day, but Owls fans needed to wait a little longer before hailing their team's success that season. The campaign 'firmly established the Owls in the top echelons of the English game', as Brodie and Dickinson's *Complete Record* puts it. There was plenty for Owls supporters to celebrate after the season's final whistle.

I was born in 1975, attending my first matches at Hillsborough during the promotion season of 1983/84. The Owls teams that took on Division One under Wilkinson are those of my formative years as a supporter. This book is my attempt to tell the story of those years. It will consider the matches and the team, along with the perspectives of fans and others involved with the club. The book provides new insights, new interviews, long-hidden photographs and a look at the memorabilia and other ephemera that survives to this day.

It considers the views of the press about the tactics employed by Wilkinson's team – *The Guardian*, for example, which said: 'Sheffield Wednesday, who bear the same relation to the beautiful game as Rambo to the Sisters of Mercy.' It also considers how far Owls historian Daniel Gordon is correct to argue that 'Wilkinson's success was largely built around two types of player: those of lesser talent who took the eye with non-stop commitment; and the "rescued" player, who had been discarded by his club or who had shown promise earlier in his career only to have then faded.'

A team playing ugly football, populated by committed discards? We will see. This book is the story of how Sheffield Wednesday returned to the highest level for the first time in 14 years and took on the elite. This is a team that did not give up. This is the Owls: *Back in the Big Time.*

The Cast

The Club: Sheffield Wednesday. Founded in 1867. Relegated from Division One in 1970. Promoted back to the top flight in 1984.

The Chairman: H.E. (Bert) McGee (1975–90)

Directors: M. Sheppard, S.L. Speight (OBE), C. Woodward, K.T. Addy, E. Barron, G.K. Hulley

Club Secretary: Dick Chester

The Manager: Howard Wilkinson (1983–88)

Management and Coaching Staff: Peter Eustace (Assistant Manager), Alan Smith (Physiotherapist), Michael Hennigan (Youth and Reserve Team Coach), Clive Baker (Scout)

Other Club Staff: Steve Ellis (Photographer), Bob Gorrill (Marketing Manager), David Barber (Groundsman), 'Stevie Splash' (Club DJ), Dennis Woodhead (Commercial Manager), Steve Woodhead (Commercial Assistant)

Players: Twenty-eight played for the first team during our period.

The Fans: Huge numbers at some home and away games. Sheffield Wednesday's support increased during a period in which attendance nationally was falling.

1.

Context

SHEFFIELD WEDNESDAY were relegated from the top flight of English football in 1970. The 14 years that passed before their return to Division One were often difficult ones for the team and its supporters. In the early 1970s, the team produced a series of mid-table finishes under the management of Derek Dooley before a collapse in form at least partly related to a mystery virus led to his sacking on Christmas Eve 1973.

Dooley's successor, Steve Burtenshaw, helped keep the team up that season, but led them to an ignominious relegation the following year. Burtenshaw was in turn replaced by Len Ashurst, who helped avoid a disastrous relegation to the fourth tier in 1976, the team winning the final game of the season against Southend to stay afloat, before achieving an eighth-place finish in Division Three in 1977.

When Ashurst was sacked after a poor start to the following season, Owls stalwart Ken Knighton was placed in temporary charge.

After one game with Knighton as caretaker, Jack Charlton was offered and accepted the job. Charlton was a legendary figure in the game – a World Cup winner with England in 1966 – and had recently left his first managerial position at Middlesbrough. He had led the Teessiders to promotion from Division Two as champions in his first season, 1973/74. Boro were presented with the trophy in advance of their final home game, ironically an 8-0 victory over the Owls.

Charlton was also presented with the manager of the season award, the first time it had been given to somebody outside the top division. Charlton remained in charge of Middlesbrough for three more seasons, achieving a series of respectable finishes in Division One, before leaving the club at the end of 1976/77, arguing that four years was the optimum time to spend in any position.

He then applied for the vacant England manager's job when Don Revie quit the role to work in the Middle East. After not even receiving a reply, Charlton swore never to apply for a job again, and instead would wait to be approached. England's loss was Wednesday's gain. In his autobiography, Charlton relates how he was approached for the post at S6. He chose to watch the team in action ('they were bloody awful'), but before the day was out he had taken the position. 'Perhaps it was the realisation that we could move only one way that attracted me,' he said. Legend has it that sitting among Owls fans that day, seeing and hearing their devotion to the club, ensured Charlton could not turn the job down!

Charlton's appointment was a major turning point in the Owls' move back towards the big time. It was not an immediate success, though, as Charlton battled to find a route to success in Division Three. 'The only gambit that I thought might work,' he said, 'was to throw the ball into the box and take it from there.' The Owls finished safely in 14th in his first season but were humiliated by non-league Wigan Athletic in the FA Cup. To add insult to injury, the club's coach got stuck in the mud trying to leave the ground after the game.

There was another lower mid-table finish the following season, 1978/79, a campaign that was famous for the epic FIVE games that the club played against Arsenal in the FA Cup third round. A series of replays eventually ended with defeat for the Owls at the neutral venue of Filbert Street, Leicester. In January of that season, Charlton made the audacious signing of Terry Curran, persuading him to drop two divisions to sign from Southampton.

Curran's signing provided the momentum that the team needed. The following season he scored 22 league goals in 41 appearances as the Owls finished third in Division Three, finally gaining promotion back to the second tier. One of Curran's goals was in the Boxing Day Massacre of city rivals United, the Owls' 4-0 victory helping provide the push needed for an excellent second half of the season.

Charlton then led the team to a series of top-half finishes in Division Two. The Owls' first overseas signing, Ante Miročević, joined the club in time for the 1980/81 season. A number of players also came through the youth system to become regulars in the first-time squad, including Mark Smith, Mel Sterland, Peter Shirtliff and Kevin Taylor. In 1981/82 the team finished fourth in the table, one point and one place away from promotion. This was the season in which a system of three points for a win was introduced. Ironically, under the previous method of two points for a win, the Owls would have been promoted.

The next season, 1982/83, was Charlton's last as Owls manager. The team finished sixth in the league and reached the FA Cup semi-final. A rare Miročević goal was not enough to prevent a 2-1 defeat to Brighton & Hove Albion. The team had topped the table earlier in the season but ended the campaign with, as Charlton put it, 'nothing to show … except a series of hard-luck stories'.

Despite the board's best efforts to persuade him to stay, Charlton chose to leave that summer. Nearly six seasons was somewhat longer than the optimum of four that he had suggested when he left Middlesbrough. The Owls had returned from the brink, with renewed confidence and vigour. They had not yet, though, returned to the top table.

The man who was responsible for overseeing promotion back to the top flight was Howard Wilkinson. With the assistance of former Owls player Peter Eustace, he saw the team to a 15-match unbeaten start to the 1983/84 campaign. With goals coming from all round the team – eight players netted five or more times – the team lost only six league games all season. Twenty-six victories and 88 points were enough to see the club promoted in second place, losing out on the championship to Chelsea only on goal difference.

The team lost a League Cup replay to Liverpool at Anfield in January 1984, when the Owls fans sang, 'We'll be back.' Come the following season, the Owls were back. Wilkinson had completed a 14-year rebuilding process. The Owls had dropped to their lowest ebb in the mid-1970s. By 1984, the club was back in the big league.

2.

1984: August to December

AUGUST 1984 saw the Owls begin their first top-flight season since 1969/70. Howard Wilkinson had not come to make up the numbers, though. When the club was promoted in the spring, he said, 'We have a ticket to the ball. Now we have to go out and show we can dance.'

Wilkinson immediately began to revamp his squad in readiness for the team's attempt to tango with the big boys. Lee Chapman, Andy Blair and Brian Marwood all arrived during the close season. Tony Cunningham, Gary Bannister and Gary Megson, stars of the promotion campaign, all departed. Cunningham was seemingly the most frustrated of the three as, despite gaining a pay rise in moving to Manchester City, he missed out on the prize of Division One football. The Football League fixture computer gave the Owls a home game to start the season. Nottingham Forest were the visitors in what proved to be a classic tie.

Key Game: Sheffield Wednesday 3-1 Nottingham Forest, 25 August 1984

The fixture fell, with a hint of darkly ironic timing, at the peak of the 1984/85 miners' strike. The National Union of Mineworkers (NUM), led by Arthur Scargill, had called a national strike in March 1984 in protest at planned pit closures. The vast majority of those in South Yorkshire were still out. A ballot was held in Nottinghamshire, and miners voted to continue working.

According to the National Coal Mining Museum, only a quarter of the county's miners joined the national strike. In July 1984 the Nottinghamshire miners split from the NUM and formed the Union of Democratic Mineworkers (UDM). Their members continued to work – breaking the national strike. There was a certain degree of antagonism between Nottingham and Sheffield, which played out in the crowd at Hillsborough that day.

The relentless chanting of 'scabs, scabs, scabs' from some Owls followers started well before kick-off and continued for much of the game. In return Forest's end was heard chanting 'we're getting paid' and, 'Arthur Scargill – what a w*****'. Some of this can be heard on the TV footage of the game. As Richard Crooks put it in *What Was Football Like in the 1980s?*, the atmosphere was 'venomous'.

The nine-year-old me knew none of this. Sat in the South Stand with my dad and brother, I remember a tremendous atmosphere and noise, but not the antagonism. It may well be that my dad put his hands over my ears at opportune moments, of course! There is a possibility of selective memory as well. The miners' strike was and still is a hugely divisive issue. It may be convenient to ascribe political motives to the supporters on the day, many of whom no doubt wanted to watch a game of football and cheer their team to victory. Derren Francis, who was a ball boy in front of the Nottingham Forest fans, told me that he remembered a tremendous atmosphere but 'no animosity, no politics'.

Wilkinson named the following team:

1. Martin Hodge
2. Mel Sterland
3. Peter Shirtliff
4. Mark Smith
5. Mike Lyons
6. Nigel Worthington
7. Brian Marwood
8. Andy Blair
9. Imre Varadi
10. Lee Chapman

11. Gary Shelton
Sub) John Pearson

The team had room for all three of Wilkinson's summer signings. Sterland was passed fit and so teenager Lee Coombes' chance of a debut passed by. Brian Clough had no place for Wednesday old boy Megson in his team. Hillsborough did see the first glance of Clough's £300,000 summer signing from Real Madrid – Dutch international Johnny Metgod. A ghost from Wednesday past also featured: Ian Bowyer, whose two goals for Manchester City sent Wednesday down from Division One in 1970.

The game itself was a great spectacle. The Owls pegged Forest back for the entirety of the initial stages. After 20 minutes, Marwood was fouled by Steve Sutton in the box. Up charged Sterland, with his trademark long run-up, to take the penalty. He scored, but the referee spotted Gary Shelton encroaching and ordered a retake. After what felt like an age, and some gamesmanship from Forest's players to delay the retake, Sterland ran in from distance again. And scored. Again.

Forest equalised on 36 minutes. Trevor Christie turned Peter Shirtliff brilliantly and fed Peter Davenport, who shot past the outrushing Martin Hodge. The Owls keeper later took responsibility for the goal. It was 1-1 at half-time and the crowd applauded the Owls team from the pitch.

Imre Varadi's 58th-minute goal was a classic that still features among my favourites of all time. It also rightly featured as one of the greatest Owls goals in a 2020 survey in *The Athletic* online magazine. The *Sheffield Telegraph*'s report described the strike as follows: 'Taking Shirtliff's headed clearance from a Forest corner, Varadi set off on a head-long 70-yard dash and finished off with an unstoppable 20-yard shot.'

Shirtliff was careful to tell me that he still claims the assist. 'I headed the ball away from a corner and Ray ran 70 yards to score, but I'm having the assist!' he said, laughing at the thought, in 2021. Shirtliff has fond memories of the fixture. 'It was a tremendous atmosphere,' he commented. 'There was some animosity between the fans of both teams as it was the time of the miners' strike and the Nottinghamshire miners had gone back to work. The result was the right one and it was a great performance and a great day.' Varadi was also happy with his goal. 'I have scored some good goals,' he said after the game, 'but that has to rank as one of the best.'

John Pearson took up the story of the third and clinching goal with me in early 2021. 'It was a Brian Marwood cross,' he told me. 'It dipped just under the keeper's left arm, I was sure he was going to stop it. The ball flew at me and hit me right on the knee. I was sure it was going over the bar. Missing from a few yards out – in front of the Kop! Luckily, though, it flew into the top of the net. A fluke really! On reflection, I wish I'd run towards Howard Wilkinson as he'd dropped me in favour of Lee Chapman, but I just stood there – I wasn't sure what to do!'

That goal came on 82 minutes after perhaps the only black mark of the Owls' day. Pearson had replaced skipper Mike Lyons, who went off suffering with an achilles problem.

The local and national press made little mention of the antagonistic atmosphere. Clough accepted defeat with the terse but fair comment: 'They murdered us; they deserved the lot.' The headlines in the local press focused on Varadi. 'Quicksilver Varadi' was the *Sheffield Telegraph*'s option, while the *Green 'Un* went with 'Varadi Cracker' and the *Sheffield Star* with 'Great Varadi Goal'.

In what was perhaps an oblique reference to the rivalry between South Yorkshire and Nottinghamshire that was on display that day, Marwood commented afterwards: 'The crowd were brilliant. I have never known anything like it in my life!'

The £5 letter in the following week's *Green 'Un* from D.M. of Sheffield took issue with the chanting of 'a minority of Wednesdayites' as it was 'abusive and totally out of place at a football match'. That feeling was not shared by Owls fan Paul Taylor, who is quoted by *The Athletic* as saying 'Ultimately it was a hollow victory in terms of the outcome of the [miners'] strike, but at the time it felt like a massive vindication.'

In many ways, the game was a vindication. For Varadi, who returned to Division One after three seasons away. For Pearson, who scored after initially being dropped to the bench. For Wilkinson, who had promised to stick to Wednesday's breathless, high-energy style – only better. In a neat way, the presence of Bowyer in the Forest team also exorcised the ghost of the Owls' 1970 relegation.

'I paid good money to watch what turned out to be an excellent football match, not listen to political chants,' wrote D.M in *The Green 'Un*. Sport and politics do mix, though, and this was a particularly political time in South Yorkshire and Nottinghamshire. In August 1984, D.M.'s views were certainly not shared by everyone. Many Owls fans had good reason to feel vindicated.

Politics or not, it's a game that is commonly recalled by fans from the time. Owls supporter Thomas Hartley told me that it was his first-ever game, and one that he was 'blessed to have experienced'. For the atmosphere, the politics, the goals, the result and the return to the big league, I agree with Thomas!

* * *

The victory over Forest got the Owls' season off to a good start ahead of two tricky-looking away fixtures at Newcastle United and Stoke City. The games proved as difficult for Wednesday as they looked on paper, with the Owls finishing on the wrong end of a 2-1 scoreline in each. Chapman scored his first goal in an Owls shirt at Newcastle, with Nigel Worthington notching at Stoke.

Both of Stoke's goals were set up by wing play from future Owl Mark Chamberlain. Despite Paul Dyson's sending off for seemingly headbutting Chapman, the Owls were unable to gain anything from the game. Wilkinson described the start to the season as 'a little bit like a Chinese takeaway – sweet and sour'!

Wednesday soon had chance to add a more positive flavour to the start of their season with a midweek home fixture against Southampton. The Owls had faced the Saints in the FA Cup in the previous campaign – losing a replay 5-1 after drawing 0-0 at Hillsborough. Wilkinson was looking forward to 'another memorable occasion … with a better result'.

The result was a positive one for Wednesday. Goals by Varadi and Shelton either side of a Joe Jordan equaliser saw the team to a 2-1 win. The Owls dominated the game, with the *Daily Mirror* saying: 'The Saints were strictly second best.' True as that was, the victory was hard-earned in the end – Peter Shilton saved a Sterland penalty and the winning goal came in the final minutes of the game.

The win took the Owls to eighth place in the early-season table ahead of another home game against Tottenham Hotspur. This was another difficult-looking game against a team that would finish the season third in Division One. The Owls had not played against Spurs in the league since two 1-0 defeats in 1969/70 and not at all since a 4-1 FA Cup defeat in 1971.

The Tottenham team of 1984 were managed by future Owls boss Peter Shreeves and featured a host of internationals. The Wednesday squad were celebrating two international call-ups of their own in advance of the game, with Worthington joining the Northern Ireland squad and Sterland gaining his inclusion in the Three Lions squad to face East Germany.

The Owls team started the match at full speed. Varadi, Marwood and Shelton had all missed serviceable chances before Chapman flicked on a free kick for Varadi to slip past Ray Clemence in the 16th minute. Spurs surprisingly levelled after 24 minutes, Mark Falco knocking the ball past Hodge despite Shirtliff's last-ditch lunge.

The winner came before half-time as Blair's corner was knocked on by Varadi to Marwood, who notched his first goal for the club at the far post. The Owls continued to dominate the game, but the scoring was finished. As the *Sunday Express* put it, 'Spurs won't need me to tell me how lucky they were to escape a real thrashing.' Wilkinson was a little less impressed. 'Our naivety frightens me a bit,' he said. 'We think we have to play at 100 miles an hour.' Wednesday had certainly made a rapid start to the campaign, resting in fourth place after five games.

The Owls had a week's break before an awkward trip to The Hawthorns to face West Bromwich Albion. It did turn out to be a tricky game for Wednesday, who went a goal down when future Owl Garry Thompson planted the ball in the bottom corner after only five minutes. Despite much Wednesday pressure, and both Marwood and Chapman hitting the woodwork, the score remained at 1-0 until the 56th minute. Unfortunately for the Owls the second goal was again scored by Thompson, who doubled the Baggies' lead with a well-placed shot.

Three minutes later the Owls were back in the game through Varadi's shot after a quick one-two. The Owls then laid siege to West Brom's goal, urged on by a large and loud away support. Reward finally came in the 84th minute when Varadi's cross was headed home by Shelton. As the *Sunday People* put it, Wednesday 'ran Albion silly to pull back from two down'. Wilkinson was pleased enough with the performance, saying that the players were 'acquiring a veneer of quality'.

The following Saturday saw the Owls return to Hillsborough to face Ipswich Town. Another tough game ensued. The Wednesday team were put under pressure early on with Lyons clearing a Romeo Zondervan effort off the line. Russell Osman later hit the bar for the Suffolk side, and it was no surprise when they took the lead four minutes before half-time.

From a short free kick, Eric Gates blasted the ball past a surprised and maybe unsighted Hodge. Much of the remaining excitement in the game came in the last 15 minutes. Marwood equalised for the Owls, squeezing in a header off the post and keeper's body from Varadi's cross in the 75th minute.

Chapman almost immediately put Wednesday in front, lobbing the keeper after the Ipswich defence failed to deal with a long through ball. Ipswich then countered, with Varadi clearing off his own line before Gates scored his second – and the equaliser – from Zondervan's cross on 81 minutes.

Mark Brennan and Gates missed further chances, but the Owls hung on for the point. 'It was a disappointing performance,' suggested Wilkinson after the game, 'but we got something from the game because we kept going.' The point that Wednesday picked up from the fixture kept them in fifth place in the table ahead of the most formidable fixture of all: a trip to Anfield to face the European champions Liverpool.

Key Game: Liverpool 0-2 Sheffield Wednesday, 29 September 1984

The Owls had lost a Milk Cup fifth-round replay at Anfield in January 1984. Wednesday fans ended that game singing loudly and en masse that, 'we'll be back'. Many thousands of Wednesday supporters did make their return to Anfield for this game. Estimates of the Owls' support vary from 5,000–8,000, maybe even more.

Those fans were captured by ITV's cameras and made up part of a large crowd of 40,196. As well as being the kings of Europe, Liverpool were the current English champions and Milk Cup holders. They were also rated as favourites by the bookies, with William Hill offering 9/2 against an Owls victory.

Wilkinson was forced into some changes to his line-up for the game. Worthington had left the field with a groin injury in a midweek Milk Cup victory over Huddersfield Town and was unavailable. Wilkinson had also been active in the transfer market that week. Pat Heard joined Jack Charlton's Newcastle United in a swap deal for the 22-year-old John Ryan. 'I see him as a very sound addition to our first-team squad,' said Wilkinson.

Ryan was immediately named in the team for the Anfield clash, somewhat to the frustration of the young defender Dylan Kerr, who told me recently that he'd hoped to make his debut that day. Shelton was available again after a minor hamstring injury and Lawrie Madden was on the bench for his first appearance in the matchday squad since the defeat to Tottenham at the beginning of the month.

Wilkinson named the following team:

1. Martin Hodge
2. Mel Sterland
3. Peter Shirtliff
4. Mark Smith
5. Mike Lyons

6. John Ryan
7. Brian Marwood
8. Andy Blair
9. Imre Varadi
10. Lee Chapman
11. Gary Shelton

Sub) Lawrie Madden

Wednesday won the toss before kick-off and opted to change ends. The massed Owls support gave immediate noisy backing to the team, attempting to drown out the chants of 'Everton reject' aimed at Hodge. The Liverpool Kop did roundly applaud Hodge, though, when he assumed his position in front of their fans. The good-humoured banter between both sets of fans continued as the Owls fans called for Bob Bolder, Liverpool reserve keeper and ex-Owl, to replace Bruce Grobbelaar. The Liverpool keeper in turn applauded the Wednesday supporters.

Liverpool fans may have wished that Bolder was in the team when, in the eighth minute, Grobbelaar raced out towards a ball that reached him at the edge of the area. It came from a long clearance by Shirtliff, and Grobbelaar had plenty of space to control or clear it. The keeper opted to hit the ball first time. It struck Varadi and bounced to his right. With lots to do, and still well over 30 yards out, Varadi was able to slot the ball home. 'Sing your heart out for the lads' was the ecstatic response of the Wednesday followers.

Liverpool had named a strong team, with Kenny Dalglish and Mark Lawrenson both returning from injury. Ian Rush, the previous season's top scorer, was missing though. It was no surprise, therefore, when Liverpool stormed back later in the half. Paul Walsh saw a header rebound off the post and Dalglish fired a shot wide. Alan Kennedy did have the ball in the net, but the whistle had already gone for offside. The Owls defence was resilient, however, and the away supporters could be happy with a solid first-half display.

The second half began with the Owls on the offensive. Blair soon played in Varadi, who shot just wide from distance. Blair's corner a couple of minutes later just flashed by Sterland when he was well placed in the box. Liverpool soon began to pressurise the Owls again. Wednesday survived a strong penalty appeal when Walsh went down under a heavy Lyons challenge in the box. The Owls were fortunate again when a John Wark effort rebounded off the post.

In the 68th minute, Wednesday doubled their lead. Marwood slipped the ball to Sterland, who strode into the box before firing in a powerful low shot. Grobbelaar blocked it but Shelton followed up and tapped in the rebound.

'I was at the right place at the right time,' Shelton told me in 2021. 'The goal was at the Kop end, but I can still remember the noise of the Owls fans down the other end. They were singing about how pleased they were to be back after we'd lost a cup tie there the previous season.'

Wednesday saw out the rest of the game with relative ease. Chapman even came close to a third with a header that was touched over by Grobbelaar. The Owls' support was revelling in the play and upcoming result by this stage. 'What's it like to be outclassed?' and, 'We said we'd be back – we are, we are,' were both chanted relentlessly and at high volume in the final few minutes and after the final whistle. The Liverpool Kop kept the positivity by staying behind to applaud the Owls team from the pitch.

The convivial atmosphere in the ground was not entirely maintained at the end of the game. One Owls supporter was slashed with a razor-type knife as he left a toilet at Anfield. In the following week's *Sheffield Star*, he described being surrounded by a group of around 50 Liverpool followers. The *Liverpool Echo* described a 'tattooed maniac' who stabbed two Owls fans after the game, leaving one needing 60 stitches and the other lucky to survive after the knife just missed his kidney.

Wilkinson later referred to these incidents as 'vile behaviour not representative of football supporters'. The *Star* ran the headline 'Punish The Savages', giving Wilkinson's view in more blunt terms. Perhaps more representative of Liverpool supporters was the lady who rang Wilkinson the following week to praise the

Owls fans, several of whom shared their hot drinks with her before and after the game.

The result was the Owls' first away win and clean sheet of the league season. Ex-Evertonian Lyons took particular pleasure as it was his first victory at Anfield in 12 attempts. Lyons also praised the Owls' huge following, saying, 'That was the best part of the match for me.' Immediately after the game, Wilkinson kept his feet on the ground. 'I am delighted with the result,' he said, 'but fortune favoured us a bit.'

By the time of his next programme notes he was more effusive, saying, 'Our victory at Anfield was perhaps the best result since I arrived at Sheffield Wednesday last season.' He revealed in those notes that the team had been awarded the Fiat performance of the week by a panel of managers including Bobby Robson, then England supremo.

The *Liverpool Echo*'s headline was 'Reds Gift Day for New Boys.' The *Green 'Un* went with 'Champion Owls' and the *Sheffield Telegraph* with the more circumspect 'Wednesday Pass the Anfield Test'. However reported, it is clear that the Owls did pass a test that day. The team were certainly 'back'!

* * *

After the drama of the Owls' visit to Anfield, the next league fixture was back on home soil against Sunderland, managed by ex-Wednesday boss Len Ashurst. This was not the team's next game, though, as in the interim a strong-looking Wednesday squad travelled to Sweden to mark the Swedish FA's 80th anniversary.

Lyons was not expecting a holiday. 'It's a nice fresh country,' he said, 'but we will be doing a lot of running wherever we are!' Tore Elofsson, chairman of Halmstads BK, commented in his programme notes, 'We are very happy to have got a winning ticket in meeting well-known Sheffield Wednesday in today's friendly game.' There was no victory for either team as the fixture finished 1-1, Chapman scoring the equaliser late in the game.

Only three days later did Chapman score again, his 13th-minute header from Blair's corner putting Wednesday ahead against Sunderland. Chapman also helped set up the second goal on 42 minutes, heading the ball on for Marwood to score at close range. That was as good as it got for the Owls, as two goals in seven minutes, both set up by ex-Owl Rodger Wylde, brought Sunderland level. Paul Atkinson and Clive Walker were the recipients of excellent passes from Wylde before the hour mark.

The last half hour saw Wednesday lay siege to Chris Turner's goal. The other ex-Owl in the Sunderland ranks performed heroics in keeping the ball out with some superb goalkeeping. 'It was like the Alamo at the Kop end,' commented a relieved Turner afterwards. The draw pulled Wednesday up to fourth place in the table, ahead of a trip to Kenilworth Road to face future Owls boss David Pleat's Luton Town team.

Shirtliff had been substituted due to injury at half-time in the Sunderland game. He missed the midweek cup game with Huddersfield that followed and was still out for the Luton fixture. His replacement in the usual three centre-back system that Wilkinson used was Gavin Oliver. The match was Oliver's Division One debut. It was not to be a happy one, as he was substituted with a calf injury after only three minutes to be replaced by Worthington.

The game saw a return to winning ways for the Owls. Chapman put them ahead in the 35th minute, crashing a powerful shot off the far post. Lyons increased the lead eight minutes after the break, turning in the box and belting a shot past Luton keeper Andy Dibble. Luton ensured a grandstand finish, though, when ten minutes from time Frankie Bunn buried a left-foot shot inside Hodge's near post.

Vince Hilaire still had time to see Hodge desperately claw his long-range effort around the post, but the Owls held on. 'The sharp and lively men of Sheffield swept across Luton like a hurricane,' reported the *Sunday Mirror.* Howard Wilkinson was less impressed. 'Make no mistake, we were worth our win,' he said, 'but we know we can do better.'

The win lifted Wednesday to third in the table, and remarkably was the seventh league game in a row in which the Owls had scored two goals. That run was to change dramatically in the next fixture, a home game against Leicester City. The build-up to the game saw Sterland and Worthington called up for their respective international squads, with Shelton also in action as captain of the England Under-21 team. That honour was described by Wilkinson as 'just reward for his perseverance, unselfishness and above all, playing ability'.

All three men made the starting XI for the Owls against the Foxes. The game was effectively over by half-time as the Owls raced into a two-goal lead. By full time, Wednesday had scored five goals without reply. The goals included a hat-trick for Varadi – his third scored after a brilliant solo run – and the only goal scored in an Owls shirt by recent signing Ryan. The win put the Owls second in the table ahead of a trip to Highfield Road to face Coventry City.

Coventry were the lowest goalscorers in Division One going into the game, with a mere eight goals in 11 games. They did, though, have a strong defensive record and a keeper in Steve Ogrizovic who often seemed to save his best games for his appearances against the Owls. It was no surprise, therefore, that the opening stages were cagey. Coventry, though, took the lead in the 27th minute, with Peter Barnes beating the defence and crossing for Dave Bennett, who nodded down for Terry Gibson to shoot home.

Wednesday saw plenty of the ball in the rest of the half and had a decent appeal for a penalty given only as a free kick on the edge of the box. The second half began with Wednesday still dominating possession but unable to create much in the way of chances.

That changed in the 75th minute when Varadi was adjudged by referee Lester Shapter to have been fouled in the area. Sterland's penalty, though, lacked the usual power and was saved relatively easily by Ogrizovic. Coventry saw out the rest of the game without any further threat of note.

A disappointing result for the Owls, as Lyons put it afterwards in a nod to the noisy contingent of supporters who made the trip:

'When you have fans like ours, it is extra demoralising when you lose.' The penalty miss was Sterland's second of the season. Unlike the Southampton game, though, there was no reprieve for Sterland and the team, and the game was the first in which the Owls did not score that season. Coincidentally, this was the 14th game of the campaign, the Owls scoring in the first 13 games for the second season in a row.

The Owls were at home for their next fixture as they aimed to return to goalscoring and winning ways. Norwich City were the opposition. In the week leading up to the match it was announced that Howard Wilkinson was to take charge of England's B team in a game against New Zealand the following week – on his birthday of 13 November, in fact. The Wednesday team were unable to offer Wilkinson a present of any points. The windy and very wet November weather fooled City keeper Chris Woods, who missed Blair's cross-shot only to be rescued by future Owls boss Steve Bruce heading it away from under the bar.

John Deehan put Norwich ahead in the 22nd minute, shooting past the advancing Hodge. Five minutes later Wednesday were offered a glorious opportunity to equalise as Chapman was fouled in the box. Given Sterland's two earlier misses it was no surprise to see Blair step up to take the kick. The penalty was saved by Woods, who looked to many eyes like he had moved before it was taken. 'How else does a keeper save two-handed at the foot of a post?' asked the *Daily Mirror.*

Wednesday continued to put pressure on Norwich for the rest of the half, and into the second period, but with limited end product. The Owls did force a series of corners, and Varadi came close with a long-range effort, but otherwise there was no way through the defence of Bruce and Dave Watson.

In the 80th minute, the inevitable happened as Louie Donowa scored Norwich's second after a quick breakaway. It was not the end of the scoring, though, as Sterland pulled one back in the 86th minute with a powerful volley following a goalmouth scramble.

There was still time for Pearson to send a header inches wide in the dying moments, but the score remained the same. Two defeats in succession for the Owls. Peter Eustace commented afterwards, 'We are still in the learning process, but we know where we went wrong.'

The following week saw the Owls travel to West London to play on the artificial surface at Loftus Road, home of Queens Park Rangers. The Rs featured ex-Owls striker Bannister in their line-up but had omitted future Wednesday sharpshooter Stainrod from their squad. Wednesday featured the returning Oliver as a replacement at the back for the injured Sterland, with Marwood dropped to the bench to be replaced by Pearson.

The game was something of a non-event in terms of goalmouth action. The Owls had a decent penalty appeal turned down by referee Alan Robinson as Shelton tumbled under a challenge in the area. In the last minute Pearson almost stole the game for Wednesday with a header that just clipped the crossbar. QPR had a late chance through Wayne Fereday who shot wide with only Hodge to beat. Otherwise, both sides created little.

The *Sunday Mirror* named Shelton man of the match, saying, 'His non-stop commitment was mainly responsible for Wednesday's point.' Wilkinson said, 'It was a very effective performance from us.'

The Owls travelled south again for their next fixture the following Saturday. This time the Wednesday team were to face Watford at Vicarage Road. The Owls team saw Marwood return for Pearson, while the Watford side featured the exciting talents of John Barnes and Luther Blissett.

Watford were managed by future England boss Graham Taylor, who was developing a reputation for playing a very direct game. Indeed, as the *Daily Mirror* put it in advance of the game, 'The jokes are flying about the meeting of long-ball specialists Watford and Sheffield Wednesday, the most popular being that spectators won't see the ball if there's any low cloud about!'

The game started very quickly with Blissett putting an early rebound wide before Watford took the lead in the 13th minute. George Reilly's shot struck Mark Smith's leg, looping over Hodge for Barnes to add the simplest of finishes. Hodge needed to make further first-half saves from Blissett and Worrell Sterling, and the Owls probably counted themselves lucky to be only one goal down at half-time. The second half saw further Watford pressure with Barnes landing a chip on the top of the net before his tricky footwork set up a chance that Sterling could probably have done better with.

It was not all one way, though, as Marwood latched on to a loose ball and unleashed a fierce strike that cannoned against the far post and back into the relieved arms of keeper Tony Coton. Shelton had two further efforts saved by Coton as the Owls looked the more likely team to score in the closing stages. Watford, though, held on.

The *Daily Mirror* accepted the error of their earlier statements in saying, 'For all the scathing condemnations of both teams' style of play … the fans recorded rip-roaring approval at the end.' Wilkinson said that it was 'a pleasure to be associated with the match … everyone got value for money'. The Owls did not pick up any points, though, with their stuttering form of only one point in four matches seeing the team fall from second to seventh in the table.

Wednesday had an opportunity to get back to winning ways against Arsenal at Hillsborough, with a Sunday 2.35pm kick-off catering for the ITV *Big Match* audience. It was the Owls' first live televised game of the season. Wilkinson expressed his reservations about televised matches in the programme for the game, concluding that 'football needs television, but in my opinion, television also needs football'.

The Owls named an unchanged starting XI from the Watford game and the midweek Milk Cup victory over Luton Town. Ryan returned to take the substitute's spot for the first time since his goal in the 5-0 win over Leicester six games previously. The game started at pace, with Chapman seeing a header go inches past the post before Hodge saved from Paul Davis as the Arsenal man was put clear. Wednesday went ahead after only 15 minutes. A superb cross from deep by Oliver took a slight deflection before it was met by a diving header from Chapman.

Wednesday dictated much of the play for the remainder of the half, Chapman seeing another header go close and a Marwood shot hitting the inside of the upright. The second half continued at a similar pace, with Varadi missing two decent chances before Arsenal had good efforts of their own from Paul Mariner and Tony Woodcock.

Arsenal then equalised against the run of play as Shirtliff, who had an otherwise excellent game, miscued horribly in the box to give Woodcock the simplest of tap-ins. Shirtliff only needed to stew on his error for two minutes before his centre-back partner Smith put the Owls back in front. Smith jumped above a crowd of players to glance Blair's free kick inside the post and score his first goal of the season.

Woodcock forced a magnificent save from Hodge in the dying moments, but the win and the three points were in Wednesday's hands. As Chapman put it after the game, 'When we pound teams as we did this afternoon, there are not many who will live with us.' The win moved the Owls back into sixth place ahead of a trip to table-topping Everton.

The trip to Goodison Park involved a return to their old stomping ground for Lyons, Varadi and Hodge. Missing out for the Toffees was ex-Owl Terry Curran, who was not enjoying the best of times in Liverpool and was serving a two-match suspension following his sending off against Watford earlier that month. Wednesday named an unchanged squad from the Arsenal game.

The Owls made an excellent start, with a goal after only eight minutes. Oliver did very well down the right flank, firing in a rapid cross that deflected off Everton defender Kevin Ratcliffe into the path of Blair, who shot home.

Smith snatched at an excellent opportunity a few minutes later, skying the ball when well placed. On 23 minutes came the first part of the most controversial incident of the game. Marwood came flying in extremely late into a tackle on Adrian Heath. To 21st-century eyes it would have been a clear red card. In 1984, it earned Marwood only a yellow. Heath was badly hurt and would not play again that season.

In the 29th minute, Blair snatched at an attempted clearance in his own box, punting the ball into the air. Trying to make good his mistake, Blair went into the back of Everton striker Graeme Sharp. Penalty. Sharp took the spot-kick and sent Hodge the wrong way.

Just before half-time came the concluding part of the earlier controversy as Peter Reid seemingly took his revenge on Marwood with a savage tackle. Marwood was stretchered off but fortunately for him would not miss any further games.

The second half descended into a scrappy encounter, with limited chances for either side. The Owls were probably the happier of the two teams with the result. As Hodge said, 'It was a great feeling to go back to Goodison and get a good result.' The incidents with Marwood, Heath and Reid left a sour taste, though. As one Owls fan put it to me, 'I always hated Peter Reid after that,' while an Evertonian felt that Marwood's initial tackle was simply 'horrific'.

Wilkinson cooled tensions in his programme notes for the next game by saying, 'Let us hope that the unfortunate incidents are now forgotten ... no one here will be allowed to carry any ill-feeling ... I, and all the players, wish Adrian Heath a speedy recovery.'

Wednesday moved on to a home fixture against Chelsea. The game was the Owls' 2,000th in the top flight of English football. Remarkably, a draw would be the club's 450th stalemate in Division One, while a win would be the 1,300th in all league games. The game proved to be a scrappy affair. The Owls had a penalty appeal turned down as Joe McLaughlin handled in the area as he fell – the referee ruled it unintentional.

Paul Canoville's speed proved an issue, but one that was smartly marshalled by the Owls defence. The second half saw Canoville curl a shot wide and force Hodge into a sharp save. Marwood hit a first-time volley wide, and Chapman saw a header go over the bar in what was proving a game of few chances.

Chelsea finally broke the deadlock on 80 minutes. Nigel Spackman put Pat Nevin through, and he crossed for Gordon

Davies to plant a header home past Hodge. The scoring was not over though, as in the 87th minute the Owls levelled. Marwood crossed, Chapman headed it back and Varadi put his header into the bottom corner to score his first goal in seven games.

There was still time for chances at either end for Nevin and Worthington, but as the final whistle went, the Owls could mark that milestone of draws. Wilkinson was pleased enough with the result. 'It was very competitive,' he said. 'Chelsea battled for a result, and I give them every credit.'

Wednesday's final game before the start of a busy festive period involved a trip to London to face West Ham United. Remarkably, the Owls' starting XI was unchanged for the sixth game in succession.

Sterland, who had missed all those games through injury, was fit enough to make the substitutes' bench. The game featured on that evening's *Match of the Day*, with the producers presumably hoping for some excitement and plenty of goalmouth action to entertain the viewers.

There was plenty of action in the first half as Wednesday dominated. Smith saw an excellent header cleared off the line and Shelton hit a fierce shot which Hammers keeper Tom McAlister could only fumble before the ball was hacked clear. Oliver had two attempts blocked in quick succession before Shelton had another shot stopped. West Ham must have been grateful to reach the break with the game still scoreless.

The second half was more end-to-end, with Worthington blocking Alan Dickens as he went towards goal before Marwood fired a shot just wide. In the 55th minute Shelton went down injured and was stretchered off to be replaced by the returning Sterland. Smith soon also went down injured and was clearly in some pain, although he remained on the pitch.

West Ham put the Owls under consistent pressure for the remainder of the game. Dave Swindlehurst skied a shot over the bar, Shirtliff blocked a seemingly goalbound effort from Tony Cottee and Hodge made a series of fine saves. The Owls held out for a 0-0 draw. The TV audience got value for money from the 20 minutes or so of highlights of a game which Howard Wilkinson described as 'a hard, but not a dirty match'.

The games flowed thick and fast, with four fixtures due to be played in 11 days over Christmas and the new year. The first of those was a home tie against Stoke City. The Owls dominated the first half, with Oliver seeing a 25-yard effort crash against the bar, before Varadi put Wednesday ahead by heading in Chapman's cross. Stoke equalised against the run of play just before the break, Steve Bould the scorer.

Wednesday kept up the pressure in the second half and were rewarded with the winning goal, Chapman diving in bravely among a crowd of players to notch the goal. Wilkinson was pleased, as 'it was a hard game, but we played well and created plenty of chances'.

The next fixture four days later was a Boxing Day tie at Hillsborough against Aston Villa. A crowd of over 30,000 turned out to watch. Nigel Spink made an excellent double save from former Villain Shelton early on before Paul Rideout broke away in the 41st minute to open the scoring.

Shelton had two further efforts in the second half, striking the bar and forcing another fine save from Spink. As time was seemingly running out, Lyons stole in to claim the equaliser in the 88th minute. It was no more than the Owls deserved with a corner count of 17-1 showing their domination. Lyons said that 'my goal was so important … it kept our nice run ticking over'. The game marked the halfway point of the league season, with the Owls sitting ninth in the table. There was now only a three-day break before the Owls travelled to The Dell to face Southampton, managed by ex-Wednesday coach Lawrie McMenemy.

Sterland returned to the starting XI, having come on as substitute in the previous three games. Oliver took Sterland's place on the bench. The game proved to be a one-sided affair as England keeper Shilton made early saves from Shelton and Marwood. Chapman put the Owls in front in the 34th minute with an opportunistic effort before two goals in three second-half minutes sealed the game for Wednesday.

Blair crossed for Chapman to head home on 51 minutes before a mistake by Mark Wright let in Marwood, who set up Varadi for a simple finish. Shilton made several further saves and the Owls were good value for their 3-0 victory. McMenemy made light of defeat by saying, 'I've had my Christmas turkey and now my team were well and truly stuffed!'

The Owls finished the year in sixth place in Division One. They had won at Anfield and seen famous victories at Hillsborough over the likes of Tottenham Hotspur and Arsenal. They had begun to prove that they could mix it with the big teams. The next fixture was against one of the biggest clubs of all, a New Year's Day trip to Old Trafford to face Manchester United.

3.

An Interview with Mike Lyons

MICHAEL (MIKE) Lyons was the Owls' captain for much of our period. Born in Liverpool, and originally a centre-forward, he moved back into central defence during his time at Everton. Lyons played for Everton for 13 years, including eight as captain. He moved to Hillsborough to sign for Jack Charlton in 1982. Across our two seasons Mike played a total of 60 games, scoring seven goals. In his career with the Owls, he played 164 games and netted 16 times. His professional career saw him play over 600 games.

Mike moved into management and coaching after leaving the Owls in a career that eventually took him to Australia. It was from Western Australia that he spoke to me by video call and the wonders of modern technology. We chatted for a while about my reasons for writing the book and football more generally, before discussing Mike's career with the Owls.

What made you decide to sign for Sheffield Wednesday?

I'd been at Everton for a long time, and really enjoyed it there, but sometimes it's just time for a change. I heard that Sheffield Wednesday were interested and I came over to have a look round. Everyone at the club was so kind to me, it seemed like the sort of place I'd like to play at. And of course, Jack Charlton was manager. He was a World Cup winner so playing for him also appealed. I kept my house in Liverpool but moved over into digs in Sheffield, so it suited that way as well.

Tell me about your first season under Jack Charlton (1982/83).

We reached the FA Cup semi that year, and it was a great disappointment that we didn't get to the final. We also finished sixth in the league, and again [that was] a disappointment as Jack wanted promotion. I enjoyed playing though, and I enjoyed working with Jack. I was very privileged with all the managers I played under during my career. Harry Catterick, Billy Bingham, Gordon Lee, Jack Charlton and Howard Wilkinson – they were all top-class managers in their own right. I learned lots from all of them, and as I say, Jack was a World Cup winner. I really enjoyed working with him.

Did things change much when Howard Wilkinson took over for the following season?

Well, Howard got us to be the fittest team in the league! Every Monday in training we would be running. He'd have us running up and down hills for an hour or more non-stop. He ran our bollocks off! I loved it though. I'd always loved running, right back from being a kid in Liverpool. I used to love running the 800 or 1500 metres and winning those kinds of races. It got us fit for the games.

We also played with three centre-backs, which was new. We weren't the first team to do that, but it suited the squad we had. Mel Sterland and Nigel Worthington could get up and down the wings in that system. I remember Mel absolutely bombing up and down the wing. It was great to play in. And of course, it worked, as we were promoted!

Did Howard Wilkinson change much following promotion?

We still worked on fitness. Monday morning, we'd still be going for a run. We still played in a similar way with the three centre-backs. The preparation for games seemed even more professional, though. We spent time every week, usually on a Friday before the game, practising set pieces. We would spend 45 minutes or an hour going over every detail. We scored plenty of goals from set pieces, and there was a sense of pride in that. We all enjoyed coming into training and I think that also showed in the success that we had on the pitch.

How would you describe the dressing-room ethos at the time?

Just simply as a great bunch of lads. We all got on really well. If there was a night out we all went, not just some of us. There were a couple of ex-Evertonians, which helped me. I used to share a room with Martin Hodge on away trips, for example. There were some talented players in that team as well.

As captain my job was to get the team psyched up and organised. We used to come running out of the tunnel for the game after playing head tennis or similar in the dressing room. We were ready, you know.

If I needed to tell someone off, I'd do that, but it didn't affect the spirit. During the game, the manager's on the side, and it was my job to get people going. I relished being captain, both at Everton and Wednesday. I was so proud. It was a tremendous honour for me.

The team were sometimes accused in the press of playing too much of a long-ball game. What were your feelings on that?

Well, it got us promoted! No one could have a go at us, really, because it was successful. And if a way of playing is successful, why not play that way? We loved it if other teams 'fannied about', passing around at the back. We'd press and press, get the ball off them and score! We had some good players as well though, you know. Hodgie was a great keeper. Chappy up front, Mel at the back and up and down the wing. We weren't just journeymen, though Howard did mould us into a team.

Are there particular games you remember that season?

You know, at my age, after playing so many games and heading the ball so often, there are a few things I forget! I remember a 4-4 draw against Chelsea in the cup – I scored in that one, though it was a very strange game. I also remember my 500th professional game, which was a win against Manchester United. I was really proud a few weeks later when Everton came to Hillsborough. Wednesday and Everton had combined to present me with an inscribed watch. The presentation was done on the pitch and all four sides of the stadium were clapping. That was a great moment.

Into the following season, you played the opening few games but moved on to Grimsby in October as player-manager. What brought that move about?

I'd always wanted to move into management. I just thought it was a great opportunity. They were in Division Two at the time, but I was fine with that. Howard Wilkinson was supportive; he knew that I also had ambitions to be a manager. It was a case of taking the opportunity when it came.

Talking of opportunities, I know that your career later took you to Brunei, Singapore and Australia. What took you so far from home?

The plane! (Laughs) Seriously though, I've been really lucky with the opportunities I have had and the career I've had. I'm grateful for everything that football has given me. I was lucky to be offered the opportunity to manage the Brunei national team and from there it wasn't too far to Singapore and on to Australia, which is why I looked for opportunities over here and eventually settled here.

Thanks Mike. A few questions from fans now.

Go for it!

Are the stories of you playing on through injury true?

I just loved being on the pitch. If I was injured, I wanted to get back on there. So as far as possible if I could I'd tell the physio that I was all right and get back on the pitch. It's what I did!

You mentioned the squad's morale before. Is it true that on one night out you were tricked and appeared in fancy dress?
(Laughs) Yes, I think that's true. I remember, I think, being dressed as Hagar the Horrible – a Viking – with everyone else in smart gear. I think it was probably Mel Sterland who set me up for that!

Finally, is it true that you broke your nose in the pre-match dressing-room warm-up, but played anyway?
I broke my nose a couple of times. I don't remember doing it in the dressing room – but it's possible I suppose. We used to head the ball about, off the walls and off each other. It could have bounced and caught me on the nose. I probably would have played on!

Thanks Mike. Finally then, what keeps you busy in retirement now in Australia?
I keep my hand in, I coach an under-12s team. Twice a week coaching and a game at the weekend. I really enjoy that. We've been luckier over here with Covid-19 than perhaps you've been in England. We're not in a lockdown, so I've been able to get out and about and occasionally down to the pub!

When I look back at my career, I feel tremendously lucky for all I've been able to do. I think I did all right, you know. I've been watching a bit of football without the fans there. I remembered from that how much we appreciated the supporters at Wednesday. They were always on our side. Even if someone made a mistake, they'd be urging us on. I'll always be very grateful for that.

Thanks Mike, I really appreciate your time.
No problem, good luck with the book!

* * *

As this book was being prepared for publication, Mike's family announced that he is now living with dementia, an issue that he relates back to regularly heading the ball during his career.

4.

The Players

HOWARD WILKINSON'S teams were remarkably consistent across the two seasons covered in this book. Twenty players featured in the first team in 1984/85, a number that rose to only 22 the following season. In total, 28 were used across the two campaigns. Nine players featured in more than 30 games in the first of the two seasons; ten players reached that milestone in 1985/86.

No player featured more consistently than goalkeeper Martin Hodge, who played in every game across both campaigns – those 104 appearances formed part of a 214-game unbroken run in the first team. At the other end of the spectrum, Simon Mills made two substitute appearances in 1984/85.

There are numerous other players who played more of a cameo role. in this period. The names of Siggi Jonsson (11+2 games) and Ian Knight (four appearances) will be well remembered by Owls supporters, for example. Perhaps the most notable character, though, is Mark Chamberlain who, after signing early in the 1985/86 season, went on to make three appearances in the starting line-up with an incredible 24 further sightings from the bench.

This section picks a fantasy XI from the players that featured in these seasons. It discusses and describes their careers at Hillsborough and elsewhere. I surveyed supporters from the era, and the most popular players from that survey are included – although I have needed to make my own executive decisions to select the final line-up!

Fans' memories of the players are also included along with some discussion as to how accurate it is to describe these players as committed discards from other teams. In a 2017 interview, Hodge described the players of this era as the 'dirty dozen' and as 'journeymen' who Wilkinson moulded into a winning team.

This team is a fantasy XI, as despite all the players making many appearances across the two years of the book, they never appeared together in the same team. It is for the reader to decide how successful they may have been if that were possible and whether the descriptions used by Hodge and others are fair.

This team plays in a roughly 4-3-3 formation. This does not necessarily match Wilkinson's preferred tactics and formation but does allow for discussion of the merits of some of the most memorable players of the era. Again, readers may decide whether this team, in this formation, would have been successful!

The *Back in the Big Time* Fantasy XI

1. Martin Hodge
2. Mel Sterland
3. Nigel Worthington
4. Mike Lyons (captain)
5. Mark Smith
6. Gary Megson
7. Gary Shelton
8. Andy Blair
9. Lee Chapman
10. Imre Varadi
11. Brian Marwood

Sub) Carl Shutt

Martin Hodge

Martin Hodge is a Southport-born goalkeeper who originally signed on loan from Everton prior to the 1983/84 season. He was already an experienced player at that stage, having played in an FA Cup semi-final for the Toffees, along with loans to a string of lower-league teams.

Hodge had cost Everton £135,000 in signing from Plymouth back in 1979. Having failed to fully establish himself at Goodison, with stiff competition from Neville Southall and others, the Owls paid £50,000 to bring him to Hillsborough. Hodge seems, therefore, to fit the description of a committed discard from another club.

Although it has been said that he was signed initially as cover for the Owls' other new keeper that season – England Under-21 international Iain Hesford – Hodge suggests that Wednesday had worries about the suitability of Hesford and that he was always expected to start in the first team. Regardless of the truth of the matter, Hodge was in goal for the first game of the 1983/84 campaign. This was the first of a record 214 consecutive league and cup games – beating the record of pre-war hero Mark Hooper.

Hodge was, therefore, an integral part of the team that gained promotion in 1983/84, keeping an outstanding 22 clean sheets in league and cup games. He remained as first choice throughout the two seasons covered by this book. The 104 matches he played formed a large part of Hodge's run of consecutive games. Hodge had a specific role in the team, both as an excellent shot-stopper and by playing as almost a sweeper.

Hodge took most free kicks in his own half, feeding into Howard Wilkinson's direct tactics. Hodge remained in excellent form throughout both of our seasons. His performances were so impressive that he was called up for the England squad in advance of the 1986 World Cup. He was to go instead of Manchester United's Gary Bailey.

At the last minute Bailey passed a fitness test, and Hodge was left behind. He recently described how that decision affected him – talking of how it 'still hurts', how it felt like 'someone had dropped a big lead weight on my head' and how it 'wrecked me'.

Hodge's outstanding form saw him keep 11 clean sheets in 1984/85 and a further 16 the following season. His bravery earned plaudits from fans, players and managers alike. One such occasion was when Hodge was knocked unconscious after an awkward fall on a hard pitch during an FA Cup match at Derby County in 1986.

After lengthy treatment from physio Alan Smith, Hodge completed the game. Hodge became known for his heroics in saving penalties during his time at Hillsborough, keeping out spot-kicks from Liverpool's Jan Mølby and Manchester United's Gordon Strachan among others in our period.

Hodge was dedicated and hard-working. He was known to be the first player in the ground on matchdays and believed in the positive effect of hard work. Fans who responded to my survey remember him as 'heroic', 'by far the most consistent Owls keeper of my time', and 'the best and toughest goalie we've had at Wednesday'. He is also well remembered for having time to speak with fans, to sign autographs and, in the case of one supporter, replying to her fan letter with a signed picture that stayed on her wall for years!

Hodge fits the criteria of being a committed, hard-working player who made a success of his career at Hillsborough after struggling for game time elsewhere. He was an integral part of Wilkinson's team with terrific ability between the sticks, his distribution from free kicks and controlling the space behind the defence. Hodge continued to play for the Owls until 1988, later returning as goalkeeper coach in the 1990s and as first-team coach under Terry Yorath in the early 2000s.

He has remained in the game ever since, working at Cardiff and Watford as match analyst, and most recently at Burnley as head of recruitment. Owls fans will remember him most fondly, though, for the years where he helped establish the team back in the big time.

Mel Sterland

Melvyn 'Mel' Sterland is a Sheffield-born former full-back and occasional striker who played for the club's nursery side, Middlewood Rovers, before signing apprentice forms with Wednesday in 1978. He went on to make his first-team debut in 1979 before fully establishing himself in the team in the early 1980s.

By this stage he had been moved more permanently to full-back and was making a name for himself with his rampaging charges from the back, which, combined with his long curly hair, earned him the nickname of Zico from Owls fans – after the Brazilian superstar.

Mel grew up on the tough Manor estate in Sheffield, and despite rumours to the contrary, has confirmed in recent years that he has always been an Owls supporter. Mel played a total of 78(+4) games across our two seasons, scoring an impressive 17 goals. Sterland was a regular goalscorer over the years, having begun as a striker.

He was also an impressive penalty taker – his lengthy run-up often leading to him lashing the ball home with great pace and power. Perhaps his most famous penalty was the one which sealed the Owls' promotion back to Division One in securing a 1-0 win against Crystal Palace in April 1984.

Sterland was a key part of the team that won promotion in 1983/84 and kept his right-back slot as the team returned to Division One in the following campaign. Although he suffered with injury as the season progressed, Sterland contributed to some famous moments – including a goal from the spot in the opening-day victory over Nottingham Forest and a late penalty to rescue a 4-4 draw against Chelsea in the League Cup.

He maintained his position in the team as the 1985/86 season began and kept his place for most of the campaign, contributing another 11 goals. That haul included the winner in two successive 1-0 victories in March against Coventry and Leicester City to maintain the Owls' push for a top-six place.

Howard Wilkinson's formation, which regularly used five at the back, allowed Sterland the freedom to push forward. This freedom was rewarded with another nickname – that of the Flying Pig. The name was originally bestowed on Sterland by Jack Charlton, who caught him eating the leftovers from another player's plate the night before a game. It was soon taken on by Owls fans in honour of Mel's buccaneering approach.

Mel gained a hatful of England Under-21 caps in his earlier years at Hillsborough, before gaining an England 'B' cap in 1987 and one for the Football League in the same year. He finally gained a full England cap in 1988. This recognition came in what was Mel's last season at Hillsborough. A row over the captaincy with then manager Peter Eustace led to him being made available for transfer.

He was sold to Glasgow Rangers soon after new manager Ron Atkinson replaced Eustace. Mel stayed in Glasgow for enough time to win a Scottish championship medal, before reuniting with Wilkinson at Leeds United.

What if … may be the thought of Wednesdayites, as the Wilkinson/Sterland combination helped Leeds to the Division One title in 1992. Owls fans certainly remember Sterland fondly; nearly two-thirds of supporters who completed my survey on the period included him as one of their three favourite players. Comments included that Sterland was 'hard as nails and couldn't half smash a ball', that with his 'running up and down the wing he epitomised the Wilkinson style', and that he showed 'total commitment'.

Mel retired from the professional game after a series of injury problems forced him to stop playing in 1994. He did return as player and player-manager at Boston United and continued to play amateur football throughout the 1990s. Mel found his sudden retirement from the professional game hard to take – and discusses eloquently in his autobiography and subsequent interviews how he nearly came to take his own life after he finished playing.

He does not fit the category of being picked up from another club, but he was certainly committed to the Owls cause and was a major contributor to the team's success on their return to Division One. He spent ten years as a professional for the club and it was fitting that on retirement a testimonial game was held between Leeds United and the Owls. Mel still attends games at Hillsborough and writes a regular piece in the club programme for each home game.

Nigel Worthington

Playing at left-back in our fantasy XI is Ballymena-born Nigel Worthington. The Northern Irishman followed Howard Wilkinson to Hillsborough from Notts County, signing in time to play in the final 14 games of the 1983/84 season. He continued to play for the Owls for over a decade, becoming the club's most capped player during that time – appearing 50 times in the Northern Ireland team.

Worthington played as left-back for our period, often in a five-man defence. He was known for his consistency and unflappable nature under pressure. Worthington was consistent, reliable and hard-working. Although not as likely to power forward as Mel Sterland on the other flank, he did aid the attack at times, and indeed later in his career with the Owls moved forward to play as a left-sided midfielder.

Worthington was imaginatively nicknamed Irish by Owls fans of the period. His playing colleagues preferred to use Barney, though, given his supposed resemblance to the cartoon character from the *Flintstones*! Worthington played regularly in the first of our two seasons – appearing 46(+1) times in the 1984/85 campaign and contributing one goal (the consolation in an early-season 2-1 defeat at Stoke).

He found appearances harder to come by the following season as injury took its toll. He turned out on 16 occasions in that campaign, scoring one goal. That goal was a memorable one, though, as he cracked home from the edge of the box with his lesser-used right foot to help set up a 2-1 win in an FA Cup quarter-final tie against West Ham United.

Worthington found his time out of the team somewhat frustrating, being quoted in the programme in March 1986 as saying: 'I had a bad start to the season … my fitness was only about 50 per cent and I've been picking up niggling injuries ever since.' Worthington also faced competition from new signing Glynn Snodin. Despite his frustrations in 1985/86, Worthington stayed and fought to regain his regular place in the team.

He gained the first of his Northern Ireland caps with the Owls at the end of the promotion season of 1983/84. He continued to appear regularly for his national team and was selected for his country's squad for the 1986 World Cup in Mexico. Despite his injury-hit season beforehand, Worthington was fully fit for the World Cup and played in two of the side's three games. He remained a regular in the Northern Ireland team during and after his time with the Owls, gaining a total of 66 caps.

Worthington stayed at Hillsborough until 1994 before moving on to Leeds United. He later played for Stoke City and made a handful of appearances for Blackpool as player-manager before hanging up his boots to concentrate on management. Worthington had a lengthy management career, including spells as boss of Norwich, Leicester and York City. He also assisted Wilkinson with the England Under-21 team and had a lengthy spell in charge of the full Northern Ireland squad.

Worthington is highly regarded by Owls fans who recall the era. Comments from those who were there include that he was a 'cracking player', along with discussion of his 'consistency, class and attitude' and that, in one supporter's opinion, Worthington is 'the best left-back the club has had in last 50 years'. Worthington was popular with his manager, players and fans alike.

He was commonly called upon to represent the club at functions and events, given his reliable and positive nature. He would be found at Q&A sessions with the supporters' club or presenting awards to the Young Owls, for example. Worthington does not fit the category of being a discard. He was highly rated as a youngster in Northern Ireland, and the Owls paid a £100,000 fee to bring him in from Notts County. He was certainly committed, though, being dedicated to the Owls' cause for over a decade, earning a testimonial game in 1993.

Mike Lyons

The centre-back positions in the *Back in the Big Time* fantasy XI were among the most difficult to fill. Not because of a lack of choice, but rather the opposite. Wilkinson often played with three centre-backs in a five-man backline. The defenders he played include some of the finest in the Owls' long history. Five players appeared more than 30 times each in the central-defensive positions across our two seasons. Only two players will fit in the fantasy team, though. The first of those is Liverpool-born Michael 'Mike' Lyons.

Lyons was already past his 30th birthday when he arrived at Hillsborough in the summer of 1982. Jack Charlton paid £80,000 to bring him to Hillsborough from Everton. Lyons had spent his entire 13-year professional career with the Merseyside club at that stage, including eight years as captain. Lyons was also made Owls captain on his arrival and led the team to an FA Cup semi-final in 1983 and to promotion in 1984. By this stage Lyons was nearly 33 years old, but despite his advancing years, Wilkinson offered him a two-year contract with the newly promoted Owls. His new role included the captaincy and work with the youth teams.

He was a regular in the team in the 1984/85 season. After missing a handful of early-season games through injury, he went on to play 47 games in league and cup – contributing six goals to the Owls cause. Those goals included two in the club's League Cup run that season – including the Owls' opener in the epic 4-4 draw against Chelsea.

Lyons was known for his rock-solid defending and commitment to the team. He was famously pictured leaving the field bloodied and battered on more than one occasion. The *Liverpool Echo* jokingly suggested in 1985 that Lyons might perform his famous daredevil routine in the club's Christmas pantomime – by running through a brick wall!

Wilkinson brought in Paul Hart on a free transfer in the summer of 1985 to offer further competition for the centre-back slots. Despite this, Lyons kept the captaincy and his place for the early matches of the season. Wilkinson was quoted at the time as saying the Lyons would be captain for 'as long as he remained at the club'. Wilkinson knew that Lyons had management ambitions.

After being left out of the team for Hart following a minor groin injury in October 1985, Lyons returned for one final league game. The Owls' 3-2 victory in that fixture against Leicester City saw them climb to third in the Division One table. He appeared one last time at the end of the month in the Milk Cup at Swindon before leaving to take up the manager's position at Grimsby Town. He played 13 games for the Owls in 1985/86 and contributed one further goal.

Lyons' initial efforts in management were not hugely successful – he was dismissed as Grimsby manager after the club was relegated in 1987. After a spell back at Goodison as reserve-team manager and coaching posts at Wigan and Huddersfield, he made the somewhat left-field move of becoming the coach of Brunei's national team! Further jobs in East Asia and then Australia followed for the now globetrotting Liverpudlian.

Owls supporters remember Lyons as a fearsome competitor who gave everything he had for the team. He was named by nearly half of those who completed my online survey as one of their three favourite Owls players of the time. Comments about him include that he was simply 'dominant', and that he 'turned Wednesday into winners, his experience and determination carried the day in many games'. Lyons' bravery is also well remembered. As one supporter put it, 'He seemed to have no regard for personal safety as he put everything on the line.' Another fan told me how he recalled that Lyons 'played as though his life depended on it'.

Lyons does fit the definition of a committed discard in some ways. His efforts for the Owls are unquestionable. He had a successful top-flight career with Everton before joining the Owls and was a regular in their team until the latter stages of his final season there. On leaving Everton, he was quoted as saying that he had 'loved every minute of it, the club have been great to me … when I leave the club will be gaining another supporter'. Everton manager Howard Kendall wanted to 'thank him for his magnificent efforts … his attitude and character are first class; Sheffield Wednesday have got a player who can inspire them'.

It is difficult to argue, therefore, that he was discarded, although Kendall did clearly feel it was time for him to move on. The Owls certainly did find a player to inspire them. Lyons is the Captain Fantastic of this fantasy team. Mike talks through his time with the club elsewhere in the book.

Mark Smith

The second centre-back spot in the team took a great deal of thought. Howard Wilkinson put great stead by his choice of players in defence. As we know, he often played three centre-backs. Playing more than 30 times across the two seasons and with great credentials to be picked as part of this fantasy team were Paul Hart, Peter Shirtliff and Lawrie Madden. With my 4-3-3 formation, though, there can be only one. Sheffield-born Mark Smith is the player to make the final cut.

Smith trained with the Owls from an early age and played for the club's nursery side, Middlewood Rovers, before signing apprentice forms in 1978. Youth-team coach (and ex-Owls player) Ken Knighton moved Smith from midfield to centre defence around this time. It did not take long before then boss Jack Charlton noticed Smith's ability – giving him his debut towards the end of the 1977/78 season.

He soon became a regular in the team, playing 50 games in the promotion season of 1979/80 and scoring 11 goals. Remarkably, all 11 of those goals were from the penalty spot – including, famously, one in the Boxing Day Massacre triumph over city rivals Sheffield United.

Smith remained a regular in the team throughout the seasons after this, through promotion back to Division One and into the first of our two seasons. He played 42 times in the first campaign back in the top flight, scoring two goals. One of those goals was a header from an Andy Blair free kick that sealed a famous 2-1 victory over Arsenal in November 1984.

Though Smith missed a handful of games over the Christmas period and early new year, he returned to the team in late January and remained ever-present in the league from February until the end of the season. Smith found appearances harder to come by the following season, making only 13 league appearances and 21 in total. A mixture of injury and Wilkinson restructuring the backline at various times meant that Smith was in and out of the team.

His one goal that campaign was the equaliser against West Bromwich Albion in a third-round FA Cup tie at Hillsborough. The goal kept the Owls in the competition and set up a run that went all the way to the semi-final. Smith was granted a testimonial in 1986 – perhaps the highlight of which was the game between the Owls and Sheffield United in September.

He remained at the club for one further season before moving on to Plymouth Argyle. Further spells followed with Barnsley and Notts County before Smith hung up his boots after one final season with Lincoln City in 1993/94. By that stage he had amassed over 500 first-team appearances across his various clubs.

Smith is well remembered for his efforts across his time with the Owls. One supporter felt that he 'would have played for England if he had gone to a bigger club'. Other fans mentioned that he was 'reliable, consistent and kept his head in difficult situations' and that he 'took his privileged position very seriously'. He is described as 'Mr Reliable at the back', though one fan remembers him as having 'simply the best slide tackle I have ever seen!'

He commonly came up among the three favourite players of the era from those supporters who completed my survey. He does not fit the category of a discard, making his career at Hillsborough from a schoolboy to the upper reaches of Division One – picking up England Under-21 international caps on the way.

Smith went on to enjoy a varied and extensive coaching career – including a one-game stint as the Owls' caretaker manager in 2004. He was certainly committed to the Owls, making 63 appearances in our period, from a total of 350 for the club over ten seasons. In the words of one fan, he was simply a 'lovely player'. Mark talks through his career with me elsewhere in the book.

Gary Megson

Gary Megson was a fixture of the Owls' midfield for much of the 1980s. He only featured on 25 occasions in our period, though. Megson could be described as Owls royalty. His father was Don Megson, who played 442 times for Wednesday between 1959 and 1969 and captained the team in the 1966 FA Cup Final.

Gary spent his teenage years in the south-west after his family moved there, with his father taking the manager's seat at Bristol Rovers. He signed schoolboy forms at Plymouth Argyle in 1975, breaking into the first team two years later.

His excellent form at Argyle saw him earn a £250,000 move to Division One Everton.

Megson found the move from Division Three to the top flight tricky, commenting six months after his move that 'down there you are one of the stars in a small place, whereas here there are lots of big-money men'. He did, though, say that it 'suits me this way and playing in the First Division is my ambition'. He did not fully secure his place, though, with a mixture of injury and stiff competition for places meaning he was in and out of the team.

He soon stepped down into Division Two as Jack Charlton signed him for the Owls in the summer of 1981. Megson immediately became a first-team regular at Hillsborough – making 148 appearances and scoring 20 goals over the next three seasons, up to and including the promotion season of 1983/84. It was a surprise, therefore, when Megson left the Owls in the summer following promotion and signed for Brian Clough at Nottingham Forest.

Despite the £170,000 fee, Clough never picked him for the first team, supposedly saying that Megson 'could not trap a bag of cement'. Five months later Megson was shipped out to Newcastle, picked up by his former Owls boss Charlton. Charlton soon moved on and Megson found himself surplus to requirements again. So, in December 1985, he jumped at the opportunity to temporarily rejoin the Owls.

The initial loan deal to Hillsborough was soon turned into a permanent transfer. Megson was quoted in the Newcastle press at the time as saying: 'It's been a case of many ups and downs, mainly downs since I left Sheffield Wednesday … I have to get myself back on the rails. It was a nice surprise Wednesday coming in for me.'

Wednesday's loan move supposedly beat a bid from ex-Owl colleague Mike Lyons, who was looking to persuade Megson to drop down the leagues and sign for Grimsby Town. Signing for Wednesday, though, did allow Megson to get back on those rails. He was a virtual ever-present in the Owls team for the remainder of the season, racking up 20 league appearances and a further five in the FA Cup.

Megson scored on his return to the side, helping the Owls to a 3-2 win over Manchester City, and played his part in an exciting 2-2 draw against his parent club Newcastle in the second game of his return. He scored a further two goals that season, the second one coming after Paul Hart headed on Brian Marwood's corner against Aston Villa in April. Megson's goal helped set up a 2-0 win and maintained the team's position in the top six.

He remained as a player at Hillsborough until January 1989, taking his total appearances for the club to 283(+3). His playing career continued at Manchester City and Norwich before short spells in 1995 at Lincoln City and Shrewsbury Town. Megson had already taken charge of Norwich City for a brief period by this stage and soon embarked on a managerial career – as boss of the Canaries again – in 1996, and managed a further eight clubs between then and his final post (to date) at West Bromwich Albion in 2017/18.

One of those posts was back at the Owls, where he stayed in the hot seat between February 2011 and February 2012 – firstly steadying the ship in League One and then readying the team for a promotion push. A wobble in results saw chairman Milan Mandaric sack Megson, his final game a 1-0 victory in the Steel City derby. Megson was famously pictured pointing at the club badge on his jumper in celebration of that victory.

Fans remember Megson's dedication to his boyhood team. Although only returning for the later stages of our second season, one supporter told me how the team immediately benefited from Megson's 'dedication and commitment'. Another fan told me how he felt Megson's return 'boosted the team just when we needed up and helped us storm to the cup semi-final'.

Megson does fit that description of a committed discard in many ways. His wholehearted efforts in supporting the Wednesday cause are clear as player, supporter and manager. His career was somewhat nomadic anywhere other than Hillsborough. His two spells as a player for the Owls were lengthy ones which coincided with some successful times for the club. It's not too much of a cliché, I hope, to suggest that the Owls' midfield in the mid-1980s is Gary Megson's spiritual home!

Gary Shelton

Nottingham-born Gary Shelton slots into the middle of our midfield three. Shelton had some experience before joining the Owls – having played first-team football for Walsall, Aston Villa and Notts County from as early as 1976. The 1980 loan spell in Nottingham came after Shelton had fallen out of the first-team picture at Aston Villa.

Shelton needed to wait a while longer for his move to Hillsborough, though, which was completed in March 1982 for the fee of £50,000. Shelton settled quickly into the Owls' line-up, playing regularly in the teams that reached the FA Cup semi-final in 1983 and gained promotion in 1984. He was named the club's player of the season in the promotion campaign.

A highlight of that campaign for Owls supporters was Shelton's match-winning goal at Newcastle United, a spectacular overhead kick. The 1-0 victory kept the Owls top of the division in mid-April and moved them one step closer to promotion glory.

Shelton remained a regular in the Owls team when they returned to Division One. He played 49 games in 1984/85, scoring five goals. Shelton scored early-season goals to help the team to a 2-1 victory over Southampton and to fight back to a 2-2 draw with West Bromwich Albion. Perhaps most famously, though, he scored the Owls' second goal as the team defeated Liverpool 2-0 at Anfield in September. Wednesday had lost in the League Cup at Anfield (a replay) the previous January. Wednesday fans had sung 'we'll be back'. After Shelton's goal had helped ensure victory, fans sang, 'We said we'd be back, we are, we are.'

He continued to play a major role in the team the following season, playing 35(+2) games and scoring one further goal. That came in the penultimate match of the season and helped the Owls to a 3-2 win over Southampton. The victory kept the team in the top six.

Shelton was called upon as an over-age player to captain the England Under-21 team in October of 1984. He skippered the team to a 2-0 victory vs Finland but was stretchered off after an hour with a suspected broken leg. Luckily for Shelton, it was only a bruised and bashed shin. Shelton came to have the double nickname of Shelly and Stretch among the other players, Stretch for the number of times he was stretchered off in games only to be back in the team the following week!

He remained with the Owls until the summer of 1987 – signing then for Oxford United for £135,000. Wednesday made a tidy profit on the sum they paid for his services over five years earlier. Two years later Shelton was on the move again. This time an exchange deal for future England manager Steve McClaren saw him swap Oxford for Bristol City.

Shelton spent nearly five years with the Robins, before winding down his playing career with Rochdale and then Chester City. Shelton has since held several coaching roles, perhaps most notably alongside fellow fantasy XI midfielder Gary Megson where, as assistant manager and reserve-team boss, he helped West Bromwich Albion to promotion to the Premier League – twice!

Owls supporters who recall Shelton's efforts in midfield remember him very fondly. To them he was 'a quality player', 'a brilliant player', 'an absolute steal' who 'could go unnoticed but only as far as the opposition were concerned and not us in the stands. He had a wonderful touch and held his own against some huge sides.' He is perhaps best described by one fan who remembers him as 'a terrier in the middle but skilful too!'

Shelton does fit the archetype of Wilkinson's committed discard. His career was seemingly drifting when he was picked up by Jack Charlton for Wednesday. He was fully committed to the Owls' cause from then on, appearing in two FA Cup semi-finals, gaining promotion and helping the team to its highest finish since the 1960s. His playing style was tenacious yet silky, committed yet calm. He is rightly at the centre of this fantasy team. Gary discusses his time with the Owls later in the book.

Andy Blair

Filling the final berth in the midfield is the Scottish-born, but Midlands-bred, Andrew (Andy) Blair. He had made well over a hundred appearances for the West Midlands trio of Coventry City, Aston Villa and Wolverhampton Wanderers by the time he arrived at Hillsborough in 1984. The bulk of those appearances were in an impressive spell at Coventry, which earned him a £300,000 transfer to Aston Villa.

Blair's spell at Villa Park saw him play at Wembley in the Charity Shield and gain a European Cup winners' medal (as a non-playing substitute) in 1982. He was never able to fully nail down a place in the Villa team though – he played just 33 games in a three-year spell. Howard Wilkinson spotted the potential in Blair and brought him to Hillsborough in a £60,000 swoop in the summer of 1984.

He made an immediate impression in Sheffield during the club's first season back in Division One. He missed only one league game all season and made a total of 51 appearances, scoring six goals. Three of those goals were a famous hat-trick of penalties to help secure the Owls a 4-2 League Cup victory over Luton Town in November 1984.

As the competition was sponsored by the Milk Marketing Board at the time, Blair was photographed afterwards celebrating with the match ball and a pint of milk! Blair's other goals that season included one in a 5-0 thumping of Leicester City in October which saw the Owls go second in the table.

Blair found his second season at Hillsborough more frustrating, playing in 24 games and scoring one goal. He was injured and substituted in the opening-day draw with Chelsea, not returning to the team until the end of September. He held down his place for a few weeks after that before drifting in and out of the team as December moved into January.

In February 1986, Blair started the FA Cup fifth-round tie away at Derby County. He misplaced a pass in the first half which immediately led to Derby's opening goal. A furious Wilkinson substituted Blair at half-time, and never picked him for the first team again. Within three weeks of that game Blair was sold to Aston Villa, with the Owls picking up a fee of £120,000 – twice what they paid for him less than two years earlier.

His career never really picked up after that – a serious knee injury meaning he spent over a year on the sidelines at Villa Park, before dropping down the leagues with Barnsley and Northampton Town and having a spell in the Maltese game. He ended his playing career at Kidderminster Harriers before retiring in 1990. After his retirement Blair opened a successful sports shop in Coventry which still trades to this day.

Blair fits the category of committed discard. He had lost his way at Villa after a successful spell with Coventry at the start of his career. He was quoted in the autumn of 1984 as saying that the best two decisions of his life at that stage were firstly getting married in the summer, and secondly joining Wednesday!

He went on to say that he 'needed someone to have faith in my ability, Mr Wilkinson has done that'. Although Wilkinson's faith in Blair declined as 1985 turned into 1986, Blair was a linchpin of the midfield for much of the early part of our period. Fans remember him as 'talented', 'calm, collected and could pick a pass', and as 'the guile to the brawn of Megson and others'. His three-penalty salvo will also live long in Owls folklore! Andy talks through his time at Hillsborough elsewhere in the book.

Lee Chapman

Taking the coveted No.9 shirt up front in the fantasy XI is Lee Chapman. Born in Lincoln, Chapman had turned professional with Stoke City in 1978. He made a very promising start to his professional career – topping the goalscoring charts in the Potteries for two seasons in a row as Stoke returned to top-flight football in the early 1980s. This brought the first of several big-money moves in Chapman's career as Arsenal took him to North London for £500,000 in the summer of 1983.

The transfer was not a success and, after only 23 appearances and four goals, Arsenal cut their losses and sold Chapman on to

Sunderland for £200,000 in December 1983. Again, the move cannot be described as a success and, after only 15 appearances and three goals in an injury-hit spell over the next season and a half, Chapman's career was seemingly at a crossroads. Stood at that metaphorical T-junction was Owls boss Howard Wilkinson, who stepped in to bring the talismanic striker to Hillsborough in the summer of 1984.

Chapman talks in his 1992 autobiography of how he took a cut in wages to sign for the Owls but that he 'was impressed by the manager, his desire to do well and the enormous potential the club seemed to have'. He went on to say that 'it was a chance to join a club whose fortunes had been similar to my own – we had both experienced hard times, but now there was chance to re-establish ourselves among the elite'. Chapman certainly took that opportunity, playing in a total of 90 games over the next two seasons and scoring an impressive 34 goals.

He made 49 of those appearances, scoring 19 goals, in the first of the Owls' campaigns back in Division One. He was a consistent goalscorer throughout the season, with strikes as early as the second game. As the season progressed, Chapman scored goals to help seal famous wins against Arsenal (2-1) and Manchester United (1-0). He also scored in the epic 4-4 League Cup draw with Chelsea.

Chapman became well known for his bravery in Owls colours. 'I got more stitches than goals last season,' he is quoted as saying in September 1985. 'Knocks don't hurt when you're in the thick of the game … I don't know whether it's bravery or stupidity!'

He continued his goalscoring exploits as the following campaign began. New strike partners Simon Stainrod and Garry Thompson had replaced Chapman's previous foil, Imre Varadi. Despite this, Chapman maintained his position up top and regularly notched goals as the season progressed. His goals included the winner against Manchester United in November with a trademark thumping header from a corner. The goal marked United's first defeat of the season and moved the Owls up to third in the table.

He found appearances harder to come by after Christmas as a mixture of injury and the emergence of Carl Shutt saw him in and out of the team. Chapman's final goal of the season was in a 5-1 demolition of Birmingham City on 8 March. He did continue to appear in the team, including in every game of the club's run to the FA Cup semi-final, and ended the season with 15 goals from 41 appearances.

Chapman remained with the Owls until the summer of 1988, being named player of the season in 1986/87. He left the club in somewhat bizarre fashion, signing for the obscure French team Niort for a fee that was decided by a transfer tribunal at £290,000. Niort seemingly could not afford the fee, and immediately sold Chapman to Nottingham Forest for £350,000, pocketing a tidy profit on the deal. Some Owls fans may have been somewhat suspicious of the legitimacy of all this, especially as a £600,000 deal with PAOK of Greece had apparently fallen through just beforehand.

None of this should outweigh Chapman's contributions in Owls colours, though – by this stage he had scored 79 goals in 186 games for the club. An impressive record. Chapman continued to be a consistent goalscorer on his return the English game, scoring regularly in his two seasons at the City Ground before rejoining his old Owls boss Howard Wilkinson at Leeds United. At Elland Road he won both Division Two and Division One title medals and scored a famous hat-trick against the Owls in an ignominious 6-1 defeat in January 1992.

Chapman continued to play at a high standard, making Premier League and Division One appearances for Portsmouth, West Ham United, Southend United and Ipswich Town before a final two-game loan spell with Leeds in 1995/96. Short spells with Swansea City and Strømsgodset in Norway followed before Chapman hung up his boots in the summer of 1996. He has since gone on to enjoy a successful business career as a bar owner and restaurateur along with his wife, the actor Leslie Ash.

He is very fondly remembered by Owls supporters from the period. He is named by nearly half of those who completed my survey as one of their three favourite players of the period. Descriptions of him include: 'big target man who bossed the centre halves!', 'fantastic in the air and great goalscorer' and 'a real handful for defenders and knew where the net was'.

Chapman is, in many ways, the epitome of the talented and committed discard from elsewhere. His career had hit a standstill after a failed move to Arsenal and injury and a change of manager at Sunderland. He found just the place to rekindle his career under Wilkinson at Hillsborough and gave everything he could for the cause. In the words of one fan: 'He scored the goals, and that's what mattered to me then!'

Imre Varadi

Chapman's strike partner in our fantasy team is London-born Imre Varadi. Born to a Hungarian father and Italian mother, Varadi was already well travelled in football when he joined the Owls in the summer of 1983. Varadi had a slow start to his career, playing non-league football for Letchworth Garden City and training two nights a week with Luton Town while working as an asphalter. After unsuccessful trials with Tottenham Hotspur and Cambridge United, Varadi returned to playing for Letchworth Garden City.

Varadi then had a stroke of good luck as the manager at Luton Town, Harry Haslam, moved to Sheffield United and offered him the chance to sign for the Blades in 1978. Varadi made an impressive start at Bramall Lane and after four goals in ten games he was on the move again – this time signed by Division One Everton for £80,000. Although he did not fully establish himself at Goodison Park, he did enough to earn a trial at Portuguese giants Benfica and then a £100,000 move to Newcastle United in 1981.

It was as St James' Park where Varadi really made his name, scoring 42 goals in 90 games over two seasons. Howard Wilkinson saw his talent and potential and paid £130,000 plus attacking midfielder David Mills to bring him to Hillsborough in the summer of 1983. Varadi was quoted in the Newcastle press as not being happy with the move to Hillsborough. There were also small protests outside St James' Park about his departure.

Wilkinson was pleased with his purchase, and in a sign of the club's thrifty nature in transfer dealings was quoted as saying that Varadi took a wage cut to join the Owls. All's well that ends well, however, as Varadi quickly settled into the Wednesday team, scoring 19 goals as the team were promoted back to Division One. Newcastle United were also promoted that season.

Varadi remained as a mainstay of the team as the Owls returned to Division One. He made 45 appearances in the 1984/85 campaign and scored 21 goals. His haul included severable memorable goals, such as the one in the first game of the season against Nottingham Forest – running from inside his own half and burying his shot in the top corner to help the team to a 3-1 victory. He also scored at Anfield in September, rounding keeper Bruce Grobbelaar, who had raced out of his area, and firing home from an acute angle to set the Owls on the way to a famous victory.

Varadi's hat-trick at home to Leicester City in a 5-0 demolition of the Foxes saw the Owls go second in the table in late October. His early-season form had seen him score eight goals in the first 11 league matches. The goals slowed a little after this, though Varadi did score both goals in a famous New Year's Day victory at Old Trafford and another hat-trick in a 5-1 thrashing of Oldham Athletic in the FA Cup third round.

A mixture of lack of form and injury saw Varadi in and out of the team as the season reached its climax. His final goal of the season came in March as he and the team dropped away slightly towards the end of the season, eventually finishing eighth.

Owls fans faced further disappointment when Varadi refused the offer of a new contract in the summer of 1985. Wednesday were faced with losing their star striker but hoped for a large sum in return. West Bromwich Albion offered £175,000 for Varadi – the Owls held out for £450,000. A Football League transfer tribunal decided on a final fee of £285,000 plus a third of the profits on any future transfer.

The sale went through and Varadi was top scorer for the Baggies the following season. As the team were relegated, though, he moved again – to Manchester City – only to be the leading scorer in another relegated team.

Wilkinson then brought Varadi back to the Owls in September 1988 in an exchange deal involving Carl Bradshaw. Varadi's second spell was not a success. Wilkinson was soon replaced by Peter Eustace, who froze Imre out of the first-team picture. A further spell under Wilkinson, and a Second Division championship, at Leeds United followed before a nomadic period, involving a dozen further clubs, saw Varadi drop down the leagues and into non-league before eventual retirement from the game in 1999.

Following his time playing football, Imre set up and runs a successful football agency – representing players whose names may be familiar to Owls fans, including Richard Wood and Chris Eagles.

Although Imre only played for the Owls in the first of our two seasons, he is well remembered by supporters. One fan recalled his 'desire and flair', another how he 'wasn't afraid to take players on – often followed by a lethal shot!' Varadi's goals stick long in the memory: the 'bullet header' that won the game at Old Trafford, the 'lung-busting belter' against Nottingham Forest or the 'calm, collected stroke home from 30 yards' at Anfield.

Varadi does not fit the discard category, with the Owls needing to pay a hefty fee to prize him away from a successful spell at Newcastle. He was certainly committed, though, using his pace and energy to chase lost causes and to do all he could for the team. The fans remember him fondly, and as Imre told me in a Twitter exchange in 2020, they are 'great memories' for him also!

Brian Marwood

Providing much of the ammunition for our front two is north-easterner Brian Marwood. He is a goalscoring winger who had spent his entire professional career with Hull City before joining the Owls in the summer of 1984. A fee, set by tribunal, of £115,000 brought Marwood to Hillsborough, with Howard Wilkinson seeing off great competition for his signature.

Marwood had played with great success in the lower leagues at this stage – helping Hull to promotion from Division Four with 19 goals in 1982/83 and finishing top scorer again the following season as the Tigers consolidated in Division Three. It was a jump of two divisions, though, that Marwood made in joining the Owls.

In his 1990 autobiography, Marwood told of the importance to him of being a Division One player and how he had turned down the offer of a bigger salary from Sheffield United to join the Owls and play at the top level.

Marwood immediately got the chance to play against the top teams. He made his Owls debut in the first league game of the 1984/85 campaign (a 3-1 win against Nottingham Forest) and was almost an ever-present for the remainder of the season. He missed just one league game, amassing 51 appearances and scoring 12 goals.

His first goal in Owls colours secured a 2-1 victory against Tottenham Hotspur in September 1984. Other goals that season included one in the thrilling 4-4 draw against Chelsea in the League Cup and one to hold Liverpool to a 1-1 draw at Hillsborough in front of a huge 48,000-plus crowd.

He initially found the physical demands of the Owls' playing style difficult to maintain – being substituted four times in his first six matches. Marwood knew that his role was not just to score goals; rather it was 'to give Wednesday width up front and pursue free areas'. This he did with aplomb, providing cross after cross for the centre-forwards.

Marwood maintained his regular place in the team in the 1985/86 season, appearing a further 45 times and notching 15 goals. These goals included several from the penalty spot and the only strike of the final game of the season, which guaranteed the Owls fifth place and effectively relegated Ipswich Town. Marwood did miss the FA Cup semi-final against Everton, though – which, as more than one supporter has told me, may have cost the Owls the game.

Marwood suggested in a 1985 interview that his success was partly down to hard work but also to the free role granted to him by manager Howard Wilkinson. 'The boss wants me creating and scoring goals,' he is quoted as saying in the match programme. 'He lets me roam around the front two. That's marvellous for me!' That roaming of position is well illustrated by the goal against Ipswich Town, which saw striker Carl Shutt turn provider, whipping in the cross which Marwood gleefully stabbed home.

Owls fans remember Marwood with great positivity. He was 'an excellent player, who created chances consistently and scored goals' said one supporter, with another remembering how 'his crosses were some of the best I've seen from a player in a Wednesday shirt' and one more simply saying that he must have been 'Chapman's dream!' Marwood also holds a unique place in the Hillsborough record books, with his strike against Ipswich being the last-ever goal scored in front of an uncovered Kop.

He stayed with the Owls until 1988, when he left in a club-record deal. Arsenal paid £600,000 for Marwood, and he was soon to win his sole England cap while with the Gunners – playing alongside Mel Sterland in a friendly with Saudi Arabia. Marwood played 31 times for Arsenal as they won the league in 1988/89.

He fell down the pecking order at Highbury at the end of the following season, however, when manager George Graham signed Anders Limpar. Marwood soon moved to Sheffield United, where injury restricted him to 22 appearances in three seasons. Further short spells with Middlesbrough, Swindon Town and Barnet followed before retirement in 1994.

Marwood had already moved into administration of the sport before hanging up his boots – he acted as chairman of the Professional Footballers' Association from 1990–93. Since retirement he has held various other roles in the game including working for Sky Sports and BBC radio, as UK marketing manager at Nike and, since 2009, at Manchester City, where he is currently managing director of their global football operation.

He does not fit the category of a reject from elsewhere, though he was certainly committed. Marwood was in high demand when he signed for the Owls. He certainly proved his worth over the coming seasons, making a great success of his time at Hillsborough and going on to win the league title and an England cap. A long way up from his humble beginnings in Division Four. Marwood was a hard-working, talented and dedicated forward player who was an integral part of the Owls team that successfully took on Division One.

Substitute: Carl Shutt

In the mid-1980s, each team was allowed only one substitute. This made choosing the extra man difficult for managers at the time, and for this fantasy team! There were several players who could have made the cut. Wilkinson's penchant for three centre-backs meant that tough-as-teak defenders Lawrie Madden, Peter Shirtliff and Paul Hart all regularly made appearances for the club – any of them could easily have been 12th man here.

International-class players such as Siggi Jonsson and Chris Morris flitted in and out of the team. Nigel Worthington was replaced for a period by Glynn Snodin, who could also easily have taken his place in the fantasy XI. Strikers Garry Thompson and Simon Stainrod joined the club for large sums and had greater or lesser success. Then there is the perennial substitute of the time, Mark Chamberlain, who despite his international quality flattered to deceive at Hillsborough.

All this leads to one man as our substitute, the Sheffield-born goalscoring sensation that was Carl Shutt.

Shutt had been on the Owls' books as a teenager but was released at the age of 16. He found form playing non-league football for Spalding United and, at the age of 23, was offered a trial with the Owls. Michael Hennigan recommended him to the club. Hennigan told me in 2021 that Peter Eustace was unsure about the signing, given that Shutt was plying his trade in non-league football, but that Hennigan was sure he'd score goals. Shutt took his opportunity with both hands, scoring eight in seven games for the reserves.

He was soon offered a contract and broke into the first team in the autumn of 1985, scoring against Coventry City on his full debut. Facing stiff competition up front, Shutt was in and out of the team in the following months. He made a huge impression as winter turned into spring, including an outstanding burst of five goals in two games in early March.

These goals included a hat-trick in a 5-1 trouncing of Birmingham City (featuring future England stopper David Seaman) and a double against Derby County to secure the team's passage to the FA Cup sixth round. Shutt continued scoring in the cup and league for the remainder of the season, including goals to help secure league victories against Arsenal and Manchester United and the Owls' goal in the FA Cup semi-final defeat to Everton. In total that campaign he played 25 times and scored 13 goals. Some introduction to professional football!

Shutt stayed at Wednesday until 1987 and enjoyed a long and fruitful professional career for teams such as Bristol City, Leeds United, Birmingham City and Manchester City. He was still playing as late as 2004 – scoring in the Conference North for Bradford Park Avenue at the age of 43.

Since retirement Shutt has spent time working in coaching and management, and, in more recent years, in the travel industry. His thrilling start to his Owls career is what is most remembered by supporters. His goalscoring prowess is what earns him a place on the substitutes' bench for this fantasy team.

* * *

This chapter began by questioning how far Howard Wilkinson's teams were populated by committed discards from elsewhere. Were they indeed a 'dirty dozen', as Martin Hodge described them? The truth, it seems, is somewhere in between. There were certainly players whose careers had gone askew elsewhere that Wilkinson brought to Hillsborough to great success. Lee Chapman, Andy Blair, Gary Shelton and, to some extent, Hodge himself fit into that category.

It is difficult to describe Mike Lyons as a discard from Everton, but his time there was judged to be up – and he was a very astute signing for the Owls. Gary Megson returned to his spiritual home after trying his luck elsewhere. Carl Shutt was another intelligent signing, making his name in non-league before returning to Hillsborough. Other players came through the ranks at S6, with Mark Smith and Mel Sterland fitting that category.

Wilkinson, though, was prepared to spend money on talented up-and-coming players, with both Nigel Worthington and Brian Marwood in great demand when they signed up to play for the Owls. Imre Varadi had already proven himself at a high level before joining the Owls for a hefty fee.

A dirty dozen? Maybe. Wilkinson certainly got the best out of the players he had available to him. There was, though, plenty of talent and genuine ability in this team, alongside the commitment to the cause which was clearly demanded of them.

5.

An Interview with John Pearson

JOHN PEARSON is a Sheffield-born striker who played for the Owls between 1980 and 1985, before making a brief return in 1995. He made a total of 80(+49) appearances for the club, scoring 27 goals. John made 5(+7) of those appearances, notching two goals, in the first of our two seasons. Over a 16-year professional career, John also played for Charlton Athletic, Leeds United, Cardiff City and others. He now works for the Owls, providing expert summaries on the club's iFollow streaming service. We chatted about the book and Sheffield Wednesday more generally before talking through John's time with the Owls.

You signed for the Owls at a young age. Tell me how that came about.

I started at Wisewood school, playing in midfield, and we went unbeaten for something like three or four years. Anyhow, when I was 14 I was asked to train with Sheffield Boys. I'd been turned down when I was nine or ten, so I was determined to succeed. Training was in the gym at Hillsborough, and I really got stuck in. It was getting towards the end of the season, and I ended up playing a few games as centre-half.

The next season I told the bloke there that I preferred playing in midfield and asked if I could go back there. He gave it a go and I scored a couple of goals. So then he gave me a chance up front! I remember scoring a couple past David Seaman for Rotherham Boys and from there I was picked for South Yorkshire Boys.

Wednesday scouted me a few times, but it was John Harris who signed me up as an apprentice. It was the happiest day of my life!

You very quickly made your debut I believe?

Yes, that was 1980 and I was only 17. I was only told on the morning of the game that I was playing. My dad, who'd taken me all around the place to matches and training when I was growing up, was on holiday in Spain. No mobile phones, remember, so he only found out I'd played and scored when he picked up the Sunday paper the next day! I played four games in a row because Terry Curran was suspended, and scored in each of them.

How was Jack Charlton as a manager?

He was brilliant. I loved playing for him. I was still an apprentice when I began, on eight quid a week, I think. I went up to 20 in the second year. Jack told me when I signed professionally that all I needed to do was knock on his door every couple of years and he'd sort my contract. That was a terrifying thing to do as a young lad, of course! There was no negotiation, that's for sure! Jack loved the club. After the FA Cup semi-final defeat to Brighton [in 1983], the changing room was very quiet and down. Jack was emotional, in tears. But it wasn't for himself, it was for the club and the players. I remember being really impressed that a World Cup winner would care so much.

Did things change when Howard Wilkinson took over the following season?

I thought it was going to change for me! I had met Howard once before. Mel Sterland and I had been asked to go and train with the England Under-21s. Jack really didn't want us to go and told us to tell England we were injured and couldn't train. We were dropped down there by the Wednesday coach as the team were playing in London. They wouldn't drop us at the training centre though, so me and Mel had to walk for miles and then get a taxi! When we arrived, I went to see Howard and told him I was injured. He didn't speak to me for the rest of the three days we were there.

I was on holiday in Benidorm when it was announced that Howard was the new Wednesday manager and my thoughts straight away were 'I'm finished' and 'it's going to be a nightmare!' As soon as I got back, I got a call from the club to go in and see the boss. I was very nervous so went to his office and tapped gently on the door. He called me in, looked me up and down and said simply, 'F****** hell, are you my centre-forward?!' He made me rap on the door again, harder(!), and then report back for training the following day. Two weeks before the rest of the team.

In those two weeks he had me running, doing biometrics, all sorts. He worked me so hard. One day the club photographer was in, and I was spewing up at the side of the pitch as the training had been so hard! It was the hardest pre-season ever, but it got me fit. We became the fittest team in the league. Mondays were always running. It was 90 minutes, like a game. Howard and Peter Eustace would set the pace and then they'd find us a hill to run up and down while they had a breather. We'd have a break in the middle, like during a game, and then be back at it. It bred confidence, though, as we knew if a game got to 75 or 80 minutes, we'd still have energy left in the tank.

Howard taught me how to be a *professional* footballer. He was ahead of his time in areas like diet, formations and fitness. He was also a great manager of people. I'll give you an example. I got injured in 1983 and had a pot on my leg. Midweek, I was out in the Park hotel in Sheffield. One of the directors saw me in there and just asked if I was going to be at the next game. Word got back to Howard and in the next team meeting he went into a long discussion about how players shouldn't be out midweek, never mind if they are injured. He didn't name me though, and just left it that players would be fined if they went too far. He made his point without embarrassing me.

He was a tough taskmaster. You didn't want to be out injured. It was harder than being fit! Alan Smith was brought in as full-time physio and would have you doing two sessions in the morning and two in the afternoon if you were injured. He'd have you in on a Sunday as well. Anyone who didn't start on a Saturday would be in on Sunday to do a run. He used to run out to Oughtibridge and back. I remember Iain Hesford would tuck a few pence inside his sock and get the bus back!

Did much change when the team were promoted?

Well, I'd been injured the previous season, and although I'd got back into the team, I wanted to be ready for the new season. I worked my bollocks off to try and get a place in the team. There'd been a few changes in the squad, with Tony Cunningham going and Lee Chapman coming in. Howard said to me before the first game that he was going to put Chappy in. He knew I'd been the best trainer all summer, but Lee was in. I was gutted but he was right. He said that Lee Chapman scored goals, in ugly ways sometimes, but he scored. I was sub for the first game against Forest but was lucky enough to come on and score. That was a dream come true, a lifetime Owl scoring in the first game back in Division One.

I knew my role that season. When I played it was as a target man to head it on or hold it up. I was a squad player who helped out when I could. The team spirit was tremendous! It was always fun to come in to training or for the games. I did score one more goal, a header against Coventry. It was my last goal for Wednesday. I'd had a right battle with Brian 'Killer' Kilcline that game and was really pleased to get one in at the Leppings Lane End.

How did the team respond to criticism about their tactics?

We knew that the press and even some opposition managers were slagging us off. Howard used it in team meetings. He'd bring in the latest match report and use it as motivation or inspiration. I thought the criticism of our tactics was really unfair. If Glenn Hoddle had been pinging 50-yard passes into the channels it would be seen as fantastic. Howard's tactics fitted the team. He played three centre-backs for example – Micky Lyons in the middle and a left- and right-footed player either side. The way we played was the way we needed to in order to win matches.

I remember one team talk, at Portsmouth I think. Howard told us that they had some speedy full-backs, a striker who would win every header, man mountains in central defence, midfielders who won every tackle and the best goalkeeper in the league. We were all muttering to ourselves about not having a chance that day. Howard paused … and said that he'd just given the team talk that Portsmouth's manager was giving to them! We felt about ten feet tall.

You moved on at the end of that season?

Yes, I moved on to Charlton. I played pretty much every minute in Division Two the next season. They were promoted to Division One and I didn't play much. I moved again to Leeds United and played regularly again in Division Two. I was lucky enough to play for Howard Wilkinson again and score a hat-trick against Sheffield United! That would only have been better if it were for the Owls! I played for a few other teams, ending up at Cardiff City.

You did return to the Owls for one final game though?

Yes, I did! That was 1995; I got a message to give Clive Baker at Wednesday a ring. I'd finished at Cardiff and, although I had a couple of other offers, I'd nothing really concrete lined up. Clive told me that Wednesday had entered the Intertoto Cup and were looking to get a team together as they didn't want to use the top first-team players. It would be a week's training and then the game against FC Basel. I thought it would be the perfect way to finish my career!

It nearly didn't happen as the club needed to sort a transfer from the Welsh FA for me. I'm pleased it did though, I'd had 16 years as a pro and started and finished my career with Wednesday. I'd had a couple of injuries by that stage, including quite a major operation on my neck. The operation had helped me get another year or two, but by 1995 I knew it was time to retire.

We still hear you commenting on the games.

Yes, I've worked for the club for several years on the iFollow service. I was asked to help by the former chairman Lee Strafford after he heard me do some bits on Radio Sheffield. I'm lucky at the minute [during lockdown] as I get to see and commentate on all the games even though the crowds aren't allowed in. From a lad who taught himself to read by going over the *Green 'Un* each week, to playing for the team, getting promoted, and playing and scoring in Division One, to now still being involved with the commentary and community work – it's been great!

Thanks John.

It's a pleasure. They were great times!

6.

1985: January to May

A NEW Year's Day trip to Old Trafford to face Ron Atkinson's Manchester United was the final league match of a congested festive period for the Owls. Sat in a healthy sixth place in the league, there seemed to be no worries about a Hogmanay hangover as the Owls took an early lead. In the 15th minute Imre Varadi outpaced the defence to plant a shot past Gary Bailey.

The United attack struggled to beat Wednesday's well-drilled offside trap and caused few problems for Martin Hodge. It was a surprise, therefore, when the Red Devils equalised on 63 minutes. Lawrie Madden's clearance took an unfortunate deflection off Alan Brazil and fell kindly for Mark Hughes to rifle past Hodge.

Eight minutes later United were awarded a penalty. Gordon Strachan, who had scored nine penalties already that season, took it but was denied by Hodge, who dived to his left and then recovered quickly to smother the rebound. Seven minutes from time the home defence left Varadi unmarked from an Andy Blair corner, and he powerfully headed in the winner.

'Wednesday are hard and efficient,' felt the United manager Atkinson. They were also the first team to win at Old Trafford that season and had earned ten points from 12 over the festive period. The win took the Owls back up to fifth in the table. 'Viva Varadi' indeed, as one newspaper headline had it.

With postponements relating to the weather and the Owls' continued involvement in the FA Cup, Wednesday played only one further league game in January. The fixture was a home game against West Bromwich Albion. Johnny Giles' Baggies team were on a good run of form and Howard Wilkinson was looking forward to the game, hoping it matched the return fixture in the West Midlands, which he described as 'one of the most exciting and high-quality draws I've seen'.

The game was again exciting, but this time it did not end in stalemate. Wednesday took the lead in the 38th minute as Lee Chapman seized on a deflection in the penalty area and tucked the ball home. Varadi had already put two snapshots wide at this stage – but he made amends in the second half, scoring his 15th goal of the season following a Chapman flick-on.

Brian Marwood and Varadi both came close before the Owls hit the woodwork twice in the closing minutes. It made little difference to the outcome, with the BBC reporting: 'It wasn't that Albion were poor, but that Wednesday were so very good. Rather like the Home Guard against a crack panzer division.' Wilkinson was looking upwards after a 12th league game without defeat. 'If you ask me straight, can we win the championship, the answer has to be – yes.'

Wednesday's next league game was a full three weeks later, when the Owls faced the daunting task of trying to record their first league double over Liverpool in 50 years. The Reds were the reigning European champions, and the fixture drew a huge crowd of over 48,000 to Hillsborough. Wilkinson was presented with the manager of the month award prior to kick-off following the Owls' unbeaten run in January, with four cup matches adding to the two in the league.

Wilkinson may have worried about the award leading to its regular curse as Liverpool's John Wark could have scored with a free header from Kenny Dalglish's early free kick. Ian Rush was set free after a Madden slip but fired wide after rounding Hodge. There was a stiff breeze blowing against the Owls, making it difficult for the team to play their usual game, and Wednesday were relieved to reach half-time with the score goalless.

In the 57th minute Wednesday's fortunes changed as Chapman flicked on a corner to Marwood, who found himself in plenty of room to bobble a shot past Bruce Grobbelaar. Liverpool continued to attack strongly; Wark shot wide and Dalglish clipped the top of the bar before the Owls gave away a free kick with five minutes to go. Dalglish pumped the free kick into the box where Mark Lawrenson was left free at the far post to head in the equaliser.

There was still time for Steve Nicol to blaze a great chance over for Liverpool just before the final whistle. Wilkinson avoided the curse of manager of the month award, but, as the *Sheffield Telegraph* put it, 'It is a measure of Wednesday's progress that a draw against the European champions is a disappointment.' The Owls dropped a place to fifth but would need to wait another three weeks before playing again in the league.

The team's next fixture was against Watford at Hillsborough. Wednesday had made a £260,000 club-record signing in the lead-up to the game, boyhood Owls fan Simon Stainrod joining from Queens Park Rangers. Unfortunately for Stainrod he was suspended for this game and the next, following a recent sending off for the Rs in a FA Cup tie against Ipswich. He was also cup-tied.

Wilkinson was clear that he would not tolerate indiscipline, saying, 'This side of his [Stainrod's] nature has too often been counter-productive. That said, we look forward to Simon demonstrating his considerable qualities over the next few years.' With Stainrod unavailable, Chapman and Varadi kept their places up front against Watford. The Owls started the game quickly, with Mark Smith's low drive being pushed away in the first minute.

As the half developed, though, Watford began to dominate with Wednesday looking sluggish. John Barnes' swerving free kick went just wide before Mike Lyons was booked for pulling Barnes back. Watford went ahead on 39 minutes, and it was Barnes who created the goal, holding off two challenges before crossing perfectly for Nigel Callaghan to drill home. Wednesday came out in the second half looking far more determined, with chances for Varadi, Lyons and Chapman before Marwood was denied a penalty when falling in the area.

Barnes was still a danger, though, putting two chances wide before an offside-looking Luther Blissett was denied by Hodge at point-blank range. Nine minutes from time the Owls got the reward their second-half performance deserved. Marwood crossed and Chapman set up Lyons to shoot home from eight yards.

The goal maintained Wednesday's record of scoring in every home match that season, but Wilkinson was not impressed with the performance. 'If we are to achieve anything this season ... there is no way that our first-half performance can come even near to acceptable.'

The Owls were back on home soil for their next fixture against Coventry City. This was the first of seven league and cup games that Wednesday were due to play in March as the fixture pile-up caused by cup runs and postponements began to catch up with the team. 'Roll on the day when no games at all are lost,' commented Wilkinson. Coventry were struggling in the lower reaches of the table but made a bright start and were unlucky to have a Cyrille Regis volley chalked off for offside. The Owls grew into the game and both Gary Shelton and Marwood had decent efforts at goal.

John Pearson, who replaced Chapman in the starting line-up, scored the only goal of the game on 36 minutes, heading in from Blair's free kick. City's goalkeeper Steve Ogrizovic was in his usual fine form against the Owls, making two further saves before the break. Coventry remained dogged in defence after the break, with chances at a premium, and very nearly snatched a point at the end with Terry Gibson firing off target from close range.

An uninspiring performance in a tie that Coventry's Kenny Hibbitt described as 'an awful game to play in'. The victory moved the Owls back up to fourth in the table ahead of a trip to Filbert Street to face Leicester City.

The game in the East Midlands saw the Owls debut of 18-year-old Icelandic international Siggi Jonsson. Recommended to the club by England boss Bobby Robson, Jonsson had signed for Wednesday at the start of the year, but a delay in obtaining a work permit meant he needed to wait until March for his debut.

Stainrod was named on the bench but would need to wait a little longer before making his opening appearance.

Wednesday had most of the play in the first half but needed to wait until the verge of half-time before breaking the deadlock. Chapman nodded down Marwood's cross and Varadi forced the ball home for his 20th goal of the season. In the second half two Jonsson corners brought good headers from Lyons and Varadi before Jonsson himself landed a cross-shot on to the bar. Then came a real turning point in the game as Peter Shirtliff's header was seemingly handled on the line. Referee Jim Borrett waved the Owls' furious appeals away.

Wednesday had been in charge until this moment, but minutes later an offside-looking Gary Lineker equalised, and the Owls collapsed with further goals from John O'Neill and Lineker inside the final ten minutes. Wilkinson was not too downhearted. 'That is as well as we have played for a long time,' he said. Wilkinson also had shared some sharp words about the referee after the game but was apologetic afterwards as 'my outburst … served no purpose other than to release my frustrations'.

The Owls' next opportunity to help Wilkinson ease his frustration was a home fixture the following Saturday against Luton Town. There was an experimental look to the Owls team, with Blair wearing the No.3 shirt but playing at right-back and Jonsson again named in midfield. Gavin Oliver, it was announced, would not play again that season with ankle ligament issues and Mel Sterland was also struggling on return from injury. Wednesday looked a little light on numbers at full-back.

Despite this, the Owls made an excellent start to the game, taking the lead in the seventh minute with Varadi slotting the ball home after Chapman's knock-on. Heavy snow made play difficult for the remainder of the half – though right on the whistle Varadi nearly added a second, his diving header cannoning back off the post.

The poor weather continued into the second half but did not stop Brian Stein hitting the post with an angled drive in the 54th minute, with Mick Harford following up to equalise with a simple tap-in. The scoring ended there and a disappointing day for the Owls was made worse when Lyons was forced to leave the field due to injury in the final minutes. 'For some reason or another we just did not perform,' commented Wilkinson afterwards.

The Owls were back in action four days later with a short trip to the City Ground to face Brian Clough's Nottingham Forest. Wilkinson named another remodelled team with Chris Morris coming in at right-back, Blair returning to midfield in place of Jonsson, and Stainrod (still to make his debut) again on the bench. Shelton was named captain on the day before his birthday. Regular skipper Lyons missed only his ninth game out of a possible 148 since he joined the club.

Another person celebrating a big day was Clough – the game marked his 50th birthday. The first half saw the Owls thwarted despite creating a series of chances. Shirtliff and Marwood had efforts cleared off the line while Shelton hit the post with a fine strike and sidefooted another opportunity wide. The second half saw the Owls remain on top but create fewer chances. 'We played very well,' said Wilkinson succinctly. Clough, on the other hand, said, 'It's my 50th birthday, but the way we are performing at home I feel more like 95!' The goalless draw kept Wednesday in sixth place in the table.

The Owls' plans to play seven games in March were curtailed somewhat by the postponement of a trip to Sunderland the following Saturday. This gave the team a ten-day break before a return to Hillsborough to meet former boss Jack Charlton and his Newcastle United team. Wilkinson was able to name a strong-looking team, including the returning Lyons. Charlton included Tony Cunningham, who was now enjoying Division One football after his move away from Hillsborough the previous summer.

The game proved to be a thriller. Marwood put the Owls ahead in the tenth minute, rising unmarked to head in Andy Blair's corner. Chapman had already missed a gilt-edged chance from a Marwood cross before Varadi set him up for a fine diving header and the second goal. Future Owls legend Chris Waddle reduced the arrears just before half-time with a header from a corner by another former Owl, Pat Heard.

The entertainment continued in the second half as a combination of Hodge and Nigel Worthington upended Waddle in the penalty area, allowing Peter Beardsley to equalise from the spot. Wednesday fired back with two goals in four minutes. The first saw Lyons head on Blair's corner for Chapman to nod in from close range. Then Varadi and Morris combined before the latter hit a beautiful cross for Shelton to tap in. Wednesday created further chances in what was probably their best home display of the season. 'It was a super game – terrific,' enthused Wilkinson.

The Owls were quickly back in action with a midweek trip to Carrow Road to face Norwich. The Canaries started well, scoring after only four minutes as Asa Hartford flicked on a John Deehan cross for Mark Barham to head past Martin Hodge. After ten minutes Wednesday were fortunate not to be two goals down when Deehan's finish was disallowed by referee Keith Miller because another player was in an offside position.

Wednesday equalised in the 31st minute, with Marwood firing in a cross that Paul Haylock turned into his own goal. Wednesday stepped up a gear in the second half and had a golden opportunity to win the game on 71 minutes. A penalty was awarded for handball in the area and up stepped Blair to take the kick. Unfortunately for the Owls he shot over the bar, gaining an unwanted double after also missing from the spot in the home fixture back in November. Stainrod made his belated debut in the final minutes, but the game petered out into a draw.

The following Saturday saw the Owls travel to Birmingham to face Aston Villa. Stainrod was named in the starting line-up for his full debut. Wednesday dominated much of the first half, with Chapman having three excellent chances, Smith heading over and Worthington foiled by keeper Kevin Poole. It was not all Wednesday, though, as Peter Withe hit the post early on before Villa took the lead on 27 minutes. Paul Rideout was the scorer, powerfully heading home from Mark Walters' cross.

The second half saw more Owls pressure before Villa scored twice more in the final 15 minutes, Brendan Ormsby notching at the far post when left unmarked from a corner and Allan Evans scoring from the spot after Hodge was adjudged to have brought down Rideout. 'The score flattered Villa,' commented Hodge after the game. Despite the heaviest defeat of the Owls' season to date, they remained in fifth place in the table and very much in the hunt for a European place. Next up was Manchester United under the Hillsborough floodlights the following Tuesday night.

The game against the Red Devils marked Owls skipper Lyons' 500th professional appearance. The Manchester team were not in the mood to give Wednesday an easy night though, dominating the first part of the game and gaining four corners inside eight minutes. It was against the run of play when Wednesday scored on 17 minutes. Blair's short free kick to Shirtliff led to a low shot from the Owls defender which keeper Steve Pears palmed out to Marwood, who laid it off for Chapman to tap home.

United continued to dominate, though, as the Owls struggled to get a handle on Danish winger Jesper Olsen. Wednesday came back into the game in the second half, with Stainrod forcing a save from Pears and Graeme Hogg almost turning the ball past his own keeper. Lyons almost marked his landmark game with a goal but headed a fine opportunity straight at Pears.

United fought back in the final minutes with further chances for Olsen, Mark Hughes and Bryan Robson, but Wednesday held on for a famous victory – and completed a league double over their Manchester rivals. The majority of the near 40,000 crowd were delighted, as was Wilkinson. 'This is probably our most welcome win of the season,' he said. 'It helps us back on the escalator.'

The Owls' relentless schedule continued four days later with a visit to Portman Road to face Ipswich Town. Chapman's winning goal against Manchester United had equalled his personal best for a season of 17. He was soon in the thick of things against Ipswich, attempting to surpass that best, with two opportunities going begging in the first ten minutes.

In the 21st minute Marwood was fouled in the area and a penalty was his reward. Marwood took the kick, scoring his first penalty for the club and his first goal away from Hillsborough. Wednesday stayed in command for the remainder of the half and for the period immediately after the interval. However, just after the hour mark, Ipswich's Dutch midfielder Romeo Zondervan made space down the left and crossed for Mich d'Avray to head in the equaliser.

Town's joy only lasted three minutes, though, before the Owls scored a bizarre winner. Smith's effort was cleared off the line only to bounce back into the net off the unfortunate keeper Paul Cooper, who was under pressure from Chapman. It was an own goal, although Chapman did claim afterwards to be 'not sure what exactly happened' and the Owls did initially credit him with the strike. He would need to wait a little longer for his personal record. The remainder of the game passed without incident, notable only for substitute Simon Mills' short appearance – his first game of the season.

The fixtures were still coming quickly and the following Tuesday evening the Owls travelled to Roker Park for a rescheduled game against Sunderland. Wednesday named an unchanged side against a Sunderland team who were struggling in the bottom three.

The match saw the Owls mostly on top, but with little in the way of clear-cut chances. Former Wednesday keeper Chris Turner made several smart saves, as did Hodge in the Owls goal as time was running out. It was not a memorable match, but as Wilkinson put it, 'We earned a point rather than lost two.' The Owls then had a week's gap before the next game, a home tie against QPR.

The game against Rangers saw two strikers face their former clubs. Stainrod started again for the Owls; up against him was Gary Bannister, who had left Hillsborough the previous summer. It was Stainrod who would finish the game the happier of the two. The first half was generally scrappy, with defences on top, until a minute before the interval. Chapman won a corner, which Andy Blair took and found Stainrod in plenty of space to open his account for the Owls with a crisp header. Bannister was involved in the Rangers equaliser after the break. His 56th-minute cross was not properly cleared and eventually found Mike Fillery, who scored with a low drive.

Only seven minutes had elapsed before Wednesday were awarded a somewhat controversial penalty when Blair was brought down in the box. Marwood took the kick and drove it home. Wednesday added a third on 80 minutes when Varadi, on as a substitute for Stainrod, raced clear to cross for Shelton. He passed to Blair, who stabbed home from close range. 'Wednesday deserved to win and I hope they make Europe,' commented Bannister afterwards. The win kept Wednesday in sixth place ahead of a trip to Highbury to face Arsenal.

Despite his goal in the QPR match, Wilkinson dropped Stainrod to the bench and replaced him with Varadi for the game in the capital. Both teams were competing for a place at the European table and there appeared some nervousness early on in a game that neither side really wanted to lose. A gusty wind made it difficult to play a passing game, or for a more direct approach to be effective. There were no chances of note in the first half for either side, nor in the opening minutes of the second period.

Wednesday almost broke the deadlock on 69 minutes when Marwood shot against the upright after rounding keeper John Lukic. Shelton had a shot which Lukic had to be at full stretch to save but Arsenal found the winner in the final minute. Charlie Nicholas and Paul Mariner combined well before Mariner drove a powerful shot past Hodge. While watching England manager Robson was impressed with the goal, a section of Arsenal fans may have been less so given Mariner's two-fingered salute in their direction after previous chants of 'what a load of rubbish' were aimed at him.

The season now entered May and the Owls still had four games remaining to play. The first of them was against top-of-the-table Everton at Hillsborough. Lyons was presented with an inscribed watch before the game on behalf of both clubs in recognition of his 500th professional game. Wilkinson recalled

John Ryan to the team for the first time since December as the Owls still struggled to fill the right-back slot.

A crowd of over 37,000 packed into Hillsborough to see Everton make the early running. The front cover of this book features a scene from this game and shows how full the Hillsborough Kop became with such an impressive crowd. There was some remaining needle from the game at Goodison Park, with Peter Reid booed every time he came near the ball. Madden clattered into Reid with an early challenge and was perhaps fortunate not to be booked. Andy Gray and Graeme Sharp both had early chances saved and blocked before the Toffees took the lead in the 26th minute. Gray crossed for Sharp to score with a seemingly miscued effort.

Despite the setback, it was the Owls who dominated for the remainder of the half. Lyons headed across goal and Morris shot straight at Everton keeper Neville Southall. It was Southall who then produced a simply incredible save to prevent Varadi scoring from six yards out. Smith tested Southall again, with Marwood crashing the rebound against the crossbar.

The Owls had further chances in the second half, coming closest to scoring with Smith's late header clipping the bar. Southall made a series of other stops in a display that the *Liverpool Echo* described simply as 'world class'. The *Sunday Express* was more effusive: 'Southall's save ... was the best I have seen all season or likely to see in the next five.' Wilkinson felt that 'apart from actually scoring we did ever so well'. Everton had brief hopes that the win would seal the championship until results from elsewhere put that to bed for another week.

However well Wednesday played, that was two defeats in a row against opposition from the top of the table. The Owls only had a two-day break before travelling to London to face another bogey team in a Bank Holiday Monday clash. That team was Chelsea, and despite the short turnaround, Howard Wilkinson made only one change to the team – bringing in Pearson for Chapman, who was still waiting for the goal he needed to beat his personal milestone.

Wednesday started well and took the lead on 13 minutes as Ryan crossed from the right for Smith to head home. The lead was short-lived, though, and as Owls fans were still celebrating, Pat Nevin launched a ball into the box for Kerry Dixon to head home the equaliser. Chelsea dominated the remainder of the half, with David Speedie hitting the post and Nevin having a shot cleared off the line. Wednesday's luck ran out in the second half as Paul Canoville set up Dixon in the 75th minute to round Hodge and score an astonishing 35th goal of the season.

There was still time for Lyons to have a goal ruled out for offside and Shelton to hit the bar with a header. There were no more goals, though, as the Owls fell to a third defeat in a row, dropping to seventh in the table and effectively out of contention for a European place.

There were still two games left of the season. The first of those fixtures was a home tie against West Ham United. The Hammers were in a relegation battle and needed points. Wednesday still had a very faint hope of a European place, and Wilkinson's competitiveness to drive them on. The manager brought Chapman back into the team, with Sterland starting for the first time since February and Worthington returning at left-back in a remodelled backline.

Wednesday took an early lead, with Blair's sixth-minute corner headed in by Chapman, who finally scored the goal to beat his personal best for one season. Just after half an hour the Owls doubled their lead, Chapman taking advantage of some uncertainty from keeper Phil Parkes to nip in front of him and nod home Madden's cross. It was Chapman's 19th goal of a fruitful campaign. West Ham had a golden opportunity to pull a goal back midway through the second half as Hodge pulled down Paul Goddard in the area. Hodge immediately made amends, though, by pushing Ray Stewart's penalty kick for a corner.

Tony Cottee did pull a goal back for the Hammers on 77 minutes, rounding Sterland and firing low and hard past Hodge. The scoring was over, though, with the Owls the victors. West

Ham had enough games left to claim the points needed to avoid relegation.

The final game of the Owls' season involved another trip to London, this time to White Hart Lane to face Tottenham Hotspur. Spurs had lost five of their last six home games, had already qualified for Europe and had lost their previous game 5-1 to Watford. Any hopes that Wednesday would have an easy ride were dashed as Tottenham took a 24th-minute lead when Chris Hughton marauded down the left before crossing for John Chiedozie to lay off for Mark Falco to finish.

The match was not a straightforward one for Spurs, either, as Wednesday remained full of fight and energy if without obvious chances. The result hung in the balance until the final minute of the game when Glenn Hoddle's skilful burst ended with a foul in the box by Sterland. Hoddle put the penalty kick past Hodge with almost the last kick of the game.

The Owls finished the season in a creditable eighth place in the table, three points shy of the European place that Southampton sat in. They had won 17 of the 42 league games, scoring 58 goals and claiming a total of 65 points. The *Green Un's* Paul Thompson commented: 'Anti-climax surrounding Sheffield Wednesday's narrow failure to qualify for Europe cannot cloud the verdict that the Owls have had a great season.'

As it turned out, Wednesday would not have played in Europe anyway following the ban given to English clubs over the summer. Wednesday, and the rest of the league, were not to know that at the time, of course. There was much to be proud of in the Owls' displays over the season. The team had an eight-match unbeaten run ended in October, and a 12-match one stopped in March. They conceded more than two goals in a game only twice all season and no club was able to do the double over the Owls.

Youngsters such as Morris and Oliver progressed into the first team and, in the main, Howard Wilkinson's signings settled impressively and improved the squad. Chapman and Varadi proved to be regular and reliable goalscorers, with many other members of the squad also chipping in – none more so than Brian Marwood, who scored a round dozen as he stepped up to Division One with aplomb. The Owls maintained a positive disciplinary record and the fans also did their bit – being named by the *Daily Star* as the best-behaved supporters in the country. The pitch that was relaid the previous summer stood up well and, as Wilkinson turned down a big-money approach from Saudi Arabia, it was clear that he and Owls supporters had much still to look forward to at Hillsborough.

7.

An Interview with Lawrie Madden

LAWRIE MADDEN was already a hugely experienced central defender when he joined the Owls in the summer of 1983. Having postponed the start of his professional career in order to complete his degree, Madden played a handful of league games for Mansfield Town before a two-year stint with non-league Boston United. He returned to league football with Charlton Athletic, playing over 100 games for the Addicks, before a move to Millwall led to another 47 appearances.

After a brief trial at Hillsborough he signed an initial two-year contract that began an eight-year spell with the Owls. He played a total of 215(+15) games for Wednesday, scoring five goals. In our two seasons Madden made 53(+1) appearances with one goal. Madden now shares his time between Spain and the UK. We spoke in the summer of 2021.

Tell me how you came to sign for the club.

It was Howard Wilkinson. I'd played with him at Boston, so we knew each other. He'd actually approached me to join him at Notts County. I was out of contract so looking for my next club. Before it was sorted, though, Howard was poached by Sheffield Wednesday. So for a little while it was up in the air. He soon asked me to come on trial at Hillsborough. I think he wanted to spend some time finding out what he'd got there in terms of the players. Before long he offered me a contract and I signed up for two years.

How did you find the training?

It was tough. There was lots of running, but we bought into it. Results helped – we were winning! Also, many of the players, myself included, had a point to prove. We perhaps hadn't quite made it elsewhere, so we were hungry and motivated for success. Howard was ahead of his time in lots of ways. In terms of his organisation, preparation, attention to detail, focus on our diets and much else, he was a pioneer.

How about the tactics?

I said that Howard wanted to understand the players he had to work with. I think in that summer of 1983 he realised what an athlete he had with Mel Sterland and that he had some great central defenders with Mick Lyons, Peter Shirtliff, Mark Smith and others. He went for the three centre-backs system with wing-backs to make best use of what he had. It was a new system to me – he hadn't used it at Boston. I think it was new to Howard as well as I know his Notts County team used to pass it around the back four before moving forward. These things go in phases or circles in sport though, and Howard knew what he wanted from the players he had. It wasn't long-ball football either. If we had just hoofed the ball forward it would have just come straight back at us. It was sophisticated, it was worked on and it was practised. Our aim in our positioning and play was to get the ball behind the defence and then squeeze. Everything was practised through drills and repeats. Those sessions, and the ones for set pieces, could last for hours! It meant that we knew what we needed to do though.

I'll give you an example. We practised zonal marking, including from corners and free kicks. I think I am correct in saying that the first goal we conceded from a set piece in the 1983/84 season was against Swansea in January. We won that game 6-1 anyhow!

How did you find Howard Wilkinson's management style?

I said he was organised. He'd break down the season into blocks of games – five-match mini-seasons. He'd work out how many points we needed to gain from each block. He was also an early adopter of match-analysis techniques – how far players had run, how long the ball spent in various areas of the pitch. As an aside, I completed my master's degree when I was with Wednesday. My dissertation was about match analysis of the 1983/84 season. It showed that there was a direct link between the percentages of getting the ball in the right areas and success on the pitch. Nowadays, of course, every team does it – through Prozone and computerised methods – but Howard was one of the first.

He was also big on motivational speeches in the dressing room. Alongside Micky Lyons, who was the heart and soul of the team, we'd really get psyched up for the matches. I played under Ron Atkinson later, who was much more relaxed about things. Both were hugely successful managers, so it just proves the point that there is more than one way to skin a cat! Howard was desperate to win something with Wednesday, by the way. I felt that the cup competitions offered the best chance of that. Ron managed it when Howard didn't quite.

You stayed at Hillsborough for eight years?

I did, and I was very grateful to Ron Atkinson for granting me a testimonial. Howard, Ron and Dave Bassett also spoke at various functions in support of that. I'm grateful to Dave also for bringing a Sheffield United team across for a testimonial game. I played for Wolves after leaving Wednesday and I'm told that I'm still their oldest-ever player!

How about nowadays, what keeps you busy in retirement?

After finishing football I ran a restaurant for a while in Crosspool, Sheffield. I also worked in the media. I wrote for the *News of the World*, reported for Sky Sports and worked pitchside for the international coverage of the Premier League. I had a bout of ill health a few years ago though, so nowadays I divide my time between Spain and back home and try and enjoy each day as it comes.

Thanks Lawrie.

No problem at all. Good luck with the book. Others might disagree with me, but I think that the period from 1983 through until the early 1990s was probably the best in Sheffield Wednesday's long history. There were some great times.

8.

The Reserves and Youth Team

THE OWLS' recruitment at youth level followed a tried and tested format. The club would scout players from the local area and sign them on youth forms while still at school. These players would often play for Middlewood Rovers during their final year in education before signing at apprentice level on a two-year contract. Five or six players would sign on those terms, and any who progressed well enough would be offered a professional deal during their apprenticeship (with pay of around £60 per week). Many players appeared for the youth team while initially on schoolboy terms.

The Owls were also beginning to make use of the government's YTS scheme in this period – with some youngsters signed on an initial one-year basis that way (they were paid £25 per week). The Owls' youth team played in the Northern Intermediate League and entered the FA Youth Cup. The reserves played in the Central League. Both the 'Central' and 'Northern' descriptions were something of a misnomer, with the reserves facing teams as far north as Newcastle United and the youth team travelling as far east as Lincoln and Grimsby.

In common with much else at Hillsborough, Howard Wilkinson encouraged a professional and effective approach in the development of young players. He registered the club as an FA Centre of Excellence for young players in 1984. This meant that the Owls could select a certain number of promising 11-year-olds to train with them for an hour a week and longer in the holidays.

Mike Lyons was given some responsibility for the scouting and coaching of the schoolboys.

By early 1985, 22 young players were selected to be part of the scheme. Coach and scout Clive Baker said at the time, 'There are some very useful lads and it's a question of keeping their development going with the right sort of practice.' Among the youngsters was Paul Smith, son of Owls physio Alan, and a future Wednesday physio himself. Baker and Lyons worked alongside Robin Wray, who combined his job as head of PE at Barnsley College with coaching the youth teams at Hillsborough. Wray also supported the coaching of the reserves and travelled with both teams.

Players would sign youth forms at 14 or 15 years old. They were often scouted playing for local boys' teams such as Sheffield or Handsworth Boys. Many young players at that age would be watched and would train with other local teams, including Sheffield United. There could be stiff competition for the signatures of the most promising players. In the earlier part of our period, Charlie Wain and John Harris were the scouts responsible for identifying players for the Owls.

Sometimes, though, some more stardust was required to encourage youngsters to sign up. Peter Rinkcavage told me how club captain Lyons came to his house to help persuade him to sign youth forms for Wednesday ahead of the Blades. In Peter's case, as a boyhood Owls fan, the decision was not too difficult to make! Some players, if they did not follow this traditional route, would be asked to come on trial. That was the case with Dylan Kerr, who was spotted playing for his dad's Saturday league team – Swinton Rovers.

On signing youth forms the players would train twice a week, with a focus on ball work and technique. Many such players appeared for Middlewood Rovers on Sundays, though they would often continue to play for their existing youth team as well. Middlewood Rovers were coached by Albert Phelan, who went on to have a lengthy career in the Owls' youth set-up – coaching the youth team that reached the FA Youth Cup Final in 1991 and remaining with the club until 2001.

Middlewood Rovers had a degree of success themselves, winning a Redgates Youth League and Cup double in 1985. Baker joined the club as coach and scout in February 1984, a job that he felt offered him the 'best of both worlds, because I enjoy coaching and I enjoy looking at matches and players'. Baker would later become the club's first academy director in 1998. In December 1984, Michael Hennigan joined the coaching staff to complete Wilkinson's support team.

Youth players who did well in training and in the Middlewood Rovers set-up were often introduced to the Northern Intermediate League while still as school. Games were usually on a Saturday morning. The youth-team line-up would often remain relatively unchanged from game to game. The reserves were more of a mix and match, with players who were stepping up from the youth team, returning from injury or out of the first-team picture all making appearances.

Both teams were relatively successful on the pitch. The youth team finished ninth (out of 15) and then third (out of 18) in our two seasons. They also reached the final of the Northern Intermediate Cup in 1986. The reserves finished sixth (out of 18) in both campaigns.

The Northern Intermediate Cup Final was a two-legged affair in the spring of 1986. Newcastle qualified for the final by beating Sheffield United, thus denying the Owls the opportunity to battle for Steel City bragging rights. Wednesday's youngsters' path to the final took in victories over Huddersfield, Middlesbrough and Rotherham.

The first game was played at Hillsborough on 24 April with the return leg at St James' Park six days later. The second fixture was the seventh game in eight days for the Wednesday reserve and youth teams, following a fixture pile-up for both squads. Newcastle had issues of their own, with six of their team in the first leg also featuring for their reserves the previous evening. Newcastle's team featured some talented players, including Paul Stephenson and Joe Allon who had already broken through into their first team.

Rinkcavage remembers the pre-match team talk featuring Hennigan mock kneeling on a couch, as if praying for heavenly assistance, before informing his team that Newcastle would be just as worried about the Owls line-up. Hennigan had a point as the Owls were facing a strong Newcastle set-up. The north-easterners had won the FA Youth Cup the previous season with a team featuring a young Paul Gascoigne and were known for their strength.

Newcastle were perhaps fortunate to escape from Hillsborough with a goalless draw. Allon was quoted as being 'quietly confident' of success in the second leg. He had reason to be confident as goals from Jeff Wrightson, Rutherford and Allon himself saw Newcastle to a comfortable 3-0 victory and dashed the Owls' hopes of cup success.

The set-up was also successful in terms of bringing players through and into the first team. The line-up for the first youth-team fixture of our period (an impressive 5-3 victory over Rotherham United) featured four players who would go on to play first-team football for the Owls: Kevin Pressman, Tony Gregory, Des Hazel and Carl Bradshaw. Later that season Wayne Jacobs, Dean Barrick and Siggi Jonsson would also play for the youth team. All would later make the first team. The addition of Ian Knight, David Johnson and Marlon Beresford the following season means that ten players from the youth squads would make their way into the first team over the coming seasons.

Beresford took the longest route, leaving the club in 1992 without having made an appearance, only to return in 2001 to play between the sticks four times. Jonsson had been signed from Iceland with the first team in mind. Work permit issues and the need to maintain fitness meant he played for the youth team before making his first-team debut.

Darren Bradshaw and Kerr never made the Sheffield Wednesday first team but did go on to lengthy professional careers elsewhere. It might be pushing the point to describe the process as a conveyor belt from youth team to Division One, but the Owls certainly had a more than reasonable level of success.

The youth and reserve teams were expected to train as hard as the first team and to follow similar tactics. Jay Maybury, who signed as a youngster in 1984, told me in 2021 that both the youth and reserve teams were 'always the fittest in our league', and that in training we 'ran and ran', with one example of an eight-mile run following two games in two days being described to Maybury by coach Hennigan as 'active rest'!

Kerr loved the running and felt that he was kept on at the club at least partly because Wilkinson recognised him as a good runner. It did not always leave him as the most popular with the professionals though – with Kerr describing to me how he 'used to get beaten up on the bus home for being the best runner!'

The reserves would often be used by Wilkinson in shadow exercises for the first team on the day before a game. Wilkinson was a 'stickler for detail', as Maybury told me, and those exercises – often practising set pieces – could last for 'hours'! Maybury described one incident where having been pushed in training all day, the reserves then faced Sheffield United. A 'knackered' Owls team lost 4-0.

Rinkcavage enjoyed the running – 'I could run all day,' he told me – but did find that the training overall 'lacked fun'. It could be a long and hard day's work for the youngsters. Gregory told me that on initially signing for the club he was living in Doncaster. A 6.15am alarm was needed to take the varying forms of public transport that would get him to Hillsborough in time for his 8.30 start. A tough day of sorting the professional players' gear, training and then cleaning up and sorting the laundry followed. The youngsters could only leave when Hennigan was happy with their work.

Gregory often left at around 5pm and arrived home at 7pm ready for a night's sleep and to do it all again. This routine took it out of him so much that one day he was found asleep in the boot room by the Owls' assistant boss Peter Eustace. He took a telling-off but was soon found digs close to the stadium along with two other youngsters, Hazel and Richard Brown.

Kerr ran through the jobs that the youngsters were expected to perform, which included: hand-scrubbing the dressing room and showers; cleaning any dirt out of the AstroTurf; ensuring that the boots of the professionals were perfect; cleaning the cars of the management on Friday afternoon and acting as ball boys during home games. This work, along with training and evening games, could mean a working day that lasted from 7am until 10pm. As Rinkcavage put it to me, the set-up was 'a hard school, designed so that only the toughest would survive'.

Hennigan was a key figure in that education. Appointed by Wilkinson to coach and train the reserves and youth team in 1984, he became a hugely influential character in the lives and careers of those he worked with. Hennigan had been on the Owls' books as a youngster but never made the first team. He did play a handful of first-team games for Southampton and Brighton before moving to South Africa with Bloemfontein. His coaching career was also varied, taking in posts at the Owls, Leeds United and Rotherham United, along with short spells as caretaker manager at Blackpool and with the Malawi national team. He was also assistant manager to Nigel Worthington at Blackpool for a time.

By the early 1970s Hennigan's football career had hit something of an impasse. He was working for the Central Electricity Generating Board and, although he was playing at amateur level and studying for his coaching badges, he was out of the professional game. The slow route back came through non-league football, with Hennigan coaching at Matlock Town before coaching and then managing at Spalding.

The Owls played Spalding in a friendly in 1984 and before long Wilkinson contacted Hennigan to offer him a job. At Hillsborough, Hennigan 'followed Wilkinson's methods to a T', according to Jay Maybury. Knight confirmed to me that Hennigan followed similar tactics to those of Wilkinson, with both the youth and reserve teams using the 5-3-2 formation that Wilkinson favoured and being encouraged to play in a similar, direct manner to the first team.

Kerr told me that 'Michael and Howard Wilkinson were basically the same person', and that 'Mick was a winner'. Dave Simpson describes Hennigan in his book *The Last Champions* as 'very much a Wilkinson disciple'. Interviewed in the same book, Hennigan admitted that 'I loved Wilkinson 'cos he brought me into football when I was nearly 43 … anybody who does you a favour like that … you're forever gonna' like 'em.'

Hennigan could certainly be a hard taskmaster. Gregory told me the story of how the youngsters were at Hillsborough until late one evening – with Hennigan suggesting to them afterwards that they should have knocked on his door to ask to go. The following evening they did just that, only for Hennigan to find some 'dust' in the freshly cleaned showers and insist that Gregory and others get changed again and run up and down the Kop as a punishment!

Kerr remembered the punishment for such infringements as even harsher: 'Five times up and down the Kop with a lap of the pitch each time.' His character was well respected by those who trained under him, with each player I talked to speaking highly of him. Kerr put it this way: 'Mick worked us hard, but he taught me what it was to be a footballer and importantly what it was to be a man.' Jon Newsome, who trained under Hennigan for the Owls as a youngster and later at Leeds United, is quoted in *The Last Champions* as saying, 'I had a massive amount of respect for Michael Hennigan.'

Rinkcavage felt that Hennigan was a 'character' doing the job that Wilkinson had asked him to do. Michael was quoted on his appointment as saying, 'I see my job as helping give the lads good habits in football and away from football, looking after them and being their football father.'

The research for this book showed me clearly what an influential figure Hennigan was. I felt it important to try and find him and talk through his times at Hillsborough. With a little detective work and the help of some of those who had been coached by him and who had spoken to him previously, a message was passed to Michael on my behalf. I was told, given his age and memory issues, not to expect a positive reply. However, a few days later my email inbox pinged with a response from Michael's partner Sonia, agreeing to arrange a date and time for me to see them. I was delighted.

A few weeks later I travelled to their house in the picturesque Sheffield suburb of High Green loaded with questions and pictures. I received a very warm and friendly welcome from Michael and Sonia. Michael greeted me with a firm handshake and looked me straight in the eye – evidence, I felt, of the kind of straight-talking coach I imagined him to have been. Sonia was friendly, attentive and clearly very knowledgeable about football, the people she had found herself among, and about Michael and his career.

Along with a steady supply of coffee and biscuits, Sonia had also arranged for Michael's friend Joe Dunn to come along. Joe had scouted for the Owls in the mid-1980s, supported the club's community work and taken his coaching badges under the tutelage of Wilkinson. Joe was intelligent, with a clear-sighted view of how Wilkinson had developed the Owls and how Michael had worked alongside him. I found myself, therefore, alongside three people with a mass of knowledge about football, the Owls, Michael Hennigan and Howard Wilkinson. I counted myself very lucky indeed.

The conversation ranged across a wide variety of topics. Sonia popped in and out, along with Joe helping fill in any gaps in Michael's recollections. Sonia recounted how Michael had joined the Owls. 'He had a call from Howard Wilkinson to see him at the club – he said he didn't know what for. So he went in his dirty overalls and had a talk with him. Turns out it was an interview for the youth job!'

She laughed at the recollection before continuing, 'Howard still says that Michael is the only person to take a pay cut to join him. He'd asked how much Michael was on so he could match it. Michael told him £7,000, but he'd forgotten the extra he got for his coaching work!' Michael stood up at this point. 'Let me show you what happened when I left Hillsborough,' he said with a glint in his eye. He walked slowly across his living room. 'Imagine this is a corridor and Howard's coming towards me.' He moved forward a few steps then copied Wilkinson's voice. 'I'm off to Leeds on Monday, are tha' coming?' Sonia and Joe both laughed at this as Michael recalled his simple reply: 'Ah.'

'Michael and Howard were very close,' Joe explained to me. 'They had this very South Yorkshire, very dry humour and would often talk in a kind of code with each other.' Joe continued, 'Michael was very helpful to Howard – he knew something in detail about every player in non-league.'

Michael interjected at this point, remembering one success. 'Shutty, I had him at Spalding,' he said. 'I recommended him to Wednesday. I remember Peter Eustace questioning it, but I knew that he would score goals at any level.' Joe continued, 'He knew the strengths and weaknesses of each player, and he was right about Carl Shutt!'

The conversation moved on to Michael's work with the youth team at Hillsborough. I had brought some pictures of various teams and players. 'Yes, remember him, I remember him, he was trouble!' chatted Michael, remembering those with whom he had worked. 'It beats working for a living,' was his response to my question about how hard he worked the youngsters at Hillsborough. 'I wanted them to understand how lucky they were to be in a job where they could earn huge amounts doing something they enjoyed.'

He went on, with a smile, 'We led from the front anyway, both me and Howard. We'd lead the running and expect the players to keep up!' Sonia reminded me of Michael's previous work before moving into football full-time. 'He'd worked in dirty, difficult jobs,' she said. 'Even in football, he'd run a team for a Rotherham pub called Joker. He'd spend Friday and Saturday nights going round the local pubs making sure the players were set for the game.' I had with me a 1984 article from the *Green 'Un* where Michael described his hopes of being a father figure to the Owls youngsters. He smiled at the thought and agreed that was what he had tried to do.

The talk of Joker led Sonia to recall some of the places where Michael had played and coached. 'I started at Wednesday,' he told me, 'but never made the team. I moved on to Brighton and Southampton and played a few games. One of them paid £5,000 for me at the time.'

Sonia took up the story, 'He moved over to South Africa next, then back to Sligo Rovers in Ireland.' Michael laughed at that thought, with Sonia reminding him that he 'fell out with the priest over there!' It was from there that Michael dropped out of the professional game before his climb back through non-league and an eventual move to Hillsborough. 'He moved to Turkey for a while,' added Sonia, 'after finishing up with Leeds. Turkey were trying to join UEFA, so Michael went over there to help train up their coaches.' Remembering the thought, she added, 'He didn't see much of the culture though – they flew him in, taxi to the training ground, hotel full of English people and plane home!'

I noticed a couple of African-style ornaments on the mantelpiece. 'He was coach of the Malawi national team for a few months,' Sonia told me. 'It was tough going though; there was corruption and, although the local FA had money, none seemed to reach the team.'

'We've met some lovely people through football,' Sonia went on. 'Michael was one of only two people from football – along with Dave Bassett – to be invited to Vinnie Jones' wedding. He's a lovely man, nothing at all like the image that's shown in the media.'

Michael could be very single-minded in his pursuit of football success as one further story shows. 'The Queen was in South Yorkshire,' Sonia told me. 'Me and a friend went to see her in Barnsley.' She continued, 'She was coming to Sheffield that afternoon and Michael told me that she was coming to the club so I should come down.' It seems that Michael had been focused on his work and was not fully aware that the Queen was at Hillsborough to officially open the new Kop roof! 'I sat in the directors' box,' continued Sonia, 'and noticed that lots of the other women were in their best outfits – hats and all.'

She went on, 'Sam Wilkinson, Howard's wife, was in front of me, and before I knew it, in came the Queen – two rows in front. She's tiny, and just like someone's gran! There's a picture somewhere of me behind the Queen, not quite dressed up enough!'

Joe added, 'He was absolutely focused on football, I'll give you an example of what he was like.' He pulled a photograph out to show me. 'Here's Michael in the close season coaching eight-year-olds as part of a summer scheme. He didn't need to do it, but he was the last off the field and first one on. He lived for it.'

By this time, I had been at the Hennigan's house for over three hours. It was coming up to time for me to leave. Sonia and Joe both kindly lent me some photographs and Michael shared another firm handshake and large smile. Michael ended by saying, 'This used to be Howard's house, you know.' Sonia confirmed as much, adding that, 'Lee Chapman used to live over the back. We used to see Leslie Ash putting the bins out, even when he denied to the press that they were seeing each other!' It seems apt to me that, given the closeness of their personal and professional relationship, Michael and Howard both lived in the same house. As Joe told me, 'They were like two peas in a pod.'

After working with Michael Hennigan, the next step for many of the youth team was into the reserves. The Central League in which the reserves featured was a man's league. It featured the second-string teams of some of the top clubs of the day, including Liverpool, Everton, Aston Villa, Leeds United and Sheffield United. Clubs used their reserve team for several reasons, including giving match practice to experienced first-team players who were out of the team due to injury or form.

This meant that youngsters coming into the team could find themselves playing against top-class opposition at imposing venues. Jay Maybury told me how his reserve debut was against a Manchester United team featuring Clayton Blackmore, Frank Stapleton and others. Maybury replaced the injured Lawrie Madden for that game at short notice and soon found himself tangling with Remi Moses. Tony Gregory remembers how Maybury gave as good as he got in that exchange!

Peter Rinkcavage remembers being 'taught a lesson' by Liverpool's John Wark. Rinkcavage was tasked with marking Wark in midfield that evening but 'never got near' the 'fit, strong and dynamic' Scot who 'beat me to the ball in both boxes and taught me a lesson about what it meant to be a professional footballer'. Dylan Kerr also remembers playing against a Manchester United team this time featuring Lou Macari. The 16-year-old Kerr put in a strong tackle on Macari. 'I nailed him,' he told me. 'Then Macari – who was an excellent player coming to the end of his career – grabbed me by the collar and told me it was a great tackle!'

Reserve-team fixtures at Hillsborough were accompanied by an official programme that was effectively a double-sided sheet of A4 paper listing the two teams with some brief information about upcoming games and ticket and travel information. Official crowd figures for Central League games seem lost in the mists of time – but supporters who were there estimate them in the 300–400 range, with perhaps 700 for fixtures against Sheffield United.

Some away fixtures had far bigger crowds – with Kerr remembering 'what felt like 40,000 at Old Trafford – they were collecting tokens to get tickets for the FA Cup Final'. Members of the club's Young Owls supporters' group could attend home fixtures for free, although, as one fan remembered, they may also have found entertainment running up and down the gangway that ran behind the uncovered seats of the South Stand.

Other attendees would include scouts from various other clubs. As my late father was friends with one such scout, I would often attend reserve games with him. At the time he would point out other scouts and ex-players. I only wish now that the young version of me had paid a little more attention to who they were!

Youth-team games gained detailed reports in the programmes of 1984/85 (courtesy of Tony Smith of the *North Sheffield Independent*). By 1985/86 the reports for both youth- and reserve-team games were much shorter and much less consistent. The local press would feature brief reports also with longer pieces for games against local rivals. The Owls' 5-2 victory over local rivals United gained a lengthy review in the *Sheffield Star*, with the headline 'Shutt Hat-Trick Settles Derby' in honour of the striker's three-goal salvo.

Gregory and Ian Knight were among Owls players to gain international recognition in our period. Gregory joined Kevin Pressman and Carl Bradshaw in the England youth set-up while Knight was soon to be capped by England's Under-21 team.

Wilkinson recognised this success, commenting in his end-of-season notes in 1986 that 'it reflects great credit on the players and my staff who have worked with them'. At the hard school Rinkcavage referred to, some of the students were beginning to graduate with honours.

The tough education was not one without any humour, though. Apprentices were given jobs to do alongside their training and matches. These jobs included cleaning the boots of the first-team squad, collecting balls in training, organising the laundry and collecting and distributing kit. All of these offered opportunities for the more mischievous among the youngsters to provide their own entertainment.

Maybury told me the tale of how some in the youth team went on the trail of a missing ball after training. The ball had been kicked over the barriers at the back of the Middlewood Road training ground, and after hunting for it for a while the youngsters decided to take the shortest route back to Hillsborough where they were due later that evening to help at a first-team game. That route was straight down the River Don!

'We decided to play army,' Maybury told me. 'We found some sticks and brushes and acted as if we were undercover soldiers!' It all seemed good fun until the group realised on their arrival at Hillsborough that one of their members was missing. Maybury and his friends hunted around the stadium looking more and more frantically for their missing colleague as time ticked round towards the evening game. Maybury picks up the story. 'Bert McGee [the Wednesday chairman] came down the tunnel showing a group of the bigwigs around and the next we hear is Sean Hardy [the missing youngster] running down the tunnel making Tarzan noises! He slipped over, presumably still wet from the river, and ended up flat on his back with his brush facing the chairman. We scarpered!' Readers might be relieved to learn that the youngsters did manage to find the missing ball, though.

Some of the fun was away from the football. Josephine's nightclub and restaurant at Barkers Pool in the city centre was a popular haunt for players of all ages. The club had provided a champagne dinner for 40 players, wives and girlfriends and club management following promotion in 1984. The fun continued into our years. Kerr admitted to me that, 'I was out maybe three or four times a week.' The mid-1980s was a time when Sheffield was a centre of pop culture and, as Kerr said to me, 'I felt both like a superstar and starstruck – I was being invited out by Joanne and Susan from the Human League, meeting ABC and Heaven 17. It was a great time.' Kerr had yet to make his professional debut and agreed that 'maybe it did affect my football!'

The players also had great fun on a trip to Bochum in the then West Germany in 1985. Bochum and Sheffield were celebrating the 35th anniversary of their 'twinning' as cities and the Owls sent a group of 12 juniors and four apprentices to play three matches on a six-day trip. The group were accompanied by Hennigan, club director Ernest Barron and various local dignitaries.

The players stayed with local families, which, as Kerr told me, was 'difficult as they didn't speak English and I didn't speak a word of German!' Despite this, and the lengthy coach and ferry journey needed to get there, the youngsters managed to have a good time. They lost 2-0 to a strong, older Wattenscheid team but won their other matches (5-0 vs Langendreer and 3-0 vs Bochum). Off the pitch the players only met twice as a group but made the most of it. One free evening was spent gaining an education in Bochum's red-light district. Alongside the strippers and sex shows, one unnamed youngster managed to get his head stuck in a peep-hole machine! On the final evening, the players were invited to a civic reception to celebrate Sheffield's ongoing relationship with Bochum. The free alcohol on offer was irresistible to some but also meant that the journey back on coach and ferry was a little 'messy'. As Kerr put it to me, 'I didn't get my head out of toilet for the whole ferry journey back!' Gregory remembers it as 'a dreadful journey from start to finish!'

Other examples of fun and games included players using the large laundry basket for collecting kit as a makeshift sledge – testing how quickly it could carry one of them down the steps in the South Stand! Taking responsibility for the first-team's boots provided further opportunity for mischief, with an unnamed youngster deliberately painting a senior pro's boots with some larger than needed stripes in advance of a televised game.

Mistakes and misdemeanors were dealt with by a 'court case' system. This involved one of the more senior youngsters sitting as judge (often with a mop on their head) and delivering a verdict on whatever punishment was deemed appropriate. The 'defendant' was effectively found guilty before being put on trial. This system worked well for minor issues as it involved some humour and team bonding.

It perhaps went a little too far when the Owls took a friendly XI to play at Lincoln United. One of the youngsters was responsible for bringing various items of kit, including shin pads. On arrival at Lincoln, it became clear that the pads were still in Sheffield. The Owls team including first-team players Mel Sterland and Siggi Jonsson made do with shin pads fashioned from the pamphlets held on the team coach advertising summer holidays! The court afterwards saw Carl Bradshaw as judge allocating a flip-flop slap on each hand – times 30 – for the unfortunate youngster who forgot the pads. One for each shin pad that was missing. 'His hands were throbbing for a week,' as one witness told me.

The harshness of the previous punishment notwithstanding, every former apprentice, youth- and reserve-team player I contacted spoke highly of the relationships and friendships they built during their time at Hillsborough. Some of those friendships have lasted a lifetime, with Maybury and Rinkcavage acting as best men at each other's wedding and godfathers for their children. Others told me about the strong bonds made between players and the positive atmosphere engendered by Hennigan and others.

Gregory illustrates that last point with a story of bringing his guitar to the club to pass the time and soon being required by Wilkinson and Hennigan to stand on a chair in the dressing room in front of all the pros and play 'American Pie' and 'Lyin' Eyes'! Hennigan was not immune to a few shenanigans of his own. Maybury told me how 'Mick had figured out that there was a hole in the false wall between the home and away changing rooms. He heard Alex Ferguson go ballistic in there after Hirsty [David Hirst] scored a late winner in 1987.' An early insight into the famous 'hairdryer' treatment, I believe.

At a time when the Owls hierarchy was keen that the club should live within its means, the youth and reserve set-up had a degree of success in terms of bringing players through to the first team. The teams were relatively successful on their own terms, with Middlewood Rovers, the youth team and the reserves all finishing in the upper echelons of their relative leagues.

Every player I have spoken to enjoyed their time at Hillsborough, whether they went on to play for the first team or moved on elsewhere. It was a hard school, but it was also a place where youngsters learned their trade with what Kerr described to me as a 'brilliant bunch' of people. Wilkinson was quoted in 1985 as being very pleased with the success of the youth and reserve set-up. 'In the future the strength of our squad will increasingly derive from home-produced talent,' he said. 'Not only is this less expensive but it's more conducive to generating club spirit.' Ten future first-team players and some great memories from those I have spoken to suggest that he was at least partly correct in his prediction.

9.

An Interview with Mark Smith

SHEFFIELD-BORN MARK Smith was a stylish left-footed defender who appeared a total of 349(+1) times for the Owls, notching 20 goals on the way. Smith came through the ranks at Hillsborough, training with the club as a youngster before working his way through the Middlewood Rovers set-up, on to an apprenticeship and through to the first team.

Smith made his debut in 1978 with the Owls still in Division Three and left for Plymouth Argyle in 1987 with the team firmly ensconced in the top flight. He earned five caps for the England Under-21 team during his years at S6. Mark retired from playing in the early 1990s before embarking on a lengthy coaching career. We spoke in early 2022 from Mark's home in the Sheffield area.

Thanks for talking to me Mark, can you tell me how you came to be involved with the Owls?

I'd been training with the club from the age of 11. Ron Staniforth used to take a group of us in the gym under the North Stand. It wasn't that serious then, more the club keeping an eye on promising youngsters. From 14 onwards it became more serious as I was aiming for an apprenticeship. Middlewood Rovers helped as well at under-16 level. It kept a group of us together. I was fortunate to be offered an apprenticeship – I think there were only three or four of us that year. It wasn't for the money! I think it was £5 a week in the first year, up to seven or eight in the second year.

I'd always played in midfield but Ken Knighton, who was coaching the youngsters by then, moved me to centre-back. I was tall, left-footed and aggressive but I'd never played in defence. I wasn't too happy about it at the time but looking back I owe him a lot. Who knows what would have happened otherwise; I might have been let go, or never made it. I have a lot to thank him for!

You made your first-team debut at a young age also?

I wasn't the first to break through. Dave Grant, who was a good player, got in before me. This was in the days before there were such large squads, so if someone in the first team got injured or whatever, the manager would look to the reserves or youth squad. I got called up for an away game at Colchester late in the 1977/78 season. I must have done all right because I was kept in the team for the next game, and then I hardly missed a game for the next three seasons. I played something like 140 games on the bounce after that.

Jack Charlton was the manager then. How did you find him?

He pushed me. He had the respect of people, so we tended to listen to him. It's funny now, but I don't remember thinking of him as a World Cup winner, although it was only a dozen years earlier. I am sure that he helped me gain the England Under-21 caps. I think he was still well thought of at the FA, so I suspect he put a word in with Ron Greenwood or Don Howe. I still have my shirts and caps by the way. I'm not one for having pictures of myself around the house though, so they are kept somewhere safe and special – probably under the stairs!

Did you come across Howard Wilkinson when you were with the England set-up?

I did, but I didn't remember much about him! Howard was assistant to Terry Venables with the under-21s. Terry had been a big draw. When Howard came to Hillsborough, and the other players asked me about him, I had to say that I didn't really remember much!

I remember feeling that I was flying in the 1983/84 pre-season. There had been some interest in me from Norwich and Aston Villa I think, and I'd been with England. I got an injury, though, and missed the first few games. Although I came back and went on to play plenty more games, including in Division One, I don't think I was ever quite the same after that. It's not good to have regrets, but I do think I could have kicked on from there. But it never quite happened.

How did you find the training under Howard Wilkinson?

We had great camaraderie. We were all in it together. We'd get in the van, up to Ewden dam or wherever, run for 90 minutes and then have a great laugh on the way back. We were a close-knit group. There used to be a nickname for us of the Wednesday Harriers as there was so much running. I'd never been so fit. I did feel that it went too far, though. We got tired later in the season sometimes. Teams that we'd beaten earlier on in the year by outrunning in them in the last few minutes were able to do it to us as we were tired. I think that Howard might have changed that in later years, especially when he went to Leeds, as I can't imagine it working with Gordon Strachan and others.

In some ways Howard was ahead of the times. We trained like a 1980s [Marcelo] Bielsa team! Three at the back, the high press, 'murder ball': we were one of the first to train and play like that – and it worked!

Do you have memories of certain games?

Some things stand out. The first game back against Nottingham Forest on a baking hot day with a huge crowd. Imre's goal was a cracker! Winning at Anfield, beating Tottenham at home, scoring against Arsenal in a televised game. At the time, though, I was focused on trying to win games of football. It's only later when I sat down at 40 or 45 years old, that I reflected on how proud I was to have been part of something.

You moved on at the end of the 1986/87 season?

I did, to Plymouth Argyle. I'd been fortunate to be granted a testimonial at Hillsborough. The game was under lights in front of the new Kop roof and 10,000 people turned up. It was testament to what I'd achieved, I think. I could have stayed but the writing was on the wall during that last season. We often played with three centre-backs, but if we were chasing the game one would be subbed. It happened to me a few times, and I remember being taken off during the last game of that season. It was a disappointing home defeat to Wimbledon, and I remember thinking that I'd had enough.

Plymouth was a completely different city to Sheffield. A rugby city, along with boats and sailing. I'm not sure it was completely the right choice for me, but my daughter was born down there, so I have happy memories as well. The training was different, that's for sure! I remember turning up for pre-season training and setting off at 100 miles an hour on the first run we did. I was told to slow down, and ease into pre-season. That never happened at Hillsborough!

I think that Wednesday had reached a bit of a turning point when I left. I'd been around since the 1970s, remember. There had been some great players under both Jack and Howard who'd helped the club return to the top. In the early 1980s there were Jeff Johnson, Andy McCulloch, Terry Curran and others. There was also the group I'd come up with, so Mel Sterland, John Pearson, Peter Shirtliff and more. We'd all learned originally from Jack, who with Maurice Setters used to come after us on the training pitch. Maurice used to play in his shoes and try and tackle us! It was no-nonsense, but there was togetherness. That stayed as the team moved back into Division One.

As I was leaving, Howard was trying to incorporate new players. The club had spent a bit of money. That brings problems with agents for example. I also wondered how easy it would be for the 'higher calibre' players to fit in with Howard's way. Those of us who'd been there a while just got on with things. I wondered if newer players would cope with his methods or question him. That's not to say that they weren't good people – Mark Chamberlain and Garry Thompson, for example, were great guys.

That's interesting, Mark. Back to the early 1980s then. You were famed for a while for taking penalties. Is there a reason you stopped?

You know, I can't remember, other than I missed a couple. I remember when I started. I'd taken a few in the Central League and scored them. In 1979 we had a retaken penalty in a League Cup game at Manchester City. Brian Hornsby had taken it and missed – but the ref ordered a retake. I found the ball in my hands and then on the spot. I scored past Joe Corrigan, I think, and it went from there. I scored ten out of ten following that, then missed one, scored one more, then missed two. I gave it up after that.

One of those penalties was a very famous one against Sheffield United.

Haha – yes it was. The Boxing Day Massacre! It still gets brought up. I worked at Sheffield United of course, they're good people – so they must have forgiven me!

How about nowadays, you are still in the game I believe?

Yes, I'm at Scunthorpe. I'm working as lead for youth development there. I've only just started and was lucky that a pal of mine – Tony Daws – is academy manager there. He's been there for 17 years and helped get me involved. I haven't been able to get near SWFC for years. It's a shame as I think I have plenty to offer on the youth front especially. But again, no regrets. As I said earlier, when I look back on my time at Wednesday it's with pride. I helped get the club back to where it should be and that's a good feeling.

Thanks Mark

No problem, I hope the book goes well!

10.

Cup Runs

THE OWLS' progress in both cup competitions across our two seasons saw the team play in some of the most memorable games in the club's history. The team had a realistic chance of reaching the final of both competitions only to fall as the last hurdle approached. This, then, is a tale of what might have been. The Owls were back in the big time and very nearly won something. A tale of failure then, or success? One for the reader to decide.

1984/85

The League Cup was first fought for in 1960/61. The Football League's general secretary, Alan Hardaker, brought in the competition to help boost the status of the English game at a time when European football was gaining prestige. Floodlights were also becoming commonplace, allowing for midweek fixtures at many grounds. The competition was not initially popular among some of the elite clubs. The Owls did not enter the competition until 1966/67, for example. However, over the coming years the tournament rose in popularity, with a Wembley final and qualification for European competition preceding entry being made compulsory for all Football League teams in 1972. The competition gained its first sponsor in time for the 1981/82 campaign – the Milk Marketing Board.

In September 1984, therefore, the Owls began their Milk Cup journey for the season with a two-legged second-round tie against Huddersfield Town. Division One clubs were given a bye through to the second round. Howard Wilkinson took the competition seriously, reflecting positively on the previous season's cup run (which ended in defeat at Anfield) and commenting: 'Wembley, like March when the final takes place, can seem almost imperceptible miles and months away, but it should require only a moment's contemplation to focus very sharply on the big prize.'

The Owls were drawn to play at home first and, in front of a good crowd of 16,139, eased to a 3-0 victory over the Terriers. Mel Sterland's first-half penalty was followed by further strikes from Lee Chapman and Brian Marwood. What seemed to be a successful evening's work was spoiled somewhat as Nigel Worthington was substituted with a groin strain which caused him to miss the next two league games.

Chapman was also (typically) tested for concussion following the game. The match was notable otherwise as being Pat Heard's final appearance in Owls colours – he was involved in a swap deal with Newcastle's John Ryan the following week.

Wilkinson commented afterwards: 'We never fired on all cylinders, and in the circumstances, the three-goal lead is very welcome.' The return leg at Huddersfield's Leeds Road ground took place a fortnight later in front of a relatively meagre crowd of 7,163. Sterland scored in the first half to see the Owls in at the break level at 1-1, Paul Jones notching the Town equaliser on the stroke of half-time. A late Huddersfield second through Mark Lillis's glancing header made no difference to the overall result – the Owls losing 2-1 on the night but progressing to the next round as 4-2 winners on aggregate. Huddersfield's manager Mick Buxton was delighted with their performance, saying, 'I am pleased that tonight we beat one of the best teams in the country.'

Wednesday's reward for beating the Terriers was a home tie against then Division Two Fulham. The Cottagers had seen off Carlisle United in the previous round. Another reasonable crowd of 15,556 turned out at Hillsborough on the night before Halloween. Wilkinson felt that the crowd 'who turned out to watch the Fulham game in appalling conditions, deserve a special mention. The day, in terms of weather, started off badly and fell away.'

It was Fulham who might have had nightmares afterwards, though, as the Owls put them to the sword in a 3-2 win. Marwood put the Owls ahead in the 24th minute with a well-driven half-volley. Fulham hit back before the break as Cliff Carr sidefooted home, only for Mike Lyons to put the Owls back ahead two minutes into the second half.

Imre Varadi seemingly put the game out of reach in the 78th minute, slamming in Sterland's cross. Fulham defender Jeff Hopkins headed home in the 81st minute, though, to make a nervous final few minutes for the Owls. Despite some intense pressure, Wednesday held on to celebrate their passage to the fourth round.

Fulham manager Ray Harford was quoted as saying: 'I'm a bit disappointed we didn't win ... We had the better chances and made Wednesday look tired.' Tired or not, the Owls could look forward to a fifth-round tie at home to Luton Town.

The game against the Hatters was certainly a memorable one. The Owls went in at half-time leading by two goals to nil. The second half saw them extend that lead to 4-0, before two late strikes by the Hatters left the final score as 4-2 to the Owls. An exciting game, therefore. What the facts to date do not say is that the first THREE Owls goals were all penalties – all slotted away by Andy Blair. This was the first (and so far, only) time in the club's existence that anyone had achieved that feat. There was also an irony in that Wednesday had previously missed three penalty kicks in other games that campaign!

Luton manager, and future Owls boss, David Pleat struggled with any irony though. 'I can't believe it, and neither can my players,' he said after the game. 'We are staggered that a referee should award such penalties ... My lads got a raw deal.' Marwood was the Owls' other goalscorer and, despite the two late consolations from Luton's Steve Elliott, the Owls were through to the quarter-final and a trip to face high-flying Chelsea.

Before the Owls could continue their campaign in the Milk Cup, they needed to begin their quest for the 1985 FA Cup.

Sheffield Wednesday have a proud history in the FA Cup. They have won the competition three times (in 1898, 1907 and 1935), were finalists in 1966 (losing 3-2 to Everton) and had been semi-finalists as recently as 1983, when they lost 2-1 to Brighton. After our period, the Owls famously beat Sheffield United in the 1993 semi-final at Wembley before losing to Arsenal late in extra time in a replayed final.

In 1985, coincidentally, the Owls were again drawn against Fulham, having seen off the London team in the Milk Cup earlier in the season. This time, though, the match was to be played at Craven Cottage.

Even more coincidentally, the score in October was matched in January as the Owls again won 3-2 and knocked the Cottagers out of a cup competition for the second time in one season. The scoring was different, however, as Ray Houghton put Fulham ahead as early as the 17th minute before two goals in three minutes from Sterland and Chapman put the Owls in front before half-time. The 11,433 crowd saw the Cottagers level in the 59th minute through Houghton again before Chapman scored the late headed winner.

Fulham manager Harford had the slightly bizarre explanation for his side's defeat that a harsh booking for striker Leroy Rosenior had upset his player's concentration and led to the two-goal salvo for the Owls. Wednesday may have had greater reason to be upset with referee Mike Dimblebee as he chalked off a perfectly good-looking Gary Shelton goal before half-time. The *Daily Mirror* may have explained matters most clearly when they said, 'Wednesday, under Howard Wilkinson's brand of ruthless realism, have developed a knack of shrugging off any adversity.' Even Harford admitted after the game that 'they stick at it all the time, never stop working and pressurising. They were better at finishing than we were. Nothing stops them.' Certainly, nothing had stopped the Owls reaching the fourth round of the FA Cup and a home tie against Oldham Athletic.

That fixture was to be played on 26 January, a mere two days before the Milk Cup fixture against Chelsea. A pivotal couple of days for the Owls' cup hopes, it seemed. The game against

Oldham turned into a formality as the Owls went two goals to the good before half-time, Varadi scoring the first in the 17th minute before Chapman notched the second. Marwood scored after the break before Varadi went on to complete his hat-trick. John Bowden scored in reply for Oldham. A 5-1 victory for the Owls, therefore. The win took Wednesday into the last 16 of the FA Cup and, as we know, they were already in the last eight of the Milk Cup. Asked if the Owls could win either competition, Wilkinson replied with typical understatement: 'Of course we can, but so can anyone else.'

The Owls' victory booked them a tie away to Ipswich Town in the fifth round of the FA Cup. Before that fixture, though, Wednesday would take on Chelsea in the Milk Cup. Victory over the Blues would book the team a semi-final place against Sunderland.

The tie at Stamford Bridge took place on a cold Monday evening in January. It attracted a crowd of over 36,000, including several thousand travelling Wednesdayites. The Owls in the crowd were the happiest after 18 minutes when, from a Blair cross, Chapman nodded the ball back for the unlikely figure of Lawrie Madden to tap the ball home. Madden remembers only really getting forward for set pieces and occasionally when filling in at left-back. 'I remember bundling this one in after a flick-on from a long crossfield pass,' he told me in 2021.

Wednesday may have considered themselves fortunate to be ahead at that stage, as Chelsea had already hit the upright and had two efforts cleared off the line. Within ten minutes of the Owls' strike, Chelsea were level. A corner from Keith Jones was flicked on towards David Speedie, who flung himself at the ball to claim the equaliser. Speedie was also involved in Chelsea's best chance of winning the game just three minutes into the second half. Referee Trevor Spencer ruled that Speedie was tripped by Worthington just inside the area and awarded a penalty.

Chelsea's leading marksman, 27-goal Kerry Dixon, took the spot-kick. He hit the ball hard and low, but too close to Martin Hodge's left side. Hodge smothered the ball and saved the penalty. Chelsea had missed their third penalty of the season, with assistant manager Ian McNeill saying of Dixon afterwards, 'He's down at the moment, but he'll probably score a hat-trick tomorrow as that's the sort of player he is.'

That follow-up game came despite a frantic finish to the tie, with Chapman then Varadi both missing chances to win it for the Owls. McNeill commented that he 'felt we were the better side, and we are still confident that we can get through'. Wilkinson for his part felt that 'we have played much better ... but we fancy our chances now and we don't fear anyone at Hillsborough'. The replay was to be played only two days later and would prove to be one of the most exciting ties in Sheffield Wednesday's history.

Key Game: Sheffield Wednesday 4-4 Chelsea, 30 January 1985

Wednesday might have felt that they had the advantage over Chelsea as the Blues went into the game missing their captain Colin Pates. The Owls were able to name an unchanged team, with Mark Smith left out of the squad despite his return to fitness in the lead-up to the game. Wednesday were unbeaten in 13 games and had won the five matches prior to the Stamford Bridge draw. Chelsea had lost only one in 12.

Wednesday had something of a Chelsea bogey to lay to rest, though. The Londoners had beaten Wednesday five times in cup ties since the Owls' victory over the Blues in the 1966 FA Cup semi-final. Wilkinson himself admitted before the game that 'Chelsea seem to bring out the worst in us'. Chelsea coach John Hollins added: 'Someone will have a lapse of concentration and both teams are good enough to pounce on one mistake.'

Chelsea's chairman Ken Bates took time out before the game to pay credit to the Owls. 'Although I dislike Sheffield's offside game,' he said, 'they also play exciting football.' The game came in the middle of a fixture pile-up for both teams – Chelsea had to play four cup games in nine days. The bookies had Chelsea as the outsiders, but it was not a foregone conclusion that either side would win.

The *Sheffield Star* reported a huge demand for tickets, causing queues and traffic jams in the Hillsborough area in the lead-up to kick-off. A huge Hillsborough crowd of 36,509 turned out to cheer the team.

The line-up for the Owls was as follows for a game that was as exciting as Bates expected:

1. Martin Hodge
2. Mel Sterland
3. Peter Shirtliff
4. Lawrie Madden
5. Mike Lyons
6. Nigel Worthington
7. Brian Marwood
8. Andy Blair
9. Imre Varadi
10. Lee Chapman
11. Gary Shelton

Sub) Pearson

The *Daily Mirror*'s report the following morning took up the story – under the headline 'Chelsea Cracker'. The *Star* added that that the game was 'surely one of the most sensational in the Owls' 118-year history – and maybe one of the all-time great cup ties'. The *Sheffield Telegraph* described it as 'one of the most dramatic nights in Hillsborough history'. The *Star's* Paul Thompson added that 'I have certainly never seen such an amazing game. It was a two-hour epic of eight goals, five bookings, controversy, incredible twists, sometimes brutal intensity and extra-time drama.' Even these headlines and comments struggle to do justice to an incredible fixture.

The bare facts show that the Owls took a three-goal lead into half-time. They were two to the good inside 22 minutes, with Lyons glancing home a Blair free kick before Blair crossed for Chapman to power in his 14th goal of the campaign. Chelsea seemed to lose their heads at this stage, with bookings in quick succession for Jones, Pat Nevin and Doug Rougvie.

Before the interval, Wednesday's players were left angered when Chelsea's Mickey Thomas seemingly flattened Blair in an off-the-ball incident seconds after Speedie hit the post. Blair was soon cautioned for a late challenge and so was Chelsea's Colin Lee after protesting too vehemently about the Owls' third goal. Marwood struck in first-half injury time – curling a beauty high into the net.

Few punters would have placed a bet on Chelsea at half-time. An enforced change – Lee being taken off with a suspected broken foot and replaced by Paul Canoville – turned the game on its head, though. Within 15 seconds of the restart Canoville was sent through the middle of a split Owls defence and pulled one goal back. Dixon soon scored his 28th of the season from a Thomas through ball. The comeback was complete when Varadi lost the ball to Nigel Spackman. He began a rapid counter-attack that ended with Nevin crossing to Thomas, who curled in the equaliser from 18 yards.

Four minutes from time it became even worse for Wednesday as Canoville tapped in Chelsea's fourth to put them in front for the first time in the tie. Wednesday seemed down and out but, with fewer than 30 seconds left on the clock, Sterland burst into the area and was tripped by Rougvie. Penalty. Sterland took the ball and from his lengthy run-up powered the ball down the middle for 4-4. Extra time saw further chances for Chapman and Marwood for the Owls before Hodge saved magnificently from Canoville. Full time of what Sterland described afterwards as 'the most exciting game I have ever played in'.

Wilkinson said, 'They will talk about this game for years. I still don't really know how it happened. It was not really a game for people with handbags. Perhaps 3-0 up at half-time we were looking forward to the semi-final with Sunderland. At 4-3 we were dead and buried but we got back in. Sterland's decision to take the penalty was his own. A little bit of bottle was involved. I can't preach to my players one thing and then start nitpicking when we lose a 3-0 lead. Our attitude is to try and win by as many goals as possible. I certainly can't say there was any criminal negligence on their part.' It was the first game of the season in which Wednesday had conceded three or more goals, however.

The goalscoring was over in the 90 minutes of normal time, and as extra time could not separate the teams, there would need to be a second replay. As both teams had played at home, the venue of that replay was to be decided by a pitchside toss of the coin between Owls chairman Bert McGee and Chelsea owner Bates. McGee lost the toss, and the Owls would need to travel to London for the next game.

The date at that stage was still to be decided, as Chelsea's fixture pile-up included their next game in the FA Cup. A poignant story related to the fixture saw Chelsea's match-changing substitute Canoville reunited with his estranged father after the game. Canoville gives an entertaining account of the game itself in his award-winning autobiography *Black and Blue*. He recalls his contribution to the game, but also how Thomas had 'bashed Andy Blair', leaving him 'laid out and needing treatment' before half-time. According to Canoville's account, Thomas had done this in revenge for the verbal treatment that Blair had been dishing out throughout the game – and did so when he knew the officials could not see what happened. What might have been – Wednesday 3-0 up and Chelsea down to ten men at half-time? History could have been somewhat different. Blair has his own say on that evening elsewhere in the book.

Peter Shirtliff told me in 2021 that the game was a 'very strange one', and went on to say how the weather had a huge impact. 'We played with the wind in the first half. The weather was horrendous, and Chelsea had the advantage in the second half, using it to help their fightback.' Madden added: 'We had a bad 20 minutes after half-time. We were bitterly disappointed, the early goal in the second half gave them a lift.' Shelton felt that 'we were cruising at half-time; Paul Canoville made the difference though'.

The match was clearly a thriller and, as Wilkinson suggested at the time, it is one that Owls supporters still remember clearly. The progress of the game saw fans run the full gamut of emotions. As Bobby Morwood told me, it was 'the best and worst game ever'! Paul Egginton remembered 'losing my brother in the melee on the Kop' after Marwood's outstanding goal on the brink of half-time. Other supporters such as Ian Fox remember making plans of how to travel to Sunderland for the semi-final and witnessing the Owls' sponsored mascot Bertie Bassett (of confectionery fame) dancing at the front of the Kop in celebration of the goals.

Some fans followed the game from afar. Richard Fidler and no doubt many thousands of others listened to the match on the radio – following Radio Sheffield's commentary. 'My dad had been giving me and my brother score updates and getting increasingly exasperated in the second half before calling us back into the kitchen to hear Zico smash home the pen!' Others followed from less common places. Neil Murdoch was in the Northern General hospital 'with a broken tib and fib trying not to jump when we scored!', whereas Darren Winnell was enjoying a night out. 'I was at Meat Loaf's gig at City Hall and when we heard the half-time score was 3-0 all the Owls were dancing about in the aisles! Got home and saw highlights on telly with disbelief at what happened in the second half … only Wednesday eh?'

Pete Lee gave credit to Chelsea's supporters. 'They started singing "Ten Men Went to Mow" at half-time,' he told me, 'and they carried on until they were 4-3 up! I think the Chelsea players must have heard them in the dressing room.'

The second half changed the course of the game and, as Simon Hill and others told me, it was a 'freezing night' which seemed to grow increasingly cold for Owls fans. Canoville's very early goal was only the beginning of the Chelsea fightback. His second goal and Chelsea's fourth was followed by wild celebrations on the pitch which, as Lee Wild told me, 'stuck with me for years'.

Sterland's late penalty of course levelled the tie but caused drama on its own in the stands. As Roland Deschain put it to me, 'We headed for the exit at 4-3, saw the penalty decision and rushed back to our seats as someone tried to stop us, saying, "You shouldn't have gone early."' Roland and his dad got back into the ground in time for the goal, as did Jay Maybury, who 'came out just before the end and heard a massive cheer, so ran up the back of the Kop just to see Mel smash the penalty in'. Gray Lightfoot also got back in to see the goal, but wondered 'how people weren't injured/killed doing an about turn that night'.

Craig took a more relaxed approach: 'I was on the Kop watching everybody leave early. I was going to join them but thought I might as well stay and get a later bus home.' He was glad he did. The final say on this game goes to the *Star*'s cartoonist Whitworth who, with characteristic wit, pictured two supporters reading a report of the game with one saying to the other: 'I can see the NUM and the NCB [National Coal Board] settling it before these two!'

* * *

The tie was settled before the end of the miners' strike. The second replay against Chelsea took place a week after the game at Hillsborough. The Wednesday evening fixture attracted another huge crowd of 36,395. Chelsea had been knocked out of the FA Cup by Millwall in the interim, so the Milk Cup was their last chance of cup glory that season. Author Richard Crooks recounts the difficulties of getting into the game alongside large numbers of other Owls fans and seemingly disinterested police in his book *What Was Football Like in the 1980s?* The near crush outside was a not uncommon occurrence at games during the period.

Inside the ground, Owls fans found an unchanged XI from the previous replay, with the only change being Chris Morris replacing Gavin Oliver on the bench. Wednesday supporters would have been happiest with the start to the game as, after only 12 minutes, Marwood backheeled the ball to Blair, who in turn fed Shelton. From that pass Shelton launched a 25-yard shot which flew into the back of the net.

Chelsea, though, soon fought their way back into the game, with Speedie forcing Hodge into two saves before notching the equaliser from a Nevin cross on the half-hour mark. The score remained at 1-1 for much of the rest of the game, with the fixture seemingly heading for another period of extra time as it went into its final stages.

Owls hearts were broken late on as Thomas scored the winning goal for Chelsea with a free header from a corner with less than 30 seconds remaining. Thomas took great pleasure in scoring the winner, remembering that Wilkinson had supposedly described him as a 'flash in the pan' after he had scored twice against the Owls during the previous season. 'I wanted to win more than anything,' said Thomas afterwards. Peter Eustace commented: 'The result was disappointing, but both Howard and I are very, very proud of the team.' The *Daily Mirror* commented that the result was 'tough on Wednesday', but the *Star* admitted that 'Chelsea just about deserved to win'.

The final whistle prompted a pitch invasion from Chelsea supporters celebrating their qualification for the semi-final. Owls fans were left to wonder what might have been. Chelsea lost the semi-final to Sunderland.

Wednesday remained in contention for FA Cup glory; their opponents in the fifth round were Ipswich Town. The fixture pile-up that had affected the early part of 1985 continued, with the game scheduled for a Monday evening kick-off in early March. The Owls were missing striker Chapman through injury, his replacement being John Pearson, who had scored the only goal in the team's league victory over Coventry City only two days earlier.

The game proved to be another thrilling one. Blair fed Varadi in the 24th minute for a neat near-post finish to see the Owls one goal to the good. Dutchman Romeo Zondervan equalised four minutes later after a corner kick bounced around in the area. Wednesday fans felt that the corner kick was dubious at best. One-all at half-time soon became 2-1 to Wednesday as captain Lyons thumped a header home following an excellent Worthington cross. The Owls held the lead until 20 minutes from time, when some fine work on the left by Kevin Wilson gave George Burley the chance to tap home the equaliser from six yards out.

Ipswich's winner came two minutes from time and was fiercely contested, with the scorer Alan Sunderland looking clearly offside. Referee Ken Baker looked long and hard at the linesman before pointing to the centre spot and giving the goal.

Sunderland said afterwards: 'I thought Mich d'Avray was offside, but I just got on with it. The referee didn't blow, it was as simple as that.' Wilkinson had to hold back a clearly incensed

Lyons at the final whistle as the teams returned to the tunnel. The *Star* commented: 'They say luck evens out over a season – if this is true then the Owls are going to need a lot from somewhere to balance this match.' The manager uncharacteristically criticised referees in the media following the next league game against Leicester. A missed handball on the line in that game denied the Owls an obvious penalty and contributed to a 3-1 defeat.

Wilkinson was in apologetic mood in the following matchday programme. 'In retrospect my outburst was ill-judged, and apologies are due,' he wrote, continuing, 'It served no purpose other than to release my frustrations.' However incensed Wednesday and their supporters were, it was the end of the Owls' dreams of cup glory for that season. Wilkinson turned his eyes to the remaining third of the league season and a possible tilt at the European places. He wrote: 'Recent disappointment has to be forgotten. We must all, fans and players together, work like hell to finish as well as possible.'

1985/86

Division One Wednesday were again given a bye into the second round of the Milk Cup in 1985. This time their opponents were to be Division Three Brentford. The Owls were drawn away from home in the first leg of the two-legged tie. A crowd of 5,352 turned out to witness an entertaining 2-2 draw between an enterprising Brentford team and what the *Daily Mirror* described as a 'woeful' Wednesday.

Certainly, the Owls struggled against the Bees. Rowan Alexander gave Brentford the lead a minute before the break with a fierce near-post header. Brentford could have scored three goals by the 50th minute. Firstly, an Alexander header was cleared off the line, then the Bees were awarded a penalty when Keith Millen was held back in the box. Robbie Cooke took the spot-kick but slammed it against the post.

This seemingly spurred the Owls into action. Chapman equalised on 65 minutes after a Glynn Snodin free kick came back off Brentford keeper Gary Phillips. Chapman then put the

Owls into the lead on 81 minutes, scoring a trademark header from a Blair free kick as the Brentford defence stood still.

The Bees were not finished, however, and equalised when Alexander volleyed home a Tony Lynch through ball. 'We were very unlucky. We scored two good goals and gave away two silly ones,' said Brentford manager Frank McLintock after the game. Wilkinson felt that 'it wasn't a classic, but we got something out of it. We are lacking a bit of confidence at the moment, but we will get it right.'

Brentford had a taste of Wembley the previous season, losing in the Freight Rover Trophy Final to Wigan Athletic. They had given the Owls plenty to consider if Wednesday were to take a step closer to cup success themselves.

As English football teams were banned from playing in Europe after the Heysel Stadium disaster, the Football League attempted to fill the void in the calendar by introducing two new competitions: the ScreenSport Super Cup and the Full Members' Cup. The Owls did not qualify for the ScreenSport competition, which was reserved for those who would have qualified for the European competitions. Liverpool eventually ran out winners against Everton.

The competition was notable for low crowds and disinterested clubs. So, even more clearly, was the Full Members' Cup. The Owls turned down the opportunity to join the competition, which, although open to 32 teams from the top two leagues, began with only 24 clubs registered. In fact only 21 teams started the competition, with Birmingham City even withdrawing on the day of their first match against Brentford.

The first season saw several teams record their lowest attendances for first-team fixtures. For example, the 12 Shrewsbury fans who made their way to Oxford for a midweek game found themselves outnumbered by stewards! The final was played in front of a 67,000-plus crowd at Wembley, who saw an exciting 5-4 win for Chelsea against Manchester City. A missed chance for the Owls? Perhaps, although the competition was widely unloved. Future cup hero John Sheridan did announce himself to Owls supporters with a wonderful solo goal in the renamed Zenith Data Systems Cup in 1989. The opposition? Sheffield United.

The second leg of the Brentford fixture was played at Hillsborough three weeks after the opening tie in front of a crowd of 11,132. The game finished as a routine 2-0 win for the Owls. Wednesday took the lead as early as the tenth minute when the linesman flagged for a penalty after what seemed an innocuous tussle between the Owls' Carl Shutt and Brentford's Roger Joseph in the box. Sterland stepped up and sent the keeper the wrong way.

Despite playing with three strikers in Shutt, Chapman and Garry Thompson, Wednesday struggled to stamp their authority on the game. Brentford created the best of the chances as the game went on, and Wednesday fans were undoubtedly relieved when Chapman headed in Blair's precise cross on 81 minutes to put the tie beyond doubt. There was still time for Steve Wignall to head over the bar for the Bees and for Hodge to be called into action to block off Brentford winger Lynch after a shaky backpass.

Wilkinson was happy with the win. 'It was a good result against a difficult, battling Brentford team,' he said after the game. He was less happy with an injury to Shelton, which saw the midfielder stretchered off after a collision with team-mate Sterland. Luckily enough, Shelton would miss only one game as a result. The Owls were through and would face Lou Macari's Swindon Town at the County Ground in the next round.

Swindon were in Division Four that season – they would finish the campaign as champions. The Owls, though, went into the fixture with some confidence on the back of two league wins since the Brentford game. Wednesday were favourites to go through and named a strong team. Swindon's largest crowd for many years, 12,110, turned up to witness the action. Swindon turned out to be no pushover – they went on to finish the season with a record number of points – and took the lead as early as the tenth minute, Peter Coyne scoring with a header after being left unmarked from a corner.

Wednesday had plenty of possession as the first half continued, but Swindon harried and fought and made life difficult for the

Owls. Shutt had two good chances, a header cleared off the line and a shot over the bar when through on goal. Wednesday continued to pressurise Swindon into the second half, although it was not all one-way traffic as the Robins' Bryan Wade had a shot blocked on the line.

Thompson replaced Shutt on the hour and he, Blair and Paul Hart at the last all had good opportunities to equalise. Swindon, though, held firm for a famous victory, marked by a pitch invasion from some in that large crowd. The *Daily Express* commented that Swindon 'playing with a completely fearless approach chased and harried Wednesday from start to finish'. Wilkinson accepted that 'you have to congratulate Swindon. After that early goal they played as if they had hearts like dustbin lids.' Wednesday were the victims of a good old-fashioned giant-killing.

Swindon's manager Macari commented: 'Cup-tie football brings out the best in the minnows.' The game was notable to Owls' supporters as the last played by Lyons before his move to Grimsby to take a player-manager position. The Owls' only remaining route to cup glory this campaign would be in the FA Cup.

That quest for glory began with a third-round tie at home to West Bromwich Albion. The Baggies were struggling in Division One and propped up the table at the beginning of 1986. The fixture was due to be played on Saturday, 4 January and was postponed TWICE more due to the weather before finally being played on Monday 13th.

West Brom were managed by World Cup winner Nobby Stiles and featured ex-Owl Varadi in their starting XI. The weather was atrocious and neither side were able to get a grip on the game in the opening exchanges. After 37 minutes, though, Wednesday took the lead, Sterland reacting quickest after heading against the keeper and smashing home the rebound.

West Brom were level only two minutes later through George Reilly's stooping header. The Owls took the lead again two minutes into the second half as Sterland flicked on Marwood's corner for Smith to head in at the far post. Marwood, Blair and Tony Gregory all had chances to extend the Owls' lead before Shutt rattled the woodwork with a shot on the turn. It was Albion who equalised in the 70th minute, however, as full-back Derek Statham raced on to a through ball and fired into the bottom corner. The Baggies could even have won the game late on but for a fine save from Hodge to deny Statham a second goal. Wilkinson was not happy with the display. 'Both I, and the players, expect criticism after a performance like tonight,' he said. They soon had chance to make amends, with the replay at The Hawthorns scheduled for just three days later.

The replay was played on a cold evening in the West Midlands. Both sides refused permission for the game to be moved in order for it to be shown on ITV. The national audience missed an exciting game. Wilkinson named another strong-looking starting line-up, with Chapman coming back into the team and Mark Chamberlain taking his place on the substitutes' bench.

Wednesday attacked from the off and were ahead after only nine minutes. Blair's cross was headed powerfully towards goal by Thompson only to be blocked by the hand of Albion's Ally Robertson on the line. Marwood took the resulting penalty and sent the keeper the wrong way. The Owls had further chances through Chapman and Marwood before Albion equalised in the 38th minute. The *Sandwell Evening Mail* described how midfielder Steve Hunt 'did his Chaplin shuffle past a defender and nonchalantly curled the ball past Martin Hodge'.

The scores were not level for long. Chapman had a well-taken header ruled out for a foul before a cross by Morris to the far post saw the big striker rise majestically to nod the ball home. Chapman's strike just before half-time was the fourth time that the Owls had taken the lead in the tie. West Brom duly equalised for a fourth time on the hour mark. Two Owls defenders hesitated as Reilly knocked on Gary Owen's cross and Mickey Thomas (remember him?) stole in to place the ball past Hodge.

The game became a little scrappy after that, with half-chances for Varadi for the Baggies and Gregory for the Owls the only moments of note as the match approached its final minutes. A late substitution changed matters, though, as Gregory was replaced by Chamberlain. In the 87th minute the Owls won a corner. Marwood took it, it was flicked on by the stork-like Chapman and Chamberlain dived in to head home at the far post.

There was still time for Varadi to hit the side-netting for West Brom, but the final whistle soon went and the Owls could finally celebrate victory. Wilkinson was relieved and delighted. 'It was a cracking match,' he said, 'and I was so convinced it was going to go to extra time that I had already ordered hot drinks for the players!' A magnanimous Stiles simply said that 'Wednesday deserved their victory'. The *Sandwell Evening Mail* felt that the Owls' performance was like 'tepid water' compared to the 'tickling champagne' that the Baggies served up at times. The *Sheffield Telegraph* admitted that the 'pace was fast and furious'. However the victory was achieved, it put the Owls into the fourth round, and a home tie against Orient.

Orient were in Division Four at the time and bossed by Frank Clark, who had enjoyed great success as a player under Brian Clough at Nottingham Forest. Wilkinson named another strong-looking team, including Snodin, who presumably was not too tired after the recent birth of his second child. Marwood had recently been placed on standby for the England squad, and he used the game to give a clear reminder to Three Lions manager Bobby Robson of his ability. Marwood set up three goals and scored the fifth in a 5-0 trouncing of the Os.

The first goal came after 59 seconds. Sterland's long throw was flicked on by Chapman for Thompson to blast home from short range. The second goal followed on 12 minutes with a perfect cross from Marwood met by a fierce Chapman header. The third strike came as early as the 26th minute with Sterland heading home following a knock-down by Thompson. Seven minutes into the second half came the Owls' fourth goal – neat work from Marwood and Gary Megson setting up Blair to drive home. Orient finally had a shot on target with 15 minutes left, as Colin Foster's drive was acrobatically tipped wide by Hodge.

Eight minutes from time, though, Marwood sealed the victory, and capped his excellent performance, by stealing the ball after a defensive mix-up and running through to drive a low shot under the advancing keeper. Wilkinson was pleased with the win, describing it as a 'very efficient, professional performance'. The Orient manager Clark admitted that 'Wednesday rarely gave us a chance'. As the *Sunday People* put it, 'The only thing Orient got right was to turn up on time!'

The day was not completely positive for the Owls, however, as Shirtliff was taken off with an injury and would miss the next two games. Wednesday, though, were through to the fifth round, and an away fixture with Derby County at the Baseball Ground.

The winter of 1986 was a cold one. The Owls managed only three games in February. The Derby County game was played at the FIFTH attempt on a freezing Wednesday night towards the end of the month. The Rams were in Division Three at the time but were flying at the top of that league. The pitch was hard but flat and deemed playable by referee Neil Midgely.

Wilkinson was party to that decision after a mid-afternoon dash down the M1 to check the state of the surface alongside the referee. Several players expressed doubts, including goalkeeper Hodge who later said, 'It was difficult to dive on and dangerous to play on.' Wilkinson, though, was quoted afterwards in the Derby press as saying, 'I thought it was in terrific condition considering the bad weather we have had.' The match was played in front of a partisan and hostile crowd. Both teams found the conditions difficult early in the game, with little effective football being played in the first few minutes. The opening goal was scored by Derby in the 23rd minute. A misplaced pass by Blair found the Rams' John Gregory, who in turn fed Bobby Davison, and he slid the ball under the onrushing Hodge.

Blair was substituted at half-time by a furious Wilkinson. Blair had had a number of previous clashes with the manager and was supposedly told on this occasion by Wilkinson that 'you'll never kick a ball for this club again'. The lead given to the Rams following Blair's mistake lasted only ten minutes, as Marwood's corner was flicked on to the unfortunate Trevor Christie, who sliced into his own net. The scoring had finished for the evening.

The drama, though, had not. In the 49th minute Hodge collected a cross from Gregory and in the process steepled over the back of Owls defender Smith. Hodge hit the floor heavily and head first. Hodge was down for several minutes and credited physio Alan Smith for his treatment. 'Three times he checked my eyes in the floodlights, but my pupils didn't react. At the fourth attempt they did, and he let me carry on.'

Hodge was later responsible for a series of outstanding saves, including from Geraint Williams and later Jeff Chandler to keep the Owls in the tie. Davison helped warm up the temperature on the pitch, firstly by pushing Hodge (for which he was warned by the referee) and later for a potentially serious collision where neither he, nor Hodge, pulled out of the chase for a through ball. Hodge needed further treatment and Davison received a booking.

At the end of the game Derby manager Arthur Cox confronted Hodge in the tunnel, accusing the Owls keeper of feigning injury. Cox was perhaps frustrated that the referee did not add an equivalent amount of injury time at the end of the game and later apologised. Hodge was certainly injured, with a cut eye, cut nose, dead leg and two clear grazed bumps on the side of his temple. Wilkinson was full of praise for his keeper, saying, 'I thought he was outstanding … he showed a lot of bravery and kept us in the tie.' The Owls had struggled to create much in difficult conditions but had done enough to earn a replay at Hillsborough.

That replay was played a week after the first game. The Owls team was altered, with Wilkinson keeping his promise not to play Blair, and Thompson also missing out. Shirtliff and Shutt came into the team to replace them. Shutt had learned only a couple of hours before kick-off that he was to replace the injured Thompson. Chapman played alongside Shutt up front and was thoroughly rested after missing the previous league game at Luton as part of a reshuffle designed to counter the effect of the Kenilworth Road artificial pitch.

The selection of Shutt turned out to be an inspired one. The Wednesday team, dressed in their all yellow away kit to avoid a colour clash with Derby, started brightly – hitting the post with a deflected Snodin free kick and feeling they had scored with a Smith header. The referee ruled that it had not crossed the line despite vehement appeals from the crowd and Owls players alike.

Shelton had a header cleared from under the crossbar and Chapman hit the woodwork with a header that had beaten the keeper. Two minutes before the break came the opening goal. A Marwood cross was not fully cleared and fell to Shutt, who was able to steady himself to rifle home from close range. The Rams immediately fought back, with Hodge saving well from Gregory and Davison missing a serviceable chance in front of goal. Derby continued to attack into the second half, with Gary Micklewhite just losing out in a one-on-one with Hodge, Chandler having a shot tipped over and a deflection off Smith going just wide.

All this Derby pressure, though, left space at the back. Shutt had a strike well saved after great work from Marwood and Sterland. He was not to be denied, however, and on 83 minutes was put in the clear by an excellent Megson header. Shutt's shot was well clear of the advancing Mark Wallington in the Derby goal and the Owls were two goals to the good.

Derby never gave up but were unable to trouble the Owls' goal after this, and Wednesday were through to the quarter-final. Derby's manager Cox felt that the wrong team had gone through. 'I genuinely believe that over the two games we deserved to go through,' he said. 'However, in football you don't always get what you deserve.'

Hodge, who shook hands with Cox on the pitch after the game, putting to bed the disagreement from the first tie, said, 'Derby are a very good side … who certainly made me work hard over the two games.' The *Daily Express* used the weather to push its metaphors to the limit in their match report: 'Wednesday emerged triumphantly from the ice age last night when they achieved the victory they needed to prevent their season going into cold storage.' Wednesday's cup run was certainly hotting up. The next game was a home tie against West Ham United.

Wednesday's fixtures were piling up again given the cold winter and the cancellations and postponements it caused. They were to play nine times in March, including the replay against Derby and the quarter-final tie against the Hammers. This game was to be played midweek but still attracted a huge attendance of 35,522 to Hillsborough. The tie was the NINTH quarter-final (including replays) since Wilkinson had taken the hotseat at Hillsborough in 1983. He had yet to reach a semi-final.

Wilkinson thought he may have been able to name an unchanged team from the tie against Derby. Shelton, though, did not recover from a knee injury in time and Worthington was brought into a relatively unfamiliar position in midfield. Both teams were in decent form, with the Owls following their victory over Derby with a thumping league win against Birmingham City. The Hammers had just won against Manchester United at Old Trafford.

It was Wednesday who took the game by the scruff of the neck in the first half. The Owls were two goals to the good inside 35 minutes. The first came in the 16th minute as Worthington, in that midfield role, struck a drive into the bottom corner from 18 yards. The shot, from Worthington's much lesser used right foot, came after West Ham's Alan Devonshire had headed a Smith effort off his line towards the Northern Irish international.

West Ham were still trying to gain a foothold in the game when Shutt scored the Owls' second of the night. Shutt raced on to a Megson pass, survived a near trip and shot low past keeper Phil Parkes. The score remained at 2-0 until half-time. Early in the second half, however, the Hammers pulled a goal back with a left-foot strike from the diminutive Tony Cottee. West Ham seemed revived and had much more of the ball in the second half. They were, though, only able to conjure up one more strike to threaten Hodge – a header from Cottee that flew just over the bar.

After a seemingly endless second half, the Owls had won, and Wilkinson had reached that first semi-final. Wilkinson credited some of that victory to Worthington playing in that midfield role. 'We needed an anchor man,' he said. 'I chose Worthington for the job. He did it for me at Notts County and it worked again.' On the same evening as the Owls' victory, Everton were playing in a replay against Luton Town for the other semi-final spot. The Toffees were victorious, with the only goal of the game scored by Gary Lineker. It was Lineker's 33rd goal of the season, and he was quoted afterwards as saying, 'I hope the semi-final is anywhere but Villa Park, it is my bogey ground!' Whether it was unlucky or not would be put to the test the following month. The Owls were to face Everton in a last four tie in the West Midlands in early April.

Key Game: Sheffield Wednesday 1-2 Everton (aet), 5 April 1986

The FA Cup semi-final was to be played at Villa Park in Birmingham. Not only was this Lineker's unlucky ground, it was also the site of one of the Owls' most famous victories – over Chelsea in the 1966 semi-final. Wednesday knew that the 1986 tie would be a huge test. Everton were league champions and favourites to win the title again. They were the European Cup Winners' Cup holders and had won the FA Cup in 1984 before finishing runners-up in 1985. Everton had beaten the Owls three times in 1985 and were unbeaten against Wednesday in THIRTEEN games since the 1966 FA Cup Final.

Demand for tickets at Villa Park was high, with both Everton and the Owls enjoying successful seasons and bucking the general trend for falling attendances. The Toffees were averaging around 31,000 at home games, the Owls just over 24,000 at this stage. Aston Villa were due 20 per cent of tickets for their own use but, in negotiation with the newly formed Football Supporters' Association, agreed to waive this and allow these tickets to be shared between the two clubs.

The tie was initially due to be played at Old Trafford but, because of what the press described as 'hooligan fears', it was moved to Birmingham. There was no love lost between the football supporters of Liverpool and Manchester at the time and Birmingham was seen as a safer neutral venue. One downside of the move was the reduced size of the stadium. Villa Park held just over 40,000 whereas Old Trafford would have fitted 55,000 supporters.

Wednesday tried to make access to tickets fair by including a voucher with entry to the previous league game against Leicester. Tickets for the FA Cup game went on general sale on the same day as a home game against Liverpool. The local press afterwards was full of complaints from fans who either missed the Liverpool game to queue, failed to get a ticket for Villa Park or both. The supporters' club secretary Rita Nettleship said she had received so many complaints that she 'had stopped counting'. Owls secretary Dick Chester defended the decision by saying, 'We have tried to be fair, but we do not have the tickets to supply our average crowd, so no matter what we do we cannot satisfy the needs of everybody.'

Those who were able to get their hands on one of the 19,000 tickets that were made available to Owls fans travelled in good spirits. There were hundreds of coaches from Sheffield, innumerable cars and three chartered trains which carried 800 supporters. Sheffield Midland station saw queues around the block as fans waited to board those trains along with the standard Birmingham-bound services. The M1 and M6 were famously filled with Owls supporters, with the cars, minibuses and coaches waving flags, dangling scarves and fluffy toy Owls from every spare window.

Wilkinson's squad were struggling with illness and injury. Chapman did make the team after recovering from a bout of hepatitis. Shelton also played, overcoming a foot injury, and Hodge recovered from a back injury and played as captain against his former team. Hodge had looked unlikely to be fit in the days beforehand, with the possibility that Iain Hesford may have made his debut in his place. Marwood did miss out with a thigh strain.

Wilkinson opted to play his regular three centre-backs formation in the following team:

1. Martin Hodge
2. Mel Sterland
3. Peter Shirtliff
4. Lawrie Madden
5. Paul Hart
6. Gary Shelton

7. Lee Chapman
8. Gary Megson
9. Garry Thompson
10. Carl Shutt
11. Glynn Snodin

Sub) Mark Chamberlain

Wilkinson took the squad to use the FA's facilities in Lilleshall in the week leading up to the match, a move that Shirtliff described to me as 'a great idea!' He told me that 'it allowed us to focus our minds for the game away from the noise in Sheffield. We had a couple of days down there and we were well prepared.'

Madden also remembers the trip to Lilleshall. 'Howard put us all up in dorms to try and make sure that no one was giving it large before the game!' he said. 'It was designed to keep us away from the pressure that was building up to give us an escape. There were also excellent training facilities, so it made sense from that point of view as well.' Thompson remembered staying at a hotel the night before and the squad being taken for a walk on the morning of the game with the aim of allowing the players to collect their thoughts. 'We were well prepared,' Shelton told me, 'Howard really did leave no stone unturned in his planning.'

There was certainly a lot of noise in the local press of South Yorkshire, with the game featuring on the front and back pages in the week beforehand and a special edition of the *Star* published the day before the game. One man who had a foot in both camps was former Evertonian and Owl, Mike Lyons. 'I wouldn't like to say who will win,' he said. 'Semi-finals are unpredictable. One of my teams will be at Wembley and I'll be sad for the one that's not.'

Members of the current Owls squad were portrayed in bullish form in their interviews. 'Thompson's in the Mood' was the headline above Garry's pre-game interview. 'This Could Be Our Year' was the take on Sterland's thoughts. 'I won't discuss the final yet, but I am confident of winning the semi-final,' announced Wilkinson in advance of the game.

The preparation, hype and mass support all focused on one thing. The match. Everton's top scorer Lineker did not pass a fitness test and was replaced by Adrian Heath. The Owls wore their yellow away strip, having lost a toss-up at FA headquarters earlier in the week. The team entered the pitch to a thunderous roar and the sight of a huge number of blue, white and yellow balloons from the massed Owls supporters.

Wednesday had the best of a generally cagey first half. The Owls won several corners and perhaps could have been awarded a penalty when Shelton was blocked in the box by Derek Mountfield. The referee waved play on. The half ended in a niggly fashion with fouls from either side. Shirtliff chopped down Heath before Peter Reid repeated the trick on Megson. The final action of the half saw the Owls remain on top, gaining their fifth corner of the game before it was cleared by Everton.

Five minutes into the second half and the deadlock was broken. After a game of head tennis around the Owls' box, Snodin nodded towards halfway – stumbling over in the process. This left Snodin out of position. As the ball came straight back, it fell to Alan Harper in the space where Snodin would have been. Hodge raced from his line to cover but Harper lobbed the Owls keeper and put Everton in front. It was Harper's first goal of the season.

A small pitch invasion of Everton fans followed before the game restarted. The ball was soon launched towards Everton's box by a long free kick from Shirtliff. It was not fully cleared and fell to Snodin on the left-hand side of midfield. He crossed to the far post where Hart was on hand to knock it towards Shutt, who nodded it past Bobby Mimms. The teams were level only three minutes after Everton's opener. Everton had some excellent chances in the second half, with Reid shooting over when well placed before Graeme Sharp had a shot well saved after a raking run forward. Sharp then shot wide from less than six yards. With no further goals, the game went to extra time.

Eight minutes into extra time and Owls' fans hearts were broken. Sharp struggled free at the far post as a diagonal ball was pumped into the box by Paul Bracewell. He caught his volley perfectly on his right boot, giving Hodge no chance. A succession of half-chances followed for the Owls as Shirtliff, Thompson and

Megson all came close without really testing the keeper. Time ran out for the Owls and Everton reached the FA Cup Final for the third year running. Wednesday were left wondering what might have been.

Shirtliff told me recently that 'we played well, so it was a disappointment we lost. It was a really tight game that they just shaded.' He went on the say that 'the fans and the atmosphere were terrific, it was a shame that we couldn't quite win it for them'. Madden felt that the Owls were 'the better team' who 'created chances that we couldn't finish' and that in extra time 'tired legs simply did for us'.

Thompson remembers thinking that the game was set up nicely for an Owls win. 'The game went by in a flash,' he told me. 'The more I think about that game, the more I think that was Wednesday's moment.' A win against Everton would have taken the Owls to a final against Liverpool, 'and who knows what would have happened then?'

During the game, Thompson attempted an extravagant overhead kick. 'I wanted to be the hero,' he told me. 'Meggo asked me what the bloody hell I was doing though!' Shelton thought that it was 'a tight game that was settled by a good strike from Sharpey. Hodgey was probably to blame for the first as he rushed out and Harper lobbed him. We soon equalised but the second goal did for us.'

The Owls players stayed on the pitch at full time, going to the Wednesday supporters to applaud them. Sterland was famously pictured leaving the pitch in tears. I shared that photograph on social media and soon received a reply from one of the fans that were pictured alongside him. Andy Clayton, who now lives in the Middle East, told me that it was he and his friend 'Big John' Crooks shown alongside Sterland in the image. Sadly, John Crooks has since passed away. Andy, though, was able to tell me the story of the day.

He, John and a group of other supporters from the Dearne Valley area had travelled down on the train early that morning. John and Andy were without tickets but managed to pick one up from an Owls supporter in the pub. With only one ticket, they managed to get into the match by quickly following each other through the turnstile, something that Andy admits 'is not acceptable these days but was a pretty regular occurrence back then'. Once in the ground, they didn't take their seat but stayed at the front, maybe on a walkway.

Andy takes up the story. 'At the final whistle we saw a couple of the Donny lads get on to the pitch and, this I remember plain as day, John said, "We'll both run at the steward and split at the last minute, so he won't know which one to grab! Come on, we're going!" And it was as simple as that. The first player we saw was Mel. I was there first, and he burst out in tears, John following up. I cannot remember how many of us got on the pitch. I do remember going to clap the Wednesday fans at the Holte End, thinking we were part of the team!' Andy and the others then made their way back to the train, meeting their friends with 'John telling everyone how I had made Mel cry and he had to console him!'

A great story, with a follow-up that may interest music fans. The Owls' kit launch for 2020/21 included the Sheffield group the Sherlocks. In the corresponding interview, two members of the band discussed how they had been taken to their first game by their uncle. It was John Crooks. Rest in peace.

The fixture is one that, perhaps inevitably, has stuck in the minds of Owls fans, both for events on and off the pitch. There is still some frustration among Wednesdayites about the lead-up to Harper's goal, with one supporter, Paul, telling me simply that 'the goal should never have stood'. Richard Crooks added, 'I've no doubt if VAR was in use then it would have been disallowed – as the ball came towards the goal Harper pushed Wednesday defender Snodin to one side … then came the goal.'

Other supporters remember the atmosphere clearly. The Owls supporters were given roughly half the tickets, including a section of the huge Holte End behind the goal. This was a standing section which was very busy, as Pete West told me: 'There were that many crammed in the middle I ended up down by the corner flag without touching the ground!'

Ken added 'I remember being worried about the overcrowding and being lifted off my feet a few times. Part of the problem was that there was rain and a lot of people crowded towards the back. I moved to the front.' The section of the Holte End was separated by netting from Everton's supporters which, as Nigel Lawes told me, meant that 'the Scouse fans, women included, were spitting at us!'

Another somewhat unsavoury incident that fans remembered was young Birmingham lads offering to 'look after' cars for money. As Owls fan Craig put it to me, 'We parked on a side road in Birmingham near to the ground and a young lad said, "50p to look after your car." It was the first time my dad and his friends, and a young me, had heard of this. We paid him and luckily the car was all OK after the match!'

Enterprising Owls supporters who could not find tickets through the usual channels found their way into the game. Richard Wells told me how he had connections in the Midlands and through Villa season ticket holders was able to acquire tickets in the Everton section. 'We recognised a few other Owls fans in that end. Villa stewards warned us to stay quiet as they felt things could get nasty if Everton lost. It was great to see and hear the Owls fans in the Holte End and, while it was good to be there, it wasn't the same being amongst the opposition.'

A final story that I enjoyed hearing comes from Jason Bate, who told me how he 'heard we were training at Lilleshall. So, on the Thursday before, I biked the ten miles from home to have a nose. Saw the squad on a training run, got scared, biked it straight back!' As the relentless chants of 'yellows, yellows' from the massed Owls support faded away, so did the Owls' opportunity of winning a trophy.

Conclusions

The Owls came near to cup glory in both our seasons. Should this be seen as evidence of success? In some ways, yes. When Wilkinson took on the manager's position, the club was still languishing in Division Two. By 1986 they were in the higher reaches of Division One, had played nine quarter-final ties and one semi-final. They were mixing with the big boys in the big time. The team were playing attacking and aggressive football and were fearless in their approach to these big games. And yet … Wilkinson had set out his stall to win trophies with Wednesday. He, and the team, did not. There is no shame in losing a semi-final to Everton, one of the best teams in the country. On another day maybe things would have gone somewhat differently.

The defeat to Chelsea after three epic games still feels the most painful. A victory here would have left Sunderland and Norwich between the Owls and cup glory. Those teams finished in the bottom three that season and were eminently beatable. What if?

Although Wilkinson was protective of his players after the 4-4 draw, there is a feeling that things could have been done differently. There is also an argument that the Owls were unfortunate with some of the key decisions made in certain games: Ipswich's winning goal from a seemingly offside position, Thomas escaping the referee's eye to lay out Blair and Harper's goal for Everton coming after a push on Snodin may all have had different outcomes in the modern age of VAR. So, bad luck, poor decisions, and determined opposition all played a role. Ultimately though, the Owls fell short of the success that Wilkinson expected and that, perhaps, the team were capable of achieving.

That is not to say that there was not much to be proud of and memories that remain until this day. As Wilkinson said in the programme notes for the game against Everton, 'It's OK to some extent losing in a final because at least you got there. If you lose in a semi-final … nothing.' He did accept, though, that the Owls would have had 'one heck of a year' whatever the result. That mixture of frustration at falling at the final hurdle, but pride at what was achieved, is perhaps the overarching feeling of Owls supporters about the time as well. It was a heck of a couple of years.

11.

An Interview with Andy Blair

ANDY BLAIR was a skilful midfielder who signed for the Owls in the summer of 1984 from Aston Villa. Born in Kirkcaldy, Scotland, he moved to the Midlands as a child and began his professional career with Coventry City before a big-money move to Villa Park in 1981. Andy's move to Hillsborough proved to be a real success as he was almost ever-present in the team in 1984/85 and, after recovering from an early-season injury in 1985/86, was again a regular in the XI. He moved back to Aston Villa in the spring of 1986.

Now into his sixties, but still running the chain of sportswear shops he set up following retirement, Andy remains in the Midlands. It was from his kitchen, overlooking a picturesque golf course, that we spoke in the spring of 2021. We chatted for a while over coffee about my reasons for writing the book, and football generally, before discussing Andy's career.

What brought you to Hillsborough in 1984?

The brutal truth is that I'd not been very good at Villa! That's despite playing against Barcelona in the European Super Cup and winning a medal in the Charity Shield. I'd only played 30-odd games in three years. They were a great team of course; they'd won the league and the European Cup. By the end of the 1983/84 season, though, I needed a change; a new challenge, a new environment. So I spoke to the manager at the time, Tony Barton, and said that to him. No agents back then, but managers did talk to each other. So before too long Tony indicated to me that Sheffield Wednesday were interested. I was delighted.

I drove up to meet Howard Wilkinson and Peter Eustace. We had a four-hour conversation. I was very impressed with both Peter and Howard. They were the perfect pair – good cop/bad cop in a way! Howard was so in-depth and analytical. He took me across to the training ground, which was deserted as everyone else was on holiday. He had me practising corners on my own. No corner flag, no goalposts – just using cones! Howard had watched me play for Villa at White Hart Lane, a game in which I managed to trip myself up and fall over – and he still liked the look of me! At a human level I was really impressed with him. I thought he was terrific. I was still a little naïve, though – I was only 24 – and I left with no mention of terms or a contract.

I heard nothing for another two or three weeks. I was beginning to worry that it had fallen through in some way, so I went back in to see Tony Barton and ask what was happening. In turned out that Wednesday needed to wait until they were able to sell Gary Megson. His move to Nottingham Forest got sorted and then my deal at Hillsborough quickly followed. I signed a two-year contract and was delighted.

And you went straight into the starting line-up for the first game of the season?

Yes, I'd signed in June, I think – ready to start on the first of July. So I took part in all of pre-season. It was exhilarating! The lead-up to the first game was fantastic. The excitement in the city was tangible. I'd played Division One football for all my career up until then, but I'd never felt anything like it before. The buzz around the ground on that first day was amazing. The atmosphere inside was great as well – a full crowd, and of course we won!

Who helped you settle into the team in those early months?

I instantly bonded with Brian Marwood; he became a great pal. On the pitch Gary Shelton and I were together in midfield and quickly formed a great partnership. The whole squad, though, were helpful and accommodating. It felt special, amazing. I stayed in the Whitley Hall hotel near High Green for three months or so and then bought a house out that way. Howard encouraged continuity, consistency and stability. Personally and professionally, it all seemed to come together for me.

The team were accused in the press of playing a kick and rush, long-ball game. Was that fair and did the tactics suit your game?

It was a great way of playing. It was thrilling. We created so many chances! The aim of any football team is to score goals and to win. The style got us into the final third of the pitch, where we could do just that. It was a direct style of football with a purpose. It suited me absolutely fine. Howard had us well drilled in the patterns he wanted us to play and what he wanted us to achieve. We played the way that Howard had organised, and it worked.

The squad has been described elsewhere as one of committed discards and journeymen. Is that fair?

Well Howard certainly put the jigsaw pieces together. It might even be fair about me. We had some great players, though. I remember the *Green 'Un* describing the three signings of Brian Marwood, Lee Chapman and myself in the summer of 1984 as 'stepping stones' for the club. I remember that Brian got a bit annoyed by it. I was proud to be a stepping stone though. We were helping the club return to the big league and I was delighted to be part of it.

Tell me more about the training and the management.

I got to see a lot of Sheffield with the running! I really enjoyed it though, no problem. The fitness training was designed to get the squad to be the best they could be. As I say, we were drilled. Howard left nothing to chance. It was organised and played to the strengths of the team. He didn't need to change things around too much in matches as we were so well prepared. Gordon Milne at Coventry was my favourite manager – he just wanted us to go out and play. Howard Wilkinson, though, was the best manager I ever had. He was an excellent man-manager and had great people around him with Peter Eustace and Alan Smith.

He got inside my head, though, in a way that ended up affecting me negatively. He asked me early in that first season whether I felt I could captain the team. We had a great captain in Mike Lyons, but I'd been skipper all the way through youth football. I told Howard that we already had a captain, but that I would love the opportunity. It never came though, as when Mike was out, Howard picked Gary Shelton as captain. No problem as Gary was a great guy, but it rankled with me as I wanted it. I suppose I wanted to prove something to Howard after that. With maturity, I realise Howard was right. I'm not sure I saw it that way at the time though.

Are there any games that stand out to you from that first season?

I remember scoring the three penalties against Luton Town! I think Mel Sterland had missed a couple earlier in the season, and I was on penalty duty. It was a fluke really. I remember reading that it was the first time it had ever been done – I don't think it was, but I do think it was the first time for Wednesday. So it's nice to be in the record books for that! I scored them past big Jake Findlay, who'd been at Villa for a while; I was pleased they all went in. I tell you what though, I think I took five penalties for Wednesday – I scored three that night and missed the other two!

Back to Howard. I remember a great example of his man-management. He was great at getting inside our heads. We played Liverpool at Anfield early in the 1984/85 season. He stood up on the coach as we were leaving Hillsborough and said, 'If anyone doesn't think we can win today, they can get off now!' Nobody did, of course, but it gave us great confidence. He stopped the coach on the Pennines for us all to have a walk about and clear our heads. Then, of course, we won!

I suppose my lowest ebb at Hillsborough was the 4-4 draw with Chelsea in the League Cup replay. There'd been a bit of needle in the first game and again in the first half between Mickey Thomas of Chelsea and a couple of our lads. It was like sledging in cricket, I suppose. Trouble is, I wasn't very good at it. I was as much to blame as anyone for it all. I said something I shouldn't have said to him, which really wasn't like me.

It ended with Mickey giving me an elbow or punch as we were lining up a defensive wall just before half-time. The ref missed it and play went on. I was in a bit of a daze in the second half about what had gone on, and the game passed me by really. I was still on penalty duties, but I think Mel [Sterland] must have realised that I wasn't really with it. So when we got the penalty and the chance to equalise at 4-3 down, he grabbed the ball off me and took the kick. He did exactly the right thing. I remember thinking that someone who wanted to be skipper wouldn't have got into that situation, so I was very disappointed with myself and the evening overall.

Into the next campaign, you were injured for a while and then moved back to Aston Villa. Was that season more of a disappointment for you?

I was injured in the first game of the season against Chelsea. David Speedie caught me across the chest and I also hurt my knee. I was out for four or five weeks but was back in the team when I recovered. Howard brought Gary Megson back to the club by Christmas time and I suspected that he was a direct replacement for me. The turning point came in a FA Cup game at Derby in March. I misplaced a pass in the first half which led to them scoring. Howard substituted me at half-time and I knew then that my time was up. It was no problem – we'd probably had enough of each other! He was the manager, though, and therefore he stayed and I went.

Howard called me in on the day before deadline day and told me that Villa were in for me. I was unsure, as I didn't really want to go back. Howard forcefully suggested, though, that I talk to them. I did just that, I went to see [Villa chairman] Doug Ellis and [manager] Graham Turner and agreed to sign. I signed alongside Steve Hunt, who I'd known from Coventry. Villa were struggling at the bottom of the table at the time. I was average for them, but Steve was brilliant and we helped keep the team up – so I was delighted with that. Unfortunately for me, my knee snapped the following season. It basically disintegrated – cruciate, ligaments, the lot. I did return to playing but I was never the same again after that.

Thanks Andy, is there anything else you'd like to add?
Just to say that to have played for Sheffield Wednesday at that time, with those players and that manager, makes me very proud. No amount of money could give you that feeling. I was able to achieve my dreams and that is a great feeling.

12.

1985: August to December

THE OWLS' first season back in the big time had been a relatively successful one. Howard Wilkinson and the club, though, were not prepared to stand still. Wilkinson said in the close season that he aimed 'to build a club with a solid structure that will live and thrive long after my departure'. Owls fans were pleased that it seemed his departure would be a long time in the future. Wilkinson, his assistant Peter Eustace and physio Alan Smith all signed new five-year contracts over the summer.

There was good news off the pitch for Wilkinson as well as he was married at Chapeltown Methodist Church. Mel Sterland also tied the knot that summer. Elsewhere at Hillsborough, the club announced record season ticket sales and that outline planning permission was being sought to put a roof on the Kop.

New signings were made, including boyhood Owls fan Glynn Snodin from Doncaster Rovers, Paul Hart from Nottingham Forest and club-record signing Garry Thompson from West Bromwich Albion. Tony Gregory made the step up to the first-team squad from the apprentice ranks. Ian Knight, aged 18, also signed on an initial trial basis having been released by Barnsley.

Players also moved out, with Simon Mills joining York City, Charlie Williamson leaving for Chesterfield and Imre Varadi preferring a move to West Bromwich Albion to a potential new contract at Hillsborough. The fee set by tribunal was £285,000. John Pearson also moved on to Charlton Athletic for £100,000 while Gavin Oliver left on loan to Brighton & Hove Albion.

The Owls returned to training on 8 July ahead of the first game of the season on 17 August. The team had already played a post-season friendly against Chesterfield (a 1-1 draw, with Varadi scoring the final goal of this spell at the club) before leaving on a pre-season tour of the Far East involving two games in Thailand. One was against a Bank of Bangkok team and the other against more homely opposition in Watford. Wednesday took a 16-man squad plus management and director representation to Bangkok for the short tour.

The game against Watford featured a rare first-team appearance for keeper Iain Hesford who, despite keeping a clean sheet and saving two penalties in the shoot-out following the 0-0 draw, could not force his way into the first team past Martin Hodge as the season began. The Owls won the shoot-out 5-3. Other pre-season games against Scunthorpe, Goole, Barnsley and Derby were all won. The Owls had planned a trip to Sheffield's twin city of Bochum in Germany but needed to rearrange those plans after English clubs were banned from playing in Europe following the Heysel Stadium disaster.

Wednesday were hit with two injury problems even before a ball was kicked in the upcoming league campaign. Siggi Jonsson was on the wrong end of a typically strong Graeme Souness tackle in a World Cup qualifier between Scotland and Iceland. It was feared for a while that Jonsson had a broken leg. Luckily the injury was not as bad as first feared, and Jonsson was back in the squad for the second game of the season. Nigel Worthington suffered a cartilage injury on the first day of pre-season training and needed an operation. With the expert help of Smith, he recovered and was fit enough to play in the first game of the season. It was a recovery which the *Green 'Un* felt was 'one of football's quickest comebacks from injury'.

The fixture computer saw that the Owls face would Chelsea in a home tie first up. The start of the season was brought forward by a week or so from previous years to ensure an earlier finish and give more preparation time for the 1986 World Cup. Wilkinson was faced with a three-into-two dilemma, with Lee Chapman,

Simon Stainrod and Thompson all hoping for a starting position up front. Thompson and Chapman made the cut with Stainrod on the bench. Wilkinson commented: 'I felt that Thompson, despite not yet being 100 per cent fit, might bring something unexpected.'

Perhaps more unexpected was captain Mike Lyons' third-minute goal for the Owls. Chapman's cross deflected to Lyons, who blasted the ball home from outside the penalty area. Wednesday forced a succession of corners in the first half hour but were unable to really threaten Eddie Niedzwiecki's goal. They were hit on the counter on 34 minutes as Andy Blair's clearance took an unfortunate deflection and fell to David Speedie, who ran through and slotted the ball past Hodge.

The remainder of the game was a somewhat dour affair with chances few and far between until the final minutes. Pat Nevin held on to the ball rather than set up the much better placed Kerry Dixon before an almighty scramble in the Chelsea goalmouth almost saw the Owls force the ball home.

The goalscoring was over, though, with both managers happy enough with a point, Wilkinson commenting that Chelsea's forwards 'will be a problem for anybody' and Chelsea manager John Hollins talking up Lyons' performance. 'Mike knows the game,' he said, 'and I expect Kerry will have learned a few things from him.'

Wednesday's next fixture involved the relatively short journey to the City Ground to face Nottingham Forest. Wilkinson brought Stainrod into the starting XI at the expense of Thompson and included Jonsson after his recovery from his summer injury. The change paid immediate dividends as Sterland charged down the right before crossing to Stainrod, who swept home a clinical finish just inside the post from 12 yards. Only two minutes were on the clock.

Forest fought back immediately with Steve Hodge bringing two great saves out of his namesake Martin in the Owls goal. Jonsson missed a header from close range as the half came to an end. Forest thought they had scored in the early stages of the second half as Steve Wigley slid in the rebound after Ian Butterworth had struck the bar. Referee David Scott had already blown his whistle for an earlier foul. There were fewer chances as the game moved towards its conclusion, though Brian Marwood looked dangerous on the wing. Stainrod was particularly pleased with his performance, saying, 'It was quite a goal … My pride was hurt when I was left out on Saturday, but the goal helps.'

The Owls faced another away trip for their next fixture, this time to Maine Road to face Manchester City. It was another changed line-up, with Wilkinson shuffling his pack up front and including Stainrod and Thompson this time. More worrying for the Owls were the injuries ruling out Gary Shelton and Blair from the midfield. Wednesday started with 18-year-old Jonsson and 17-year-old Gregory in the midfield berths. Gregory was making his debut.

There were early chances for both sides as Brian Marwood came closest with a shot that just flew over the bar. On 28 minutes the Owls took the lead, Jonsson crossing for Thompson to stab in his first goal for the club. Half-time arrived with few further chances. Five minutes into the second period, City equalised as Paul Simpson smashed a shot past Hodge.

Wednesday then needed to soak up a period of City pressure before being gifted the second as Marwood stole in on a woefully short backpass before rounding the keeper and knocking the ball into the empty net. A third Owls goal followed on 83 minutes as Marwood latched on to Thompson's flick from Hodge's long clearance for his second of the game.

Wilkinson was delighted with the performance of Gregory and Jonsson, which 'reflects great credit on them'. Lyons reminded readers of the following match's programme that Gregory was still an apprentice and would be 'cleaning boots, tidying up, laying out kit and so on' when back at Hillsborough.

Next up for the Owls was a home fixture against Watford, only two days later on a Bank Holiday Monday. Wilkinson opted for an unchanged team, with the two youngsters keeping their place in midfield. Wednesday took an early lead as Marwood's corner fell to Sterland to smash home from close range.

Hodge was kept busy in the Owls goal, making a couple of good saves before excelling himself in the 36th minute to save from the spot. Shirtliff handled on the line to give Luther Blissett the chance to score from 12 yards, but Hodge guessed right to push the ball away. Into the second half and Gregory had the chance for a dream home debut, firing straight at Tony Coton and then just over the bar – 'a sitter', as he told me in 2021!

Sterland cleared the ball off his own line before Watford equalised. A corner was flicked on to Blissett, who this time made no mistake from close range. Wilkinson brought Chapman on in an attacking move. The big striker then won the game for Wednesday by powerfully heading Marwood's diagonal cross into the net. Watford's manager Graham Taylor was angry after the game, calling the pitch 'diabolical' and feeling that work done to the Hillsborough surface over the summer had not taken, meaning that keeper Coton miskicked the ball in the lead-up to the Owls' first goal.

Taylor suggested that the pitch would be 'like a bog' come the autumn. Head groundsman David Barber disagreed and was pleased to be proved right, commenting in November that, 'Mr Taylor's comments were not fair ... the pitch is now playing better than ever'. Eustace spoke for the club after the game, keeping his comments to the fixture. 'We knew we would have our hands full today,' he said. 'Watford keep the pressure on for 90 minutes.'

The fixtures kept coming thick and fast, with a trip to Oxford next for the Owls the following Saturday. Wilkinson shuffled his pack, with Gregory and Stainrod dropping out as Shelton returned from injury into the midfield and Chapman returned up front. Carl Shutt was named as substitute. Wednesday were wearing a unique combination of blue and white stripes with Oxford's yellow shorts and socks to avoid a clash.

The first half of the game was relatively uneventful, with a couple of half-chances for Chapman and Marwood all that the Owls had to show for their efforts. The pace picked up after half-time and Wednesday took the lead on 51 minutes. The ball was not cleared from a corner before falling to Thompson, who squared for Jonsson to drive home from ten yards out. It was the Icelandic international's first goal for the Owls.

The goal seemed to spark Oxford into action and they soon had the ball in the net before it was chalked off for a foul on Hodge. Oxford had a golden opportunity to equalise on 63 minutes when a penalty was awarded after a foul in the area by Worthington. John Trewick took the kick and drove it low to the keeper's left. Hodge guessed correctly and brought off a stunning save – his fifth from the last six penalties he had faced.

The miss seemed to knock the wind out of Oxford's sails; the main chance of the rest of the game fell to Hart, who hit the post for the Owls. The game was otherwise notable for Shutt's late appearance which marked his first-team debut. Hart said afterwards that 'we were always looking comfortable', whereas Oxford manager Maurice Evans said, 'I thought Wednesday were a bit fortunate.'

Wednesday's August fixtures had seen four wins and a draw. The team were sitting pretty in second place in the early-season table. The first game of September was a Tuesday evening home tie against champions Everton. Wednesday seemingly had every reason to feel confident. The game started well for Wednesday, Thompson going close with a spectacular overhead kick before they took the lead in the 24th minute. Thompson's header was punched off the line by an Everton defender, Marwood scoring the resultant spot-kick.

Everton equalised before half-time through a close-range effort from Derek Mountfield. The second half saw an Owls collapse. Goals from Trevor Steven, Gary Lineker, Graeme Sharp and Adrian Heath put Wednesday to the sword. Wilkinson suggested afterwards, 'I feel like the captain of the Titanic!' Howard Kendall, Everton's manager, commented that 'we were a little bit special tonight'. The *Daily Mirror* had it that 'Everton stormed through Hillsborough like Hell's Angels shopping at Mothercare!'

The Owls had only a few days' respite before the first of four successive games against London-based opposition in league and cup (five if Luton count!). West Ham United were the next opponents in a Hillsborough clash. Wilkinson again shuffled his pack, with Chris Morris and Lawrie Madden making their first appearances of the season. Sterland, Hart and Shirtliff all missed out after the Everton thrashing.

The Hammers surprised the Owls with a quick start, taking the lead on nine minutes as Frank McAvennie rounded Hodge to slot home for his sixth goal in seven games. Chapman equalised ten minutes later, heading in Thompson's cross. Madden almost put the Owls ahead just before half-time with a header that hit the angle of post and bar before being hacked off the line.

Wednesday did score on 58 minutes. Jonsson's cross was nodded down by Lyons to Thompson, who scored his first goal at Hillsborough for the Owls. Wednesday dominated after that, but after missing several chances it was perhaps inevitable that West Ham would equalise. On 88 minutes, Tony Cottee took advantage of hesitation in the Wednesday backline and squeezed the ball home. Wilkinson was seemingly irritated about 'not one of our better performances'. West Ham captain Alvin Martin thought the draw was 'a tremendous result for us'.

Wednesday's next fixture was a trip to Highbury to face Arsenal. The lead-up to the game had seen more transfer action with Stainrod moving to the Midlands to join Aston Villa and England international winger Mark Chamberlain joining the Owls from Stoke City. Chamberlain took his place on the bench for the Arsenal game. The Gunners went into the game on the back of three clean sheets and it was clear why in the opening stages with defences on top.

On 29 minutes Arsenal took the lead after Ian Allinson was felled in the area by Hodge. The same player took the resultant spot-kick, leaving Hodge with no chance. Wednesday battled hard to level the scores and came close when Arsenal keeper John Lukic made a stunning point-blank save from a Thompson header. Wilkinson brought Chamberlain on for his debut at the expense of Chapman, but although he showed some good touches, he and the rest of the team created little of real note. The *Sunday Mirror* were not impressed with the game and the low crowd. 'Huge gaps on the terracing indicate disenchantment with football's version of Star Wars,' they commented. Wednesday's Mark Smith simply felt 'it was a disappointing result'.

The Owls returned to London the following Saturday to face Tottenham Hotspur at White Hart Lane. Howard Wilkinson brought Snodin into the team for his debut at the expense of Worthington. The squad was otherwise unchanged, with Chamberlain beginning to get used to what would become his customary place on the bench.

Glenn Hoddle missed an early chance for Spurs before Chapman put Wednesday ahead with a superb diving header on 20 minutes. Tottenham equalised on 31 minutes as Chris Waddle latched on to an excellent pass from Osvaldo Ardiles and gave Hodge no chance. The second half was a disaster for the Owls. Three goals in the opening 17 minutes meant the game was over as a contest just after the hour mark. Mark Falco, Waddle and Falco again were the scorers. Hoddle atoned for his earlier miss with the fifth and final goal in the dying minutes.

'Spurs were simply terrific,' commented Wilkinson. Tottenham's manager Peter Shreeves focused his compliments on Ardiles. 'Ossie was outstanding,' he said. 'He won a million tackles for us and kept us on the move.' Ardiles was perhaps lucky to have stayed on the field after an earlier disagreement with Lyons. 'I didn't punch him – he's too big for me!' said the Argentine, who was issued with a booking for his part in the incident.

After a further trip to London for a midweek cup game with Brentford, the Owls returned to home soil with another fixture against southern opposition. Luton Town were the next challenge for Wednesday at Hillsborough. Sterland and Blair had returned to the team at the expense of Morris and Jonsson for the Brentford game, and both remained in an otherwise unchanged team for the Luton tie. The opening 40 minutes of the game gave little sign of the excitement which followed, with chances few and far between for either side. Three goals in three minutes as half-time approached changed all that. The Owls took the lead when Thompson knocked on a long kick from Hodge to Marwood, who lobbed Les Sealey. The Hatters immediately equalised as Mick Harford followed up to score from close range after a Brian Stein shot was blocked. The last move of the half saw Wednesday retake the lead when Lee Chapman powered in from a Marwood cross.

The start of the second period saw Chapman go close to extending the Owls' lead before Luton were not too far away with shots from Harford and Stein. In the 62nd minute the Owls did extend their lead. Thompson's shot was handled in the area, Marwood placing the ball into the bottom corner from the resulting penalty. Once again, though, Wednesday were pegged back as almost straight from the kick-off Harford was able to stroke home following a rare mistake by Hodge.

Wednesday had the better of the chances in the remaining minutes but that was the end of the scoring. Howard Wilkinson said he was 'relieved with the result but not elated'.

The result saw the Owls end September in seventh position in the table. It also marked the end of that run of games against southern opposition. 'London has not been the happiest of places for the Owls since my arrival,' commented Wilkinson wryly. The Owls now faced four league fixtures against teams from the Midlands, the first of which was a trip to St Andrew's to face Birmingham City.

The Owls had a changed backline with Morris and Hart named at the expense of Snodin and Lyons due to injuries. Birmingham were defending a 14-match unbeaten home record and had the better of the early chances, with Andy Kennedy blasting over and then bringing a fine save from Hodge. Just before the interval, though, Wednesday took the lead. A Marwood corner found Sterland unmarked and he blasted the ball high into the net.

The Owls' second goal came within two minutes of the restart when Birmingham centre-back Kenneth Armstrong knocked the ball into his own net from a Marwood cross.

Wednesday were denied a penalty despite Chapman seemingly being pulled down by Birmingham keeper David Seaman. Despite the failure to score further goals it was an excellent performance, which Wilkinson said was 'as comprehensive a win as you are likely to see'.

Wednesday's second game against Midlands opposition involved a return to home soil for the visit of Coventry City. The Owls were again struggling with injuries and Wilkinson therefore gave full debuts to Chamberlain and Shutt. The reworked team started well, with Sterland firing an early 30-yard drive over the bar and then providing a cross which Lee Chapman just failed to convert.

Chapman made amends on 21 minutes, heading home following an excellent flick-on from Hart. Then, a minute before the break, Shutt netted with a fantastic diving header. The second half saw the game turn on its head. Wednesday missed early chances but on 50 minutes a terrible backpass left Hodge helpless as future Blades boss Micky Adams rounded him and pulled one goal back. Fifteen minutes from time Cyrille Regis crossed past a tired-looking Owls defence for Terry Gibson to shoot low into the net. Gibson therefore became the first Coventry player to score in six consecutive Division One games. There was still time for Hodge to deny Regis a winning goal in the final minutes as the Owls hung on grimly. 'It was like giving a condemned man a reprieve,' commented Wilkinson afterwards.

It was the Owls' turn to travel for their next game, to the East Midlands this time and a fixture against Leicester City. Wilkinson again needed to shuffle his pack, with Shelton and Shirtliff added to the injury list. 'We are undergoing a prolonged list of injuries, the likes of which we have not encountered before,' he commented. Jonsson returned to the starting line-up, as did Lyons and Snodin.

Despite the enforced changes in personnel, the Owls started well. In the 27th minute Smith's long free kick was knocked down by Chapman for Marwood to nip in and head the opener. There were further chances before half-time for Jonsson and Smith and

Leicester could consider themselves lucky to be only a goal down at the break.

Leicester came out of the traps much quicker in the second half. Steve Lynex soon bundled his way through the Owls defence and his angled drive took a wicked deflection and looped in for the equaliser. Lynex and Andy Feeley came close before Mark Bright crossed for Alan Smith to head the Foxes in front from close range on 67 minutes.

Wednesday seemed to gain a second wind at this stage and were level within five minutes as Chapman and Snodin combined for Jonsson to sidefoot home from ten yards out. The Owls continued to push and on 79 minutes a corner fell to Jonsson. His overhead kick was met by Chapman, who hit the bar with a header but was alert enough to knock home the rebound. The return to form since the Tottenham debacle had seen the Owls take ten points from a possible 12. 'Watch out for Wednesday,' commented the *Sunday People*.

The Owls' next fixture was their fourth in succession against a Midlands team, this time a Hillsborough clash with West Bromwich Albion. The Baggies were managed by World Cup winner Nobby Stiles but were rock bottom of the league. Wilkinson needed to reshuffle his team, with Shelton, Madden and Morris named at the expense of Lyons, Smith and Jonsson. Wednesday's defence was described as 'makeshift' in the following week's programme.

It was the Baggies' backline that was put under pressure early on, Sterland and Shutt both seeing drives go close before Marwood was desperately unlucky to see his shot strike the upright. Wednesday went ahead on 38 minutes when Snodin curled a deep cross into the path of Lee Chapman, who powered home his tenth goal of the season.

Wednesday's attacks continued. Chapman saw a header clip the bar and Sterland had a fine effort cleared off the line. The Owls were quieter in the second half but still saw Shutt glance a header wide and Chapman test the keeper. Garth Crooks came close for the Baggies in the final few minutes but any result other than an Owls win would not have reflected the play. 'Wednesday are very effective,' commented Stiles.

Wednesday travelled south for their next game, a fixture on the artificial pitch at Loftus Road against Queens Park Rangers. Thompson returned to the team up front after appearing as a substitute in a midweek Milk Cup fixture at Swindon. Shutt dropped out of an otherwise unchanged team. It was the London team who made the early running, with a series of attacks that threatened the Owls goal. A fine double save from Mike Fillery and then Gary Waddock was perhaps the pick of Hodge's several contributions in the first half.

QPR dominated the early stages of the second period also, though they were unable to create any further clear-cut chances. On 78 minutes the Owls took an unexpected lead when Blair set up Snodin to smash home from just inside the box. The Owls' lead was short-lived as Rangers quickly equalised with a great run and powerful shot from Robbie James. 'Wednesday were fortunate to leave with a draw,' commented the *Daily Mirror*. 'I don't like coming here with this pitch,' added Wilkinson.

Key Game: Sheffield Wednesday 1-0 Manchester United, 9 November 1985

Manchester United approached the game against the Owls in great form. Unbeaten in the league, they were ten points clear of Liverpool in second place and 13 ahead of the Owls in third. Wilkinson was in bullish mood beforehand. 'It's a welcome test for us,' he told the *Sheffield Telegraph*. 'They're riding the crest of a wave and we're in there with them. Now we'll find out how good we are.'

Eustace added that 'United are a team full of good players who this season have become a little bit meaner and harder'. The tie certainly appealed to the paying public as 48,105 turned out on a cold and windy November day to witness what turned out to be a hard-fought game. The crowd was boosted by a large contingent from Manchester. As one supporter put it to me recently, 'It felt like there were 17,000 of them there!'

Wilkinson named the following line-up:

1. Martin Hodge
2. Mel Sterland
3. Glynn Snodin
4. Lawrie Madden
5. Chris Morris
6. Paul Hart
7. Brian Marwood
8. Andy Blair
9. Lee Chapman
10. Garry Thompson
11. Gary Shelton

Sub) Mark Chamberlain

Lyons was on the verge of moving to Grimsby Town and despite rumours beforehand was not included in the squad to make a dramatic farewell appearance. Hodge could celebrate his 100th consecutive appearance for the Owls. Manchester United manager Ron Atkinson recalled Bryan Robson in midfield after a month out with injury. He left Gordon Strachan on the bench, commenting: 'He's a world-class player, but the way that Jesper Olsen and Peter Barnes have been playing made it a very difficult decision.' Paul McGrath started the game at centre-back with Graeme Hogg suspended.

Lyons helped with the pre-match warm-ups for the Owls, and it did not take long for the temperature of the game to also rise. A huge roar greeted the teams as they ran on to the pitch. Both sides had early chances, with Madden fouling Norman Whiteside for an early United free kick which was fired into the wall. Marwood looked lively and was denied a goal by the quick reactions of United keeper Gary Bailey.

The course of the game was altered on 15 minutes when Robson hobbled off, seemingly suffering a recurrence of the achilles issue that had kept him out previously. Strachan replaced him and United reorganised. The match kept up its quick pace for the remainder of the half. The Owls forced a succession of corners at the Leppings Lane End which United defended solidly. United broke quickly and the Owls were reliant on Sterland and Blair for vital interceptions. Half-time saw another thunderous round of applause for the efforts of the Wednesday team.

Wilkinson revealed after the game that two of his players had struggled with injury in the first half. 'Paul Hart received a very bad blow to the leg, while Andy Blair twisted his knee,' he said. 'I could have taken either player off at half-time but that would have meant jigging the team about.' Instead, he kept the team as it was for the start of the second half. The *Green 'Un's* report that evening suggested that 'the centre-back was definitely limping after the restart'.

The Owls defence had to cope with a United onslaught, with the wide men of Olsen and Barnes looking threatening. Alongside the ever-present threat from Mark Hughes, Strachan and Whiteside, that gave the Owls a daunting task. As the half developed, though, the Wednesday team began to have the better of the play. Shelton cleverly chipped the ball over Frank Stapleton and got a powerful shot away. Shelton then released Marwood with a perfectly weighted pass that needed Bailey to make a sharp save from the winger's resulting strike. On 71 minutes Thompson came agonisingly close with an acrobatic overhead kick that flew just wide of the post.

The game was decided in the final ten minutes. Wilkinson brought on Chamberlain to replace Marwood on 82 minutes, having seen that his two injury-threatened players would last the course. Two minutes later Chamberlain provided the perfect near-post corner for Chapman to glance home the match-winning header. 'Mark takes great corner kicks and that one was just perfect,' commented Chapman after the game, continuing, 'it looks like an inspired decision by the boss to bring him on.' Chapman's 11th goal of the season provoked loud and wild celebrations in the stands. 'I think we've sent a few fans home happy tonight,' commented Chapman wryly.

Madden told me in 2021: 'We deserved it, we were the best team on the day, and we were up for it.' He continued by reflecting on the importance of set pieces to the team. 'We were kicking downhill towards the Kop in the second half. We missed a number of chances through open play but as was often the case we scored from a well-drilled corner routine.' Shelton felt that it was a 'tight game against a very good Manchester United side, but one that we deserved to win'.

Not everyone went home happy. The *Daily Mirror* carried the story of how the United striker Hughes booted the ball in frustration on the final whistle, only for it to hit 12-year-old asthma sufferer David Manley full-on. Hughes wrote to Manley, a letter that was published in the Owls' match programme. He offered fulsome apologies and the opportunity for the boy and his father to watch the return game at Old Trafford and meet Hughes after the game.

Maybe happier after the game were a group of unnamed Owls players who, legend has it, placed a £100 bet on Wednesday beating United at odds of 3/1. Such bets were against FA rules and, as the *Daily Mirror* had it, they could 'expect at least a ticking off from the FA'. Wilkinson dismissed the rumours in the following day's papers.

One person who certainly was happy was Owls chairman Bert McGee. He made his first visit of the season to the Hillsborough press room to tell the assembled reporters: 'Don't anyone dare tell me that football is dead after that. We have just seen 48,000 people watch 22 footballers play their best.' He went on: 'Football has had such a belting over the last few months – this is a time to be joyous.'

Wilkinson joined in with the positivity. 'It was important to us to play giving 100 per cent and to measure ourselves against outstanding players.' The *Sheffield Star*'s Paul Thompson wrote a glowing review of the team afterwards. 'Wednesday must rightly command respect and they have the record to demand it.' He continued, 'They not only became the first team to beat United, they did so on merit.'

News of the Owls' winner sparked cheers on Anfield's Kop that day. It also saw the beginning of a fall from the top of the Manchester United team, who stuttered for the remainder of the season, eventually finishing fourth. Little of that mattered to

Owls fans that day – as one told me recently, they were simply 'brilliant times!'

* * *

Wednesday travelled to Villa Park for their next fixture. Wilkinson was able to name an unchanged starting XI from the victory over Manchester United, though Worthington did replace Chamberlain on the bench. Aston Villa featured ex-Owls striker Stainrod in their ranks.

The game started quietly but burst into life in the 22nd minute when Marwood took the first corner of the game. Hart glanced it back towards goal, and Nigel Spink in the Villa goal helped bundle it into the net. The goal was given to Hart and was his first in Owls colours. Villa reacted strongly, with Steve Hodge hitting the side-netting and Andy Gray blasting wide, before equalising in the 38th minute. Mark Walters and Hodge combined well before crossing to Colin Gibson, who powered a header past Hodge.

Wednesday needed to battle hard in the second half to keep the scores level, as Gibson hit the bar and Villa dominated possession. There were few further chances, though, until Hart nearly added a second near the end with a smart header from a Marwood cross. It was a 'run of the mill' match according to the *Sheffield Star*. It did, though, extend the Owls' unbeaten run in the league to eight matches.

Wednesday's next game was a home tie against Southampton. The Owls named an unchanged starting XI for the fourth successive game. The Owls made a rapid start, with Shelton just missing an excellent Marwood cross and then heading at Peter Shilton within the opening five minutes.

Snodin tested Shilton again with a rasping 25-yard drive before the Owls took the lead in the 19th minute. Blair ran down the right and crossed for Chapman to crash a shot past Shilton. Amazingly, this was Chapman's first non-headed league goal of the season! The Owls had chance after chance in the remainder of the half, but a combination of goal-line clearances, miscues when well-placed and Shilton's heroics in goal ensured that the score remained 1-0. Wednesday's supporters were delighted at half-time, giving the team a rousing standing ovation as they left the field.

The second half was inevitably a little slower, but the Owls still dominated and in the 70th minute they notched the second. The move started with Hodge throwing the ball to Sterland, who sprinted up the wing before crossing for Marwood to glance a header home. Southampton set up a nervy finish when Mark Wright scored from close range on 81 minutes, but it was the Owls who were attacking as the final whistle went. 'It would be difficult to top our first half display,' commented Howard Wilkinson.

The Owls travelled to Suffolk the following weekend to face an Ipswich Town side who were struggling near the foot of the table and had gone 13 games without a league win. Wilkinson named the same starting XI for the fifth game in a row, though Jonsson did take Chamberlain's place on the bench.

Ipswich were boosted by their midweek 6-1 victory over Swindon Town in the Milk Cup. The game initially seemed to be going with the league table as the Owls took a fortuitous 17th-minute lead, Town defender Frank Yallop slicing the ball into his own net following a Brian Marwood corner.

Ipswich, though, levelled within five minutes, with Mich d'Avray outjumping the Owls defence to head home Kevin Wilson's cross. Both sides had chances as the game entered the second period, with Chapman the closest with a powerful header. On 75 minutes, though, Ipswich found the winner when d'Avray scored his second of the game from a low cross.

Despite a succession of corners, Wednesday could not find the equaliser. Wilkinson was magnanimous in defeat. 'We were very disappointing,' he said, 'but don't take anything away from Ipswich who fully deserved to win.'

The Owls returned to home soil for their next game and their first in December, facing Brian Clough's Nottingham Forest. Wednesday were again unchanged, though Chamberlain returned to the bench. The game was played in foul weather conditions, with both sides finding the wind and rain difficult in the opening period.

Forest grew into the game as the half progressed, with future Owl loanee Franz Carr speeding past the Wednesday defence before shooting wide. Hodge made tremendous saves from Neil Webb and Peter Davenport (twice) before Colin Walsh swerved a shot just wide. The Owls created little of note in the first half and were relieved to reach the break on level terms.

Webb put Forest ahead on 54 minutes, following up after Hodge parried Nigel Clough's shot. The Owls equalised three minutes later through Marwood, who shot home following excellent work from Shelton and Chapman. Forest poured forward again after the goal, with Hodge saving well from Davenport and twice from Carr.

Chamberlain came off the bench on 79 minutes and forced the winner seven minutes later. The ball found its way through a mass of players in the box for Chamberlain to stab home. The *Sunday Express* were clear in their view: 'Forest at their scintillating best should have won it.' Wilkinson admitted that 'Martin Hodge was our saviour'.

Wilkinson changed the team for the first time in seven games for the following fixture, a trip to Stamford Bridge to face Chelsea. Worthington returned for his first starting appearance since September. He replaced Thompson as Wilkinson opted to return to a five-man backline. The defence initially struggled against Chelsea's experienced attack, with David Speedie blocked by Hodge when clean through, before in the 27th minute a free kick led to the opening goal. Kerry Dixon flicked on Pat Nevin's kick to Speedie, who fired home his 13th goal of the campaign.

Snodin had a good chance to equalise just before the break, but keeper Eddie Niedzwiecki saved with his feet. This was to prove crucial as three minutes into the second period Chelsea went two up, Nigel Spackman pouncing on a loose clearance and firing in off the post. Chelsea continued to charge forward with Dixon spurning THREE chances in as many minutes – Hart clearing one off the line, Hodge brilliantly saving the second and the third going wide.

Wednesday were given a lifeline on 67 minutes as Chapman was upended in the box. Marwood drilled home the penalty. The

Owls were unable to bring any real pressure to bear and their day was made even worse when Sterland was dismissed for a second bookable offence in the final seconds. Sterland's trip on Speedie followed an earlier lunging tackle on Kevin McAllister. Spackman thought that the referee had been harsh, saying, 'He didn't deserve to go, not in the last minute, it was just a trip.'

The sending off was the first for any player at the club since Wilkinson's arrival two and a half years previously. 'Stupid and inexcusable,' was the manager's description of Sterland's second booking. Wilkinson, though, took the blame for the defeat. 'I changed our formation,' he said. 'I was wrong and I accept full responsibility for the result.'

The Owls now headed into the traditionally busy festive period – four fixtures in 11 days awaited them. The first game was a home tie against Manchester City. Wilkinson had brought Gary Megson back to the club on an initial one-month loan in advance of the game. He went straight into the starting line-up, with Thompson also returning.

The rejigged team went a goal down early on as Mark Lillis shot home from close range after only 13 minutes. Wednesday soon equalised, though, as less than a minute later an excellent Marwood cross was nodded home by the returning Thompson. After 25 minutes Wednesday took the lead and this time it was a homecoming delight for Megson, who headed in following a Shelton knock-down. Just before the break the Owls made it 3-1 with Sterland scoring a header from a corner.

The second half saw City dominate throughout. They pulled a goal back on 66 minutes through Neil McNab and missed several other excellent chances. The two clearest ones were missed by Gordon Davies in the dying minutes. Manager Billy McNeill felt 'we were entitled to the three points'. Radio Sheffield agreed: 'Davies played Santa to Wednesday, gift-wrapping them three points they did not really deserve.'

The Owls and their supporters would have time to open their presents before the next fixture – a Boxing Day clash against Newcastle United. The supporters did have an earlier start than usual, though, as kick-off was at 1pm. Over 30,000 supporters made it out of bed in time to watch Wilkinson's unchanged team.

The first half was exciting and competitive but lacked composure as both sides were guilty of sloppy passing. Wednesday looked in injury trouble as firstly Hart, then Shelton and Snodin pulled up with knocks. Snodin's was a hamstring pull and forced his replacement by Chamberlain just after the half-hour mark.

The reshuffled Owls took the lead on 41 minutes, with Marwood launching a 25-yard rocket into the top corner. Newcastle turned the game on its head in the second half, with Glenn Roeder equalising on 53 minutes after Hodge parried Peter Beardsley's shot. On 72 minutes Beardsley took advantage of some uncertainty in the Wednesday defence to nip in and slot the ball through the legs of Hodge.

The Owls found the strength to equalise with ten minutes remaining. Marwood's corner was flicked on by Hart to Thompson, who slotted home. Wilkinson said afterwards that he had contemplated putting Thompson back into defence as Hart was carrying a knock 'but changed my mind and fortunately the gamble came off'.

The day was a memorable one for supporter Mark Balaiss. 'The first game I went to was against Newcastle on Boxing Day 1985,' he said. 'The only thing I remember about the day was going with my mother's cousin, who was groundsman at the time, and getting some autographs!' Perhaps it was not the most important of games, but it marked the last home game of a successful 1985.

The Owls' next two fixtures were both in Merseyside. First up was a trip to Everton. Wilkinson named an XI with a remodelled backline, including Shirtliff, Worthington and Smith and leaving out Sterland, Hart and Snodin. Chamberlain made a rare start, with Gregory being named on the bench. Ex-Evertonian Hodge was named as captain for the day, and he was regularly called into action in the first half.

He saved well from Paul Bracewell after eight minutes before Gary Stevens put the Toffees ahead after 20 with a low shot from outside the box. It was 2-0 after 25 minutes as Bracewell and

Graeme Sharp combined to set up Gary Lineker. The Owls nearly pulled one back before the break when Thompson's shot struck the post.

Wilkinson brought on Gregory for Smith at half-time. The Owls soon pulled a goal back, Thompson pushing Blair's cross towards goal, where it went in despite Stevens' best efforts on the line. Thompson soon saw a header bounce down from the underside of the bar but, despite strong shouts from the Owls that the ball had crossed the line, Everton survived.

The Toffees then added the killer blow with four minutes to spare, Lineker nodding home from Kevin Sheedy's inch-perfect cross. 'We had our chances to settle the game,' felt Wilkinson afterwards, adding the following week that 'we turned in one of our best away performances for some time'.

The defeat to Everton, combined with the Newcastle draw, saw the Owls drop a position to sixth in the table. This was their lowest placing since September. Despite this, the *Green 'Un*'s Paul Thompson was bullish about the club's prospects in 1986. In an article titled 'Owls Are Equipped for Anything Now!', Thompson argued that the team were now a 'strong, respected force' in the top flight and that despite 'not having played as well as last season, they have looked solid and have the base on which to make more progress'.

Wilkinson seemed to agree with those thoughts, commenting in his programme notes for the Newcastle game that he hoped that '1986 sees the acquisition of our first trophy for the club and that the progress we've made during our time here continues'.

The Owls were in the same position in the league as 12 months previously. In common with the early part of the previous season they had achieved some famous victories. This time round there had also been a couple of trouncings. With new players now bedded into the team – and the established players having over a year of top-flight experience – Owls supporters did have some cause to agree with Wilkinson's optimism. Anfield beckoned for the first game of 1986.

13.

An Interview with Peter Shirtliff

PETER SHIRTLIFF was a 6ft 1in centre-half whose Owls career stretched to 356(+3) appearances in two spells, with 13 goals. Shirtliff was a boyhood Owls supporter and joined the club straight from school, making his debut in 1978 as a teenager. He was in and out of the team as a youngster before cementing his place in the early 1980s, becoming a mainstay of the team that won promotion to Division One in 1984.

Shirtliff remained a regular in the team for the two seasons covered in this book before moving to Charlton Athletic in the summer of 1986. He returned for a second spell at Hillsborough under Ron Atkinson in 1989, being part of the team that won promotion from Division Two and the League Cup in 1991. He remains among the top 20 appearance makers of all time for the Owls. We spoke in the summer of 2021 from Peter's home on the north-west coast.

Tell me how you came to sign for the club.

I signed as a schoolboy. George McCabe had me watched, I think, and brought me in on trial. I played for Middlewood Rovers for a year, and then signed apprenticeship forms.

You made your first-team debut at a young age?

I was 17. It was a League Cup tie away at Doncaster in 1978 and the first game of the season. I had an inkling it was coming because we'd done some preparation in the week and I knew that Ray

Blackhall, the first-choice right-back, was injured. So I filled in for him. I also played in the return leg and then a couple of league games, all pretty quickly and all at right-back. In fact, that first season I played nearly 30 games, I think, all in the same position.

The manager back then was Jack Charlton. What are your memories of working with him?

Jack was a great coach and a great manager. His man-management was excellent. I was out of the team for much of 1979/80 but he told me that I wasn't forgotten and that I was in his plans. It helped make sure that I wasn't too frustrated. He was also able to pass on his experience. He was great with us youngsters at the time. He was good with detail and the little things we could do to improve our game. That was true for all positions, but he was particularly able to help us defenders given all his experience. It was a great time; there were lots of youngsters coming through at a similar time to me. When I became more of a regular in the first team again in 1980/81, we played at some big grounds, particularly down in London. I really enjoyed it.

Did things change when Howard Wilkinson took over in 1983?

It was totally different! There was a new structure and new training methods. He had a fantastic group in the season we got promoted. There were some talented players – Gary Bannister, Gary Shelton and others. Most importantly, though, they had great character which I know Howard really appreciated.

Did that remain the same after promotion to Division One?

Yes, it did. It's funny calling it Division One, because it's now the Premier League. The top level. A couple of players moved on, and new guys came in, but it was broadly the same squad. We still had a core group of youngsters who came up with me – so Mel Sterland, Mark Smith, John Pearson. They were all great players. Mel really was excellent. Howard added in some new signings, but the camaraderie, character, ability, willingness and drive all remained. We were a really good team.

Did you enjoy the training?

Well, I saw a lot of the countryside! It wasn't much fun for me; long-distance running wasn't in my make-up. I think you're either made for it or you're not. And I wasn't! I did feel fitter though, and the team were clearly fitter as well. The training was incessant, certainly in the early part of the season. Later in the season it was more playing the games and recovering, but early on it was relentless. I believe I am correct in saying that we got as many soft tissue injuries in training than we did in matches as the training was so hard. Alan Smith, the physio, was excellent. Later in my career he was superb in helping my rehabilitation from a back injury. In this period he was also great in helping me and others back from any injuries we'd suffered.

The attention to detail in training was really impressive as well. On Fridays, Howard would call us all together and give us very detailed instructions for the game. He always knew the opposition's strengths and weaknesses really well. After that we'd be back out on the training ground practising various things for the game. It was often drills around free kicks and corners. Howard would organise the reserve-team players as the opposition and then we'd practise. Sometimes for a very long time!

The team took some criticism for the tactics. How did you feel about that?

I thought the criticism was unfair. It was direct football, not kick and rush. Howard liked us to get the ball forward rather than backward or square – but it was always with a plan. He wanted us to get crosses into the box and to create chances. It was direct, exciting football. It was the kind of football that I still like to see and that I think the fans like to watch. We created lots of chances. If it was long-ball football, then it was long-ball with a plan!

We almost always played with three centre-backs. That was new to me, but we worked on it in Howard's first pre-season and from then on, so we were prepared when the games started. It served us well, as the goals-against column shows. It also allowed Mel and whoever was at left-back the freedom to get up the pitch. I usually played on the right of the three and enjoyed it there.

How did the team respond to setbacks?

Disappointment and defeat seemed to spur us on. After the FA Cup semi-final loss to Everton, we went unbeaten until the end of the season. We would have qualified for Europe if English teams hadn't been banned. And we deserved it, we played intense football right to the end.

You moved on at the end of that season?

I signed for Lennie Lawrence down at Charlton Athletic. There were a few reasons for it. I fancied a change. I'd been in and out of the team a little and at 25 or 26 years old I wanted to be a regular starter. Charlton had just been promoted into Division One and so were a team on the up. I enjoyed my time there.

You did re-sign for the Owls though in 1989?

Yes, Ron Atkinson brought me back up. I was part of the best team ever to go down in 1990! I still can't believe that a team with Roland Nilsson, David Hirst, John Sheridan and others got relegated. It was different under Ron than it had been under Howard. Ron put a lot of emphasis and responsibility on us as players to make the decisions and choices. I really enjoyed it and working under Trevor Francis afterwards. Ron, I think probably got the best out of me from all the managers that I worked with. I was lucky enough under him to play in the promotion and League Cup-winning team of 1990/91, though that's material for another book!

Thanks Peter.

No problem at all, it's great to reminisce – and you've reminded me of some things I had forgotten! Good luck with the book, I look forward to it.

14.

The Boardroom and Finances

A QUICK glance at the Owls' annual reports across our period shows a positive story. For the accounts ending 31 May 1984, the final year in Division Two, the figures showed an income of £1,899,940 and a profit of £119,931. By 1985, after a season in the top flight, these amounts rose to £2,869,913 with a surplus of £466,675. The following year income rose again to £3,248,663, though the surplus dropped back to £376,561. A rosy picture, then? Yes, in outline, though a more detailed study of the figures throws up some potential issues. In this chapter I study the figures, but also look at the characters involved and investigate what the money was used for.

This period also saw the Owls move further into the modern age of sponsorship and commercial deals. In 1986, the club put a roof on the Kop – funded, at least partly, through donations from supporters. So, a trawl through the figures, but also a story of what the finances were linked to. For the accounting fans among my readership, I am sorry that there is little reference to debentures, fixed assets, depreciation or accruals!

The board at Sheffield Wednesday remained the same throughout our two seasons. Chairman H.E. (Bert) McGee was supported by six further board members: Matt Sheppard, Stan Speight, Clifford Woodward, Keith Addy, Ernest Barron and Geoff Hulley. The club secretary, equivalent to today's CEO or similar, was Dick Chester. Commercial manager was Dennis Woodhead, a former Owls player. Marketing manager was Bob Gorrill.

McGee and Sheppard had been involved with the club since the darkest days of the mid-1970s. McGee had taken over the chairmanship from Sheppard in September 1975. Woodward and Speight joined the board earlier that year. McGee and his board had taken some difficult decisions in the intervening years, which helped the club make its slow climb back to the top table. It is not too much of an exaggeration to say that McGee and his board rescued Sheffield Wednesday from the abyss in the 1970s. By the mid-1980s the club was in a different position, with differing pressures and higher expectations.

An indication of the new demands was in the sponsorship of the club's shirts. The team's strip had been emblazoned with the logo of 'Crosby Kitchens' during the promotion season of 1983/84. The following campaign saw a much bigger deal with the Barnsley-based MHS Group. The contract with MHS was described in the club programme as 'the largest of its kind for the club' and included, for the first time, advertising rights at the ground, the use of entertainment facilities and the MHS name on both home and away shirts.

MHS's managing director Malcolm Stockdale felt that 'the success of Sheffield Wednesday, and the breadth of its support, suggested an ideal partnership'. The MHS initials first featured on the club's shirt for a home match against Ipswich in September 1984, the large-sized letters supposedly there for clarity in the presence of television cameras.

Not all supporters were happy with this. Letters in the following week's *Green 'Un* described the logo as 'ugly' and 'intrusive'. One supporter may have been happier as MHS announced their sponsorship deal with an opportunity to win a signed football for anyone who bought five gallons of petrol at one of their service stations.

Revenue at the Owls was impressive during our period. The club announced in 1985 that the club's income during the promotion season of 1983/84 put them in ninth place in the country as far as revenue was concerned. Gorrill was not prepared to rest on his laurels in terms of sponsorship, though. Gorrill, who moved to the club at the start of the 1984/85 season after holding a similar position at Chesterfield, said in the spring of 1985 that 'I am trying to create something different and in keeping with a top First Division club'.

Gorrill was determined to increase sponsorship at Hillsborough. By that summer he had already obtained sponsorship for goal nets (Roseby curtains!), corner flags and flags on top of the South Stand – and negotiated deals for ten sponsored cars for players and management. Twelve sponsored mascots were in place for the following season and plans were in place to improve the hospitality lounges. In a nod to how different the mid-1980s were, 'personality girls' looked after guests on matchday. Gorrill was pleased with his work to date. 'I have a file of letters from our sponsors who express satisfaction with the way they were looked after.'

By September 1985 more of Gorrill's plans had come to fruition, with match ball sponsorship available for £150 or £250, the mascot for the day scheme at £85 and the hire of various function rooms and suites for 'up to 200 people' with prices on request. Supporters could also sponsor a player's kit, with prices ranging from £5 for socks to £75 for the full kit. Video tapes of all matches at Hillsborough were made available to buy (on either VHS or Betamax) for £8.95. For much of the 1985/86 season the Owls' shirts went without a sponsor, with colour television manufacturer Finlux completing a deal in time for the FA Cup semi-final and final few games of the season.

My favourite piece of sponsorship for the season, though, was the announcement of the availability of Owls-branded Coca-Cola! It is difficult to ascertain how successful financially these schemes were. The accounts show 'miscellaneous income', which is further broken down into 'publicity' and 'commercial activities'. There is not a separate line for sponsorship. I believe that the sums involved are not the key here, though. This was the Owls moving into the modern, commercial, sponsored age. Driven by promotion to Division One and the publicity that brought, the club took advantage and moved forward.

It could be argued that a focus on sponsorship and commercial activity took the club away from the match-going supporter. Indeed, much of the club's spending prior to the return to the top flight was on the executive areas. The club spent around £350,000 on redevelopments to the South Stand, including a new main entrance, additional offices, a new boardroom, reception room, function room and sponsors' lounge.

There were developments that the average match-going fan would have noticed also. The pitch was relaid at a cost of £50,000, with the discovery of enough underground water to suggest that the River Don may once have flowed where the ground now stands! The new surface was described in the club's *The Owl* magazine as 'arguably the best pitch in the country'. Although some lumps and bumps were removed, there was still a one-metre fall towards the Kop end. A new electronic scoreboard replaced the obsolete one that stood on the top of the Kop and dated back to the 1966 World Cup. There was also an investment of £200,000 on turnstiles, toilets and refreshment facilities at the Kop end.

The following summer saw the Owls react to the disaster at Bradford City's Valley Parade stadium by aiming to confirm Hillsborough's safety against fire. The North Stand roof was sand-blasted to ensure a rust-free surface, along with being pushed to a nine-degree slope to match the legislation at the time. More work was needed on the South Stand, with the wooden floor covered by a sheet metal surface. Forty-two tons of metal and 32,000 screws later, the club secretary Chester said: 'We shall all remember the horrific scenes at Bradford. We are now confident that Hillsborough is now absolutely safe from this sort of incident.' Again, this work benefited the match-going supporter.

Some Owls supporters remained frustrated. Hillsborough was an excellent, modern stadium on three sides. The huge Kop was uncovered and had remained broadly unchanged in nature for decades. In the summer of 1984, the *Sheffield Star*'s Owls reporter Paul Thompson felt that cost of a roof on the Kop – even then estimated at £1m – meant that work was unlikely to begin any time soon. He did say, however, that McGee and the Owls board would love for it to happen.

Within two years the Kop had its roof and, in Thompson's words, the 'Koppites who get soaked when it rains and complain that their chants drift away into the wind' were now able to stand on the largest covered standing area in Europe. The capacity of the newly covered stand was 22,000. It was a spectacular feat of financial planning, design, engineering and building that ensured the new structure was in place for the beginning of the 1986/87 season.

The first news of plans for the Kop to be covered was revealed in the summer of 1985. Chester, club secretary at the time, told me in 2021 that he genuinely believed the board had only come to a decision to go ahead in the previous 12 months. A report in the *Sheffield Star* in August 1985 showed the outline of two plans that the club was said to be considering. Consulting engineers Eastwood and Partners had drawn up two schemes. Both covered the Kop; the second also extended and 'squared off' the back of the stand, creating capacity for an extra 5,000 fans.

By September 1985, McGee was announcing via *The Owl* magazine that the club had gone for the second option. This version of the plan included seating for families at the front left-hand portion of the Kop, with further space for disabled supporters in front of that. The rest of the Kop would remain standing. McGee said of the plans: 'This is the realisation of my ambition to have a roof over the Kop. It will improve the amenities at that end of the ground and improve the sound effects for the fans as they support their team. When the roof is completed, Hillsborough will be just about the best ground in the country.'

Howard Wilkinson was also quoted at the time giving his support to the project. 'It's my intention here to develop Sheffield Wednesday into one of the leading clubs in the country … the Kop roof is part of that programme. From a manager's point of view, it's very easy to take a very selfish, single-minded and narrow view in situations such as this but to do so, in my mind, is not conducive to the overall welfare of the club.'

Wilkinson knew the dangers of any decline in team performance being blamed on the club's expenditure on the stadium. The *Sheffield Star*'s Thompson understood Wilkinson's predicament. 'In a way he cannot win. If the team are successful, the Kop issue will be forgotten. If they start to dip, then people may ask why money was not spent on the team instead of the ground.'

The plans provoked a degree of excitement among Wednesdayites. There was plenty of work still to be done at this stage, though. Sheffield City Council gave planning permission in August 1985 for the new roof after plans for both potential designs were submitted by the club in January that year. There was the small matter of the cost to build it, and the appointment of a suitable contractor to complete the work. The cost of the work was estimated at a cool £1m.

Chester related the story to me of how the final three bidders to complete the work were invited to Hillsborough to discuss their bids. Each was told that it was £1m and not a penny more. Any work that had not been accounted for in the bid would need to be paid for by savings elsewhere. Sheffield-based building contractors Ackroyd & Abbott were the successful bidders and would begin work immediately following the end of the 1985/86 campaign. There was now the small matter of finding the money. Between 1979 and 1988 an organisation called the Football Trust allocated the Owls £431,280 for 21 different schemes on the ground. The Trust administered a fund of public money taken from the football pools companies and gave grants to clubs for improvement and safety work. A bid went into the Trust for help with the costs of the Kop roof. Eventually a sum of £595,099 was agreed. Just over £400,000 to find, therefore.

Fans went into overdrive following McGee's request that they 'help us raise the necessary money'. McGee even appealed on an LP produced by the Owls in 1985. Titled *Alive and Well*, the record featured the song 'We are the Owls', sung by the squad, along with commentary and interviews. McGee said that the scheme would go ahead or that he would die in the attempt!

A series of fundraising activities followed, ranging from 'super-supporter' Shaun Jones' sponsored run from his Chesterfield home to Hillsborough in time for the home game with Newcastle United on Boxing Day 1985 to the much larger fun run and open day at Hillsborough on 27 April 1986.

Supporters were encouraged to raise sponsorship for taking part in the run. The sponsorship form was titled 'Kop This!' and was itself sponsored by Portland's Nissan Land, Gorrill presumably not missing a trick in terms of money-raising opportunities. The five-mile run around the Hillsborough area began at 8am on a Sunday morning. It attracted around 3,000 for the run and a total of nearer 15,000 during the day. Supporters were able to tour the ground, meet players, take refreshments and attend a disco later in the evening.

All participants were given a medal and certificate. They were encouraged to collect sponsorship and to buy a commemorative T-shirt (just £4.95!). The shirt was labelled with the 'Kop This!' slogan and sponsored on the back by Portland Autos. The club's iconic Owl logo was shown holding an umbrella, and written around the side were the words: 'It's the Sheffield Wednesday FC Family Fun Run.'

The club promoted the event regularly, with the programme commenting that they hoped fans would 'give a helping hand to building the roof on one of the finest stadiums in the country'. Fans were to pay in their sponsorship money to the club over the coming days and weeks, receiving a brief acknowledgment slip for their efforts.

Anne Stokes-Moorhouse remembers the day fondly. 'We got to Hillsborough, registered and then waited quite a while to go past the starting line, as it was quite busy with loads taking part,' she says. 'Once we were on Penistone Road there were crowds of people cheering us on. I met my mum and dad on the way back and we went back into Hillsborough for the open day with a tour around the dressing room. We saw the massive bath, boardroom, trophy room and met the players and got some autographs in my Young Owls autograph book!'

Clare de Rouffignac, who lived in Australia at the time, added her efforts to the fundraising by completing her version of the fun run wearing an Owls scarf in the 70+ degree heat of the New South Wales coast. The fundraising efforts did not stop there, with a limited edition (5,000 copies) badge produced in advance of the last game on the uncovered terrace. Priced at 30p if bought from the ground or 50p if purchased in advance via postal order, they sold out. The badge again featured the umbrella-holding Owl.

The 1986 accounts show £110,296 received by the club from the development associations and as gifts towards the roof on the Kop. This was an increase from £103,872 the previous year. The development associations had been raising money for the club for decades. The new West Stand was half funded by donations from the development fund to the tune of £55,000 in 1961, for example. In the 1970s the development of a club lottery following the loosening of the law to allow such things saw donations of £144,460 in 1978 and £233,500 the following year.

Chester told me in 2021 that the total raised specifically for the Kop was in the 'tens of thousands'. Whatever the total raised, the supporters had done their bit and the roof would be built. The goodwill of some supporters was tested when ticket prices for the 1986/87 campaign were announced following the end of the previous campaign. An adult day-admission charge on the Kop would rise from £3 to £3.50, a 16 per cent increase.

Supporters' club secretary Rita Nettleship was quoted at the time as saying, 'The Kop price rise is disappointing ... it would have been nice if the club could have pegged the price.' In the club's defence, the price for youngsters and pensioners was capped and a new system of family season tickets was introduced.

Consulting engineer Dr Bill Eastwood felt that the roof would be 'worth an extra ten points a season' to the Owls given the extra noise and atmosphere it would generate. He was an Owls supporter. Peter Horsepool, who was managing director of major contractors Ackroyd & Abbott, would not reveal which team he supported at the time. His company did, though, move rapidly into action. Well before the final game of the season, they had installed a concrete track in front of the Kop and demolished a section of terracing to help create space for the huge crane that would be needed over the summer months. Norman Tate & Sons were a major subcontractor whose Sheffield United-supporting employee Vic Harris walked in for his breakfast the day after the Blades' 6-1 thrashing at Blackburn to find a Bar Six chocolate bar all that was available!

Regardless of the teams supported by the contractors, work continued apace over the summer months and the roof was completed in readiness for the opening game of the 1986/87 season. Ackroyd & Abbott hired the second-biggest crane in the country to help complete the job. A railway track was built behind the goal for the crane to lift prefabricated steelwork from lorries at each side of the ground and move it on to the Kop.

Much of the material for the roof was manufactured locally, with the steelwork coming from Parkgate and the huge pre-cast concrete blocks for the terrace being made at Ingbirchworth. The stadium's floodlights were refocused in order that work could continue throughout the night. Site agent Stan Blackwell was quoted in July 1986 as saying, 'The covered Kop will be ready for the first match, but the job will not quite be 100 per cent complete.'

Whatever snagging jobs required completion were hurried along by the announcement that the roof would be given an official opening by Her Majesty Queen Elizabeth II on Friday 12 December 1986. The Queen arrived on a cold winter's afternoon to see crowds of Sheffielders watch her entrance down Penistone Road. Turnstiles opened at noon in time for the Queen to make her entrance at 2.30pm.

The crowds were entertained in the meantime by a Young Owls football display, followed by community singing led by the City of Sheffield Girls' Choir. Her Majesty was then brought to the directors' box with a fanfare and the national anthem. The choir then returned with a series of Christmas songs, including a number entitled 'Mistletoe Carol' that was written in honour of the occasion.

The Queen was then driven around the stadium before unveiling the plaque to commemorate the opening of the covered Kop. The chairman McGee then introduced Her Majesty to various dignitaries along with then club captain Martin Hodge and the manager Wilkinson. As McGee put it in his notes for the programme for the day, it was 'a great honour to the club to be able to welcome, with pleasure, Her Majesty to open our new Kop and give us all a day to savour and remember'.

The Kop roof was clearly the most dramatic and maybe most successful use of the club's money during our period. The donations from fans and positive relationship that the club had engendered with the Football Trust meant that the overall cost to the club was less than that of a mid-range striker at the time. McGee and the Owls board were famously careful with money. A closer look at the Owls' accounts over our two years, though, throws up some suggestions that not all was necessarily rosy.

Although the club's accounts showed a healthy surplus between 1985 and 1986, the figure in the latter year was boosted by a doubling of income received from transfer dealings. The club brought in £1,187,000 from player sales in 1986, compared to £592,500 the previous year. Indeed, without the extra money, the accounts would have shown an overall loss. The club's expenses also rose in the second year back in the top flight. Wages increased from £904,335 to £1,182,004 and transfer fees payable from £667,750 to £1,021,250. One employee was shown as earning £40–45,000 and another more than £50,000. No employees were paid at that level in 1985.

This spending is indicative of Wilkinson's desire to improve the quality and depth of his squad. There is nothing in the accounts to suggest that the club could not afford the players. The question to be asked is whether the club had the wherewithal to continue spending at that level if needed. If the extra transfer income is stripped out of the figures, then the club's overall income fell by over £200,000. Much of that loss came in matchday receipts.

Attendances fell in the second season back in Division One. This was not exclusively a Sheffield Wednesday problem, as crowds fell nationally at a time of worries about hooliganism and following a series of disasters at football matches. The Owls would need to find a way of dealing with it, though, if income was to stay high. Increasing sponsorship and improving commercial opportunities was one potential way forward.

Another method was by raising the prices of tickets, as we saw above. It remained to be seen whether the draw of the newly roofed Kop would be enough to bring the supporters in at higher prices. The work on the club's finances that had effectively dated from the mid-1970s, and which had helped drive the team's success over that time, had now reached a tipping point. Should the club stay within its means, or should it look to spend and hopefully push on even further?

The answer to that question might need another book – but it is clear to me that the summer of 1986 marked a point where major decisions that would affect the club's medium- and long-term future would need to be made. The success on and off the pitch over the previous decade had reached a potential turning point. Stick or twist?

15.

An Interview with Gary Shelton

GARY SHELTON was an experienced midfielder who joined the Owls in the spring of 1982. By that stage he had clocked up over 50 first-team appearances for Walsall, Aston Villa and Notts County. Shelton signed for the Owls during the stewardship of Jack Charlton and remained at the club for over five years, making a total of 237(+4) appearances and scoring 24 goals. In our two seasons Shelton played 84(+2) games, notching six goals along the way.

His hugely committed but also skilful and creative style ensured that he was a fans' favourite. I had heard that he tended to keep himself to himself in retirement and not talk regularly about his playing days. I was very pleased, therefore, when Gary replied to my message asking to chat and even more so when he returned my call in the autumn of 2021.

Thanks for speaking with me Gary. Let's start with how you arrived at Hillsborough in 1982.

I wasn't getting much of a look-in at Villa at the time – there was one season under Ron Saunders where I only played four times. Although Tony Barton took over just before I came to Hillsborough, I thought it was time for me to move on. I'd already been on loan at Notts County, and I wanted first-team football. Jack Charlton was in charge at Wednesday. He brought an Owls team down to Villa for a League Cup game in 1978 I think – and I scored the only goal. So I don't know if he remembered me from that. I think John Harris scouted me as well. When I came up to Hillsborough, Jack sold the club to me within seconds! He was one of the best managers I ever worked for; he knew the game inside out and was a great man-manager.

He used to call me, Gary Megson and Gary Bannister the 'Three Amigos' – because we all had the same name! When I first came up the club put me up in a B&B and he asked the other two amigos to take me out for a meal and look after me. They did, and we went out for a nice meal and a few drinks – nothing crazy. They charged it to the club and when the bill come in Jack told them that he'd asked them to look after me, not to take the piss! They ended up having to pay their share of the bill out of their wages! It was a great atmosphere in those days. Terry Curran took me under his wing a little, as did Mike Lyons. Great people.

Jack could also be very generous. I was married with a very young son when I first moved up. Jack took us to his farmhouse out near Barnsley somewhere and said to me and my wife that I could have it for a few days as he was going up to the North East. I had a bit of a nosey around as you do while I was there and found a cheque on the mantlepiece – made out to Jack. It was his testimonial money from Leeds and came to over £80,000!

It must have been very different when Howard Wilkinson took over?

I was worried when Howard took over because he'd been coaching at Notts County when I was there. Villa wanted £200,000 for me and it was Howard who told me they wouldn't be signing me. I worried that he just didn't fancy me. In the first week he was at Wednesday, though, he pulled me into the office and told me that it was a clean slate and that everyone would get a fair chance. Howard was the best manager I ever worked for in all sorts of areas. His organisation and training was donc with military prccision. It was brilliant!

How did you find the fitness training?

It was scary! I was fortunate as I was good at long-distance running. They'd regularly take us up on to the moors as you know.

Sometimes they even had us doing relay-style laps in teams of four round Ewden dam. One time they took us out towards the moors at the back of Stocksbridge somewhere. We ran for miles and miles. All of a sudden we looked round and couldn't see Howard or Peter Eustace. We carried on a while longer and then decided that we had to head back. We'd passed a pub on the way out and when we got back to it we figured out that's where they had gone. They were in there and had laid on soup and sandwiches for us all as a thank you for our hard work and efforts. Great man-management!

I said that Howard was organised. I've never known team meetings like it! Each Friday before a game there would be an hour-long meeting where he'd set out the strengths and weaknesses of the opposition. We'd then practise aspects of that for hours in the afternoon. We all knew exactly what were expected to do. We scored lots of goals from set pieces, for example, as we were so well drilled.

I suppose the only negative I could pick from all the fitness training was that we were maybe a little jaded later in each season. In the promotion season of 1983/84, for example, Chelsea were able to pip us at the post for the title and that might have been because we were running on fumes after February/March time.

How about the tactics? The team were accused of playing a long-ball game. Is that accurate and did the tactics suit your game?

Howard had us playing to our strengths. I enjoyed playing in that team. We got plenty of touches of the ball in midfield and could pass it. So I wouldn't say it was long-ball. Everything we did had a purpose.

I know you had an England Under-21 call-up at this time, also?

Yes, I was over the moon! I was called up as an over-age player. Howard Wilkinson had his links with the FA and he told me that I was selected and that I was captain! I enjoyed the game, but it had a bit of a sad ending for me as I was carried off injured. I thought that I'd really damaged my knee but luckily it was only bruised. I got a further call-up for the under-23s. We'd played at QPR the weekend before on their artificial pitch. I'd clashed with the keeper and my knee swelled up to twice the size the next morning.

The England squad met at Derby and Alan Smith, the Wednesday physio, was with the national set-up. He told me that there was no chance of playing on the Tuesday night with England, so it was back to Sheffield to rest up. I still have my England shirt in a frame though – I'm very proud of it. I also have an Owls shirt up and some great pictures by Steve Ellis and others, including one of me scoring at Anfield.

Who did you enjoy playing alongside?

I was lucky enough to play alongside some great players in my career. Ray Houghton at Oxford, for example, was right out of the top drawer. At Hillsborough, though, it would have to be Meggs [Gary Megson]. We had a great understanding. He wanted me to win the ball and then he'd do the rest! We stayed in contact afterwards. When he became manager at West Bromwich Albion I was on holiday in the States. Meggs was trying to get hold of me, and when I got back home we spoke. I worked with him at The Hawthorns with the youth and reserve teams and as coach. We had some great times, including promotion and relegation from the Premier League.

You moved on to Oxford from Hillsborough?

I did, but I didn't want to leave! Howard Wilkinson wanted to make some changes to the squad. I think he was trying to buy Mark Wright at the time from Southampton and needed some funds. I'd scored against Oxford not too long beforehand, and they enquired after me. Howard pulled me in and told me that he'd accepted an offer from them, and it went from there. I stayed there a couple of years and went through a relegation. I then moved on to Bristol City and had five great years down there. I moved on to Chester and played a little before moving into coaching and management there.

Thanks Gary, is there anything else I should include about your time at Hillsborough?

Just that it was a great time for me. The fans were brilliant to me. I fed off them at times and really enjoyed the atmosphere. A few games really stand out, including the FA Cup replay against Burnley in 1983, where I scored a couple in the game that took us to the semi-final. Also big games in front of massive crowds back in Division One against Manchester United, Liverpool and the rest. They were great times, with great people. I'll look forward to reading the book about it all!

16:

1986: January to May

THE YEAR 1986 would certainly prove to be a dramatic one for Owls supporters. It began with Wednesday taking another trip across the M62 in time for a New Year's Day clash with Liverpool at Anfield. Howard Wilkinson again altered his starting XI, with Carl Shutt coming in up front and Tony Gregory starting in midfield. Shutt made an almost immediate impact. Inside two minutes Mark Chamberlain crossed, Lawrie Madden headed on and Shutt was there at the far post to nod home.

Gregory tested Bruce Grobbelaar from 30 yards, but otherwise Liverpool were on top for the remainder of the half. Ian Rush, Ronnie Whelan, Jan Mølby and Steve McMahon all missed reasonable chances, and when Whelan headed on target just on the half-time whistle, he found Martin Hodge at his best. The second half saw continued Liverpool pressure and it was no surprise when Rush equalised on 49 minutes with a simple tap-in for his first goal in nine games.

Liverpool had an excellent chance to go ahead on 56 minutes. Chris Morris brought down Craig Johnston in the area, but Hodge made a tremendous save from Mølby's resulting penalty kick. The Reds did take the lead on 74 minutes when Paul Walsh ran on to a quick through ball to put Liverpool ahead.

The Owls did not give in, though, and on 86 minutes Shutt knocked the ball on to Garry Thompson, who found space to squeeze the ball home for his fourth goal in as many games. 'Maybe we were a little fortunate,' felt Hodge afterwards.

The New Year's Day point left the Owls still in that comfortable sixth place in the league. They would not play another fixture in Division One for 17 days as the FA Cup and weather curtailed the early January fixtures. The tie was a home game against relegation-threatened Oxford United. Wilkinson was able to call on Peter Shirtliff in defence for the first time since mid-October and included Paul Hart in his backline. Hart only lasted ten minutes before limping off to be replaced by Chamberlain.

The enforced change did not knock the Owls out of their stride, however, as they opened the scoring only three minutes later. The goal was a bizarre one as Brian Marwood's innocuous cross was hacked clear by Neil Slatter, but only succeeded in bouncing off his colleague Malcolm Shotton and into the Oxford goal. Wednesday dominated the remainder of the half without producing any real chances of note.

It was still against the run of play when Oxford equalised after 53 minutes. John Aldridge sprang the Owls' offside trap and crossed from the right for Slatter to bundle in the goal. The game fell flat after that, although Shutt forced a good save from Alan Judge and Thompson fired just wide. The Owls were relieved when the winner finally came on 86 minutes. Andy Blair's long, high cross eventually fell to Marwood, who slotted in his 12th goal of the season. Owls defender Morris described it as an 'indifferent performance'. With the points in the bag, the FA Cup meant that Wednesday had another two-week wait for their next fixture.

That tie was a trip to Vicarage Road to renew rivalries with Graham Taylor's Watford. Hart returned to the team, having missed the FA Cup game in the interim against Orient. Shirtliff missed out, having been substituted through injury in that game. Wednesday went a goal down in the 19th minute, John Barnes racing down the left to cross for Colin West to poke the ball home. A few minutes later West blazed over after Martin Hodge parried an effort from Barnes.

Wednesday started the second half with more purpose, with keeper Tony Coton forced into excellent saves from Lee Chapman and Thompson. The Owls' reward came on 66 minutes when Hart knocked on a Marwood corner for Gary Megson to head home. Wednesday pushed hard for a winner but it was to be Watford who left with all three points. Four minutes from time, Nigel Callaghan's cross found Barnes, who headed in at the far post. 'I still think we can finish in the top six,' felt Peter Eustace.

The team had a three-week wait until their next game. Tottenham Hotspur were the visitors to S6, which was scattered with a thin coating of snow. Morris replaced Mark Smith in an otherwise unchanged starting line-up. Spurs, who had not scored in the league since Boxing Day, gave a debut to 18-year-old David Howells.

Wednesday had the best of the early action and Ray Clemence had already made an excellent save from Thompson before the same man gave the Owls the lead on 20 minutes. A poor Chris Waddle clearance found Blair, who passed across goal for Thompson to nip between Clemence and the defence to shoot home.

Wednesday had plenty of possession during the remainder of the half, but Spurs dominated the chances with Hodge saving well from John Chiedozie, and Blair making a last-ditch block to stop Mark Falco. Tottenham continued to trouble the Owls into the second half, with Hodge making a fantastic save to again stop Chiedozie.

On the hour mark Tottenham found the equaliser. Chiedozie sped through and lashed the ball into the bottom corner. Only seven minutes later, debutant Howells made it a day to truly remember as he hit a crisp shot past Hodge from Paul Allen's cross. Wednesday offered some pressure but created no real chances as Spurs held on to their lead and the three points. 'No excuses, we put up a poor display,' felt Hodge.

Wednesday's first fixture in March was a trip to Kenilworth Road to play Luton Town on a synthetic pitch. Wilkinson made several changes to the team to cater for playing on such a surface and to freshen things up in advance of a cup replay with Derby County the following week. Perhaps the most surprising omission was that of nine-goal striker Chapman.

Luton had lost only once at home all season. It was clear why as they dominated the early play. Mick Harford put the Hatters ahead after only 16 minutes, rising above the Owls defence to power a header past Hodge and into the bottom corner. Wednesday were determined but created little for the remainder of the half, Glynn Snodin coming closest with a free kick.

The second half followed a similar pattern; the Owls forced a series of corners but created little in the way of clear-cut chances. It was Luton who nearly doubled their advantage towards the end with Hodge saving brilliantly from Mike Newell in the closing minutes.

The Owls had laboured to their third league defeat in succession and were reported to have stayed in the dressing room for over an hour after the game in discussion about their display and the result.

Whatever was said in the dressing room seemed to have the impact needed in the next game. The Owls had already beaten Derby in the FA Cup before they returned to league action with a home tie against Birmingham City. Chapman returned to the starting line-up, up front alongside Shutt, who had scored both the Owls' goals against the Rams. Wednesday started at pace against Birmingham, with Shutt twice going close before opening the scoring after only nine minutes. Shutt's goal was a pinpoint header into the top corner from Marwood's cross.

He doubled the Owls' lead on 30 minutes after Blues keeper David Seaman dropped a high cross into his path. Chapman scored the third just before half-time after he turned and shot from Megson's pass. Into the second half and Wednesday had already hit the post before Chamberlain scored the fourth.

Shutt completed his hat-trick with the pick of the goals – taking the ball from his own half, skipping two challenges and firing home under Seaman. Birmingham did pull a goal back in the closing stages through David Geddis, but it was immaterial to the result. 'They could have scored 14,' commented Blues manager John Bond. His opposite number Wilkinson was full of praise for Shutt, saying, 'He can be justifiably proud.'

Wednesday travelled with confidence to their next league game against Coventry City at Highfield Road. The Owls had qualified for the FA Cup semi-final in the meantime, with Shutt's goal in the victory against West Ham United meaning he had netted SIX times in one week! Shutt unsurprisingly kept his place for the Coventry game with Hart replacing Smith in the only change from the Birmingham line-up.

The first half was a dull affair, livened only by Cyrille Regis' header which rattled the crossbar. Megson thought that he had given the Owls the lead on the stroke of half-time, but his cushioned header was ruled out for offside. In the 63rd minute Wednesday did take the lead. It was the recalled Hart who helped create it, nodding on Marwood's corner for Mel Sterland to head into the top of the net.

The remainder of the game passed with little in the way of goalmouth action, though Hodge did stop Regis again with 15 minutes to go. 'A match that seldom rose above the mediocre,' felt the *Sunday Express*. There was some cause for celebration for the Owls as the win was the team's first in eight away games.

Wednesday then faced a quick return to action with Leicester City visiting Hillsborough on the following Tuesday evening. Shutt dropped out of the team to be replaced by Thompson in an otherwise unchanged line-up. Leicester had most of the play in the opening stages and created the first clear-cut chance, which Alan Smith headed into the hands of Martin Hodge. The Owls took the lead on the half-hour mark with a stunning strike from Sterland. Thompson set up the rampaging full-back who lashed home from over 25 yards.

The Owls remained on top for the rest of the half, though early in the second half Hodge saved brilliantly from Tony Sealy to maintain the Owls' lead. Wednesday kept the edge on their opponents, though much of the rest of the game was scrappy. Despite an almighty goalmouth scramble in the final minutes, Wednesday could not add to their lead. Wilkinson felt afterwards: 'We looked jaded … but I expected this … we didn't half work and fight.'

The Owls travelled to London for their next fixture. The game against West Ham United gave the Hammers a quick chance to avenge their FA Cup defeat earlier in the month. Wilkinson shuffled his forward line again, bringing back Shutt at the expense of Chapman in a team that was otherwise the same. West Ham were challenging for a place in the top six but came into the fixture on the back of two successive defeats. Wednesday had won their previous five (including cup games).

Frank McAvennie scored West Ham's winner. He seized on an errant backpass after only six minutes before slotting the ball past Hodge. The Owls were grateful to Hodge and some wayward shooting from Tony Cottee in keeping the score down. A game to forget.

The Owls returned to home soil for their next game, a juicy-looking Easter Saturday tie against Liverpool. Nearly 38,000 supporters turned out for the occasion. Wilkinson tweaked his team again, bringing in Madden into the defence at the expense of Hart. Liverpool's player-manager Kenny Dalglish dropped himself from the squad, having played a full 90 minutes for Scotland midweek in winning his 100th international cap.

The game itself was a scrappy affair. Dalglish's replacement Paul Walsh came close for Liverpool when he chested down a cross and volleyed just over. Wednesday came closest on 34 minutes as Liverpool keeper Bruce Grobbelaar spilled a Sterland cross, but neither Marwood nor Shutt were able to force home the loose ball. Walsh skimmed the far post with a cross-cum-shot which beat Hodge in the flight as the first half drew to a close.

The Owls suffered an injury blow on 41 minutes as Nigel Worthington was withdrawn with a knee problem. The injury meant that the Northern Irishman would miss the remainder of the season. 'It is really unfortunate for the lad,' said Wilkinson afterwards. 'He has been playing very well for us and had a blinder for Ireland the other night.'

The second half saw even less goalmouth action, with the best chance falling to Jan Mølby, who shot at Hodge when under pressure from Snodin. The Owls had half-chances through

Thompson and substitute Chamberlain before the game petered out. It was the first time that season that the Owls had not scored at home, and Liverpool still awaited their first victory at Hillsborough since 1968. 'Few Games Promised So Much but Delivered So Little,' was the cutting headline in the *Dublin Independent* the following day. Wilkinson admitted that 'it was one of our more professional performances even though the match did not turn out as good as some in the past'.

Wednesday returned to action two days later, making an Easter Monday trip to St James' Park to face Newcastle United. Hart returned in defence at the expense of Shirtliff, while Gary Shelton returned to the starting XI for the first time in six games. It was not to prove a happy return.

Newcastle went ahead on only nine minutes, Paul Stephenson scoring his first league goal. The Owls then conceded two further goals in three minutes, Paul Gascoigne heading home when unmarked on 34 minutes and Peter Beardsley firing home a deflected effort three minutes later. Shelton was substituted at half-time, but the Magpies went four ahead a minute into the second period when Beardsley sped through to set up Billy Whitehurst.

Gascoigne missed a great chance before the Owls did pull a goal back through Shutt on 69 minutes. Wednesday remained second best, however, and were 'lucky not to suffer a heavier defeat' according to the *Sheffield Star*. Perhaps the team's mind was on the FA Cup semi-final against Everton five days later.

The Owls returned to league action with a midweek home tie against QPR. Marwood had missed out against Everton through injury, with Wilkinson naming a three-man forward line of Chapman, Shutt and Thompson. He retained the same team against QPR. On a freezing evening at Hillsborough, a crowd of only 13,157 turned out to watch an Owls team who seemed to be suffering from the after-effects of their efforts at Villa Park.

Chapman came close early on with an acrobatic overhead kick but there was little else for Wednesday fans to get excited about. Passes went astray and defenders were on top on both sides. Wednesday's best attempt of the second half was a 30-yard shot from the unlikely source of Madden, which flew just over. Gary Bannister had the best chance to win the game against his former team, but his shot hit Hodge and John Byrne struck the post with the follow-up when it looked easier to score. Wilkinson said afterwards that 'we lacked quality, pace and incisiveness'.

Key Game: Manchester United 0-2 Sheffield Wednesday, 13 April 1986

Wednesday's season ran the risk of tailing away after their FA Cup exit. Prior to the game against Manchester United, they sat in ninth place in the table. This fixture was a televised match, with a 2.35pm kick-off on a Sunday. Ron Atkinson's United sat third in the table, two points behind the leaders Liverpool.

The Red Devils seemingly had much more to play for than the Owls. Atkinson's team had dropped away in the hunt for the title in previous weeks – winning only two of their last ten games. Atkinson commented in his programme notes for the game: 'No one regrets more than me the loss of our commanding lead at the top of the table.'

Wilkinson named the following starting XI:

1. Martin Hodge
2. Mel Sterland
3. Peter Shirtliff
4. Lawrie Madden
5. Paul Hart
6. Gary Shelton
7. Lee Chapman
8. Gary Megson
9. Garry Thompson
10. Carl Shutt
11. Glynn Snodin

Sub) Mark Chamberlain

Hart played wearing a lightweight guard to protect his hand following a fracture at QPR. Jimmy Greaves helped summarise the game for ITV and began by damning Chapman with faint praise – 'good in the air but lacking ability', he felt. Chapman had half a chance to make Greaves eat his words early in the game, winning the ball well but putting his shot wide. Within a minute Shutt had a clearer opportunity, only to fire his shot at Chris Turner when he had only the keeper to beat.

Bryan Robson met Jesper Olsen's free kick with an excellent header at the other end, only to be foiled by Hodge. United did have the ball in the back of the net as the game headed towards half-time, Mark Hughes bundling both the ball and Hodge goalward. The referee gave a foul. Greaves felt it was 'good goal, a 50/50 challenge' that he 'couldn't see anything wrong with'.

At half-time, Greaves continued to bemoan the Owls' lack of imagination and need to 'replace their microchips', presumably as he felt they were playing like robots! Paul Thompson's report in the following Monday's *Sheffield Star* saw it somewhat differently. Wednesday were 'solid and well organised and put together some incisive attacking football to create chance after chance against a dodgy United defence. Wednesday could have been well in charge by half-time.'

Those chances continued to come in the second period. Thompson had already fired in a powerful shot before his determination and aggression helped set up the opening goal. On 54 minutes, Chapman headed a ball towards the box for Thompson to barge in between two defenders and steer the ball to Shutt, who powered a low drive under Turner.

Within five minutes it was 2-0 to the Owls. Sterland showed all his athletic qualities in chasing a ball into the right-hand side of the area. Turner rushed out and found he had no alternative but to bring Sterland down. Quickly dusting himself down, Sterland strode up and placed the penalty low and hard into the bottom right-hand corner.

United had little left to offer. Their only further chance of note came from a poor Sterland backpass. United's Colin Gibson rounded Hodge but then shot well wide of the gaping open goal. As the game moved into its closing stages there was still a chance for Shutt to add to his tally, but his header from Sterland's pinpoint cross was directly at Turner.

A solid win for the Owls, therefore. Hodge commented that, 'I thought we were superb', his counterpart Chris Turner in the United goal adding: 'It was a great result for my old club.' Wednesday's fans were delighted, mocking the Manchester United supporters with a chant of 'You're worse than Sheffield United!'

United's fans took out their anger on chief executive Martin Edwards, hurling abuse at him as he left the directors' box at full time. United would finish fourth in the end-of-season rankings. A long way from the expectations of earlier in the season. After keeping his team in the dressing room for 90 minutes after the game, Atkinson told the assembled press that 'we've blown it', meaning the league title, and that his team's second-half performance was 'the worst of any team since I came here'. Atkinson would survive as manager but was sacked in November that year after a poor start to the following campaign.

Wilkinson was delighted with what he called 'a very creditable victory'. In a dry aside in his programme notes for the following game Wilkinson added that he was 'only too pleased that I'm neither clever, nor sarcastic enough to be a TV football expert'. Wednesday's club DJ, 'Stevie Splash', added in his notes that it was 'a tremendous victory' and that 'the comments dished out by the commentators were very unjust'.

The *Star* added that 'Wednesday were impressive in all departments, with many impressive individuals'. They named Thompson as man of the match. The match is available in full on YouTube for anyone who might want to judge who was correct in their verdict. For my money it was a complete away performance. It also completed a 'double-double', as it saw the Owls win their fourth consecutive game against United. Four in four in our two seasons. A great record.

* * *

Wednesday's next fixture was another tricky-looking tie against an Arsenal team who were just below the Owls in the table. The midweek tie attracted a disappointing crowd of 16,344 to Hillsborough to watch an Owls team that was unchanged from the Manchester United game. Wednesday started the game quickly and Shutt was unlucky not to put the Owls in front when his lob over John Lukic was cleared off the line. On 25 minutes Wednesday did go ahead with a perfectly taken Sterland spot-kick. The penalty was awarded after Hart was held down in the box by Martin Keown.

Late in the half, Arsenal were awarded an indirect free kick inside the Wednesday area, but it came to nothing. The second half saw chances for both sides, before a loose backpass from the Gunners' Paul Davis found Shutt in acres of space to run on and fire home. The scoring was over in a game in which, as the *Daily Mail* put it, 'Wednesday enjoyed almost total domination'.

The result took the Owls up to sixth place with four games remaining. There were some rumours in the press that the European ban on English clubs might be lifted that summer. Regardless of this, Wilkinson was keen that the club 'finish in the highest position it has achieved for 21 years'. Next up in their attempt to do that was a home fixture against relegation-threatened Aston Villa.

Wilkinson shuffled his team, bringing Ian Knight into defence for his debut and seeing Marwood return from the injury that had kept him out of the previous four matches. Villa featured Andy Blair and Simon Stainrod, both of whom had left the Owls for the Birmingham club earlier in the season.

Wednesday set about Villa at pace in the opening minutes. Morris saw an early effort cleared off the line before Shutt put a serviceable chance wide from Thompson's through ball. Morris then hit the bar with an excellent shot before the Owls took a deserved lead on 30 minutes. Villa did not clear fully from a corner, leaving Hart free to chip the ball across for Megson to head home.

The Owls remained on top into the second half and doubled their lead on 64 minutes. Megson was fouled 25 yards out from goal. Sterland leathered the free kick home for his third goal in successive games and 11th of the campaign. There was little further goalmouth action at either end as the Owls secured their first win over Villa in 20 years. 'A ferocious demolition job', reported the *Sunday People*.

The Owls faced West Midlands opposition again in their next fixture, a trip to The Hawthorns to take on already relegated West Bromwich Albion. A tiny crowd of 6,201 turned out to watch. Wilkinson named an unchanged starting line-up to face the Baggies. Ron Saunders' team featured future Owl Carlton Palmer in their ranks.

The game seemed to be going to form on 11 minutes when Wednesday were gifted the lead. Paul Dyson in the Albion defence failed to move out as part of an offside trap, leaving Marwood in plenty of space to fire home from Megson's pass.

Albion's 17-year-old Mark Robinson could count himself very unfortunate not to have equalised before half-time. He twice forced excellent saves from Martin Hodge before firing a terrific long-range volley into the top corner just before the break. The 'goal' was ruled out as other Albion players were offside.

Palmer smacked a header off the underside of the crossbar in the early minutes of the second period. The Baggies eventually forced the equaliser on 58 minutes, when George Reilly scored his first league goal of the campaign from an excellent through ball. Ironically, Reilly's only other goal in his 20 games since joining from Newcastle the previous December was also against the Owls in the FA Cup. Neither team could find the winner in what was ultimately a disappointing game. Wilkinson commented that 'we took it too easy and in the end were fortunate to draw'.

Two games of the season remained and the Owls' continued unbeaten run since their FA Cup defeat saw the team remain in sixth place in the table. Wednesday travelled to The Dell for their next fixture against mid-table Southampton. Wilkinson recalled Snodin and Gregory to the starting line-up. Wednesday took an early lead when Shutt fired a shot on the turn past Peter Shilton. There were further chances at either end in an entertaining first half.

The Saints equalised on 55 minutes when Jimmy Case fired in a powerful free kick. Wednesday took the lead again nine minutes later, with Shelton forcing the ball home from close range. On 77 minutes Southampton equalised again, with Danny Wallace blasting past Hodge after David Armstrong's long pass set him clear.

The game was heading to injury time when Sterland crossed for Hart to apply the finishing touch and ensure the Owls' eighth away win of the campaign. 'It was another good performance in what has been a splendid season,' commented Hart.

The Owls had one final fixture to play, against Ipswich Town at Hillsborough. The end-of-season party atmosphere was enhanced as it was the last game that fans could watch from an uncovered Kop. Even the club's regular matchday DJ, 'Stevie Splash', could not resist joining the rank-and-file Kopites on the terraces for the occasion, leaving the tannoy system in the hands of Alan Price.

Ipswich had other pressing matters on their minds – three points would keep them safe from relegation. Wilkinson named a strong team, with Shirtliff replacing Madden, and Gregory dropping out for Megson.

Ipswich dominated much of the first half, with Mark Brennan forcing several saves from Hodge. At the other end, Terry Butcher and future Owl Ian Cranson kept the Wednesday forward line very quiet. Eight minutes from time, though, Shutt made a darting run from the right before crossing between Butcher and keeper Paul Cooper, and Marwood was able to stab home his 15th goal of the season.

The Owls had won, and Ipswich faced an excruciating 24-hour wait for the result of relegation rivals Oxford's game against Arsenal. Oxford won, and Ipswich were down.

The victory took the Owls to fifth place in the final standings. This was their highest position since 1960/61. The team had won exactly half of their 42 league games, scoring 63 goals and amassing 73 points on the way. Wilkinson described Sheffield Wednesday at the time as a 'thriving and dynamic club'. The summer was to see the stadium developed further with the huge, uncovered Kop having a roof put on. Worthington would represent

Northern Ireland in that summer's World Cup, and Hodge was on standby for a place in the England squad. Youngsters Gregory, Carl Bradshaw and Kevin Pressman were shortly to represent England Youth in a tournament in China.

This was clearly a high point in the long history of the Owls. Wilkinson, though, was still looking to improve. 'The quality of player at the club must get better,' he said. 'I must introduce even more quality to the team.' The extent to which Wilkinson was able to achieve that is material for another book. His two seasons in Division One had certainly announced that the team were 'back in the big time'.

17.

An Interview with Tony Gregory

TONY GREGORY was a tenacious and skilful midfield player who came up through the ranks at Hillsborough. Tony made his first-team debut for the Owls when still an apprentice in August 1985, going on to make 6(+1) appearances that season. In total he made 16(+5) appearances for the club, scoring one goal. He stayed at S6 until 1990 before moving to Halifax Town and later into non-league football. On retirement, Tony retrained as a chiropodist – he still owns and runs a practice in his native Doncaster. It was from Doncaster that we spoke in the spring of 2021.

How did you come to sign for Sheffield Wednesday?

I think that I have the claim to fame of being the last person that Jack Charlton signed for the club! I signed on schoolboy terms in May 1983, and he left soon afterwards. Going back a few years, I'd played for Doncaster Boys all the way through and played for Middlewood Rovers for a year. I was in a team there with Kevin Pressman and Steve Chambers, who went on to play for Mansfield. Before I signed, I trained with the club in the holidays and at half-term. There were offers for me to think about from other clubs, but I was happy to sign for Wednesday.

I then moved to a two-year YTS/apprenticeship deal in 1984. I got a bit of a shock, though, when it came to sorting out our kit. When pre-season training started the club brought a load of great-looking Adidas boots in for the first team. I was excited, thinking I was going to get this great kit. When it was our turn, though, it was picking from a different cupboard of cheap Mitre boots! It ended up with us being given £25 to go up to Johnny Quinn and Gerry Young's shop on Middlewood Road to pick another pair. Anything above that we had to pay ourselves!

How quickly were you playing games for the club?

I made my debut for the youth team in the Northern Intermediate League in August 1983. I was a regular that season even though I was still at school. I made my debut for the reserves in March 1984. The club needed to ring up my school to see if I was OK to play! That match was against Stoke City. I remember also playing against Liverpool at Anfield.

The Central League was a great league. There could be thousands at some games; teams like Liverpool and Manchester United would give vouchers to their fans to use in cup games. There would also often be some strong players. We beat Everton once for example; I beat Andy Gray at the front post to score a header. Kevin Sheedy played in that one as well I think. I'd often be playing twice a week at that stage. The reserves played midweek and the youth team on a Saturday – usually in the morning unless we had a long trip somewhere.

Who coached you in this period?

Funnily enough, for a period in 1984 between July and September there was no youth coach. Albert Phelan and Clive Baker would help. Mick Lyons as well. Mick Hennigan joined the club around September, originally as the youth-team coach, but he also helped with the reserves.

Tell me about your experiences with the England set-up.

In February 1985 I received an invite to go and train with England at Lilleshall. The coaches were sorting the teams and, after they'd handed plenty of bibs out and got some games going, there were still ten or so of us left – nearly all of us midfielders! One of the coaches must have realised that they needed a right-back for a practice game – so they asked whether any of us could play there.

I quickly put my hand up, thinking it might be my best chance to get a game – I'd never played there before in my life! No one else was up for it and I ended up playing every minute of the two practice games that followed.

In April I was picked to go with an England team down to Cannes in the south of France. I also played against Iceland in September that year. The following year, as an under-18, we travelled to China and in 1987 we went to Brazil and Uruguay. That last trip was led by the then England manager Bobby Robson and all his team, so Don Howe and others. It was a fantastic experience. I've still got my England shirts – they fit me as well!

By that stage, you'd also made your debut for Sheffield Wednesday. What are your memories of moving up to the first team?

My debut was away at Manchester City in the third game of the 1985/86 season. It wasn't a complete surprise as I'd played in a friendly against Scunthorpe a couple of weeks earlier and I knew that Gary Shelton had been struggling with an injury. Howard Wilkinson called me in on the Thursday afternoon and told me I was playing. I remember missing a decent chance in the game, but it was a bit of a blur otherwise. We did get the win though!

I played again two days later, on a Bank Holiday Monday against Watford. I remember that game more clearly. I hit a powerful shot that just went past the post and later missed a big chance that I should have scored! I was up against Brian Talbot, who was a hero of mine as I'd grown up as an Arsenal fan. I also remember Luther Blissett and John Barnes playing for them. Superstars really.

I was an apprentice at this stage, so on the Tuesday morning it was back to cleaning boots and the rest of it as if nothing had happened! I didn't get another sniff of the first team until Christmas time.

So it was back to the reserves?

Yes, and the youth team. The next time I got in the first team was a game away at Everton. I didn't know I was going to be in the squad so when the teams were pinned up for the weekend I was looking for my name on the youth-team list. I couldn't see it anywhere, so I was all set to go banging on the manager's door and ask why I wasn't even in the youth team! One of the other lads shouted across to me, 'Greggers, you're in the first team!' I was, but I could see I had been added to the list at the last minute as the 15th name.

I assumed I was there to make up the numbers, so I told my dad not to bother coming across. At 1.15 or so on matchday, though, Howard pulled me to one side and told me I'd be sub. We were in the hotel so I quickly ran to find a phone to ring my dad to see if he could make it. In the meantime the team bus left without me! I had to get a taxi to the ground and the worst thing was that nobody noticed I wasn't there!

The team played well in the game. We created loads of chances, but we came in at half-time and were 2-0 down. Garry Thompson had a header that bounced down off the bar and looked miles over the line, but it wasn't given – VAR would have sorted it! So despite playing well we were losing. Howard was furious at half-time about something. Mark Chamberlain took a lot of it. I remember Howard being so angry that he threw a teacup that smashed on the wall. Anyhow, he decided to change things around a bit. He brought a defender off, Mark Smith I think, and brought me on. We played well again, and Garry Thompson pulled one back, but Gary Lineker scored a poacher's goal near the end, and we'd lost.

A few days later and I'm in the starting line-up at Anfield against Liverpool. That was an amazing experience against some top players. Jan Mølby is a mate of mine now, but back then I was in awe of him. Liverpool murdered us that day really. Carl Shutt put us ahead early on, but they must have had about 30 chances. I had a decent shot, which was one of only three or four we had all game. Liverpool equalised and then went ahead but Thommo scored again late on, and we escaped with a point. I remember before the game us realising that our usual penalty takers weren't playing. Howard quickly asked who would be on spot-kicks if we got one – and I jumped in and said I'd do it! I would have done as well, taking one at the Kop end would have been something!

I stayed in the team for the next two games, which were in the cup against West Brom. We drew at Hillsborough and then beat them at their place in the replay. In the first half of that second game I got dead-legged. It was agony. I hobbled about afterwards and at half-time I wanted to come off. Howard told me that I was 'not letting that b****** stop me from playing' so I was staying on.

I hobbled about for another half an hour or so, before eventually being subbed anyway. Three days later I was in the Royal Hallamshire hospital with blood clots in my leg. Fans don't really hear about that sort of thing – it was reported as me having a thigh strain. There was a risk I could have lost my bloody leg though.

I got back in the team towards the end of the season for one more game – a win down at Southampton. I stayed in the squad for the start of the next season as well, and soon scored my only goal – a diving header from a Glynn Snodin cross against Chelsea in front of the Kop. I should have had five or six goals with all the chances I'd missed in various games up to that point. I'm pleased to have one though – I've got the picture up still!

How did you find Howard Wilkinson?

I thought I'd made a terrible mistake when he came in as the training was so hard! He used to take us up to Ewden reservoir and have us running up and down hills. He used to give Peter Eustace a head start and have us chase him up to the top of a hill and back over and over again. It was a bit like pre-season all the way through until January. He would run our balls off every Monday. I was young remember, so I was fit – but not 'man fit' if that makes sense. Over time I got used to it, though I don't think I ever enjoyed it!

He worked us all hard the rest of the week as well. Tuesdays would be small-sided games. Thursday he'd have us going through his plans for the weekend's game and work through some shadow exercises, for example. He'd have us out for what seemed like hours sometimes until whatever we were practising was to his standards. Fridays was set pieces.

How did you find the tactics?

I was not too enamoured with the style of play, but it got results! I fitted into it because I wanted to get into the team. I found that the direct style meant that sometimes the ball would bypass midfield. I was the type of player who liked to get my foot on the ball and look for the pass. Howard's play was more about getting it forward quickly and looking to win what he called 'the seconds'.

Even though I was young, I was prepared to say my piece. There was one game where I took the ball down on my chest and passed it to one side to Mel Sterland. It was just before half-time, and I could see Howard going mad on the sideline – he threw his notepad down in disgust. He wanted the ball knocked forward. He called me into the office the following day and told me off. He asked me why I couldn't see that he was making me into a better player. I told him that I couldn't see what I'd done wrong – as far as I was concerned I'd kept the ball.

He was ahead of his time in some ways. He was advanced on things like food, drink and supplements. He had us all drinking a green-coloured glucose drink years before Lucozade was a thing! He allowed us to drink alcohol, but not after a Wednesday. He also encouraged anyone who liked a beer or two to drink water with it. I do remember drinking tea at half-time, though, which seems incredible now!

Thanks Tony, is there anything else I should mention?

Let me tell you a story about the FA Cup semi-final. Howard took us to Lilleshall on the Monday before the game. Gary Megson was carrying an injury and all week I was going to be in the team. On the Friday, though, he'd recovered and was back in the squad. On the Saturday we only had 13 fit players. We got on the coach, and Howard named the starting XI. The two left were me and Mark Chamberlain. I spoke to Mark and asked him whether Howard had told him he was sub. He hadn't and he hadn't told me either.

We had to go up together and ask him in the changing room! Howard pointed at me first and then slowly moved his finger towards Mark. That was me out of the team, I was gutted. I'm not sure he'd thought about it before that moment.

I got on really well with lots of the other lads by the way. It was a great atmosphere. Me and Glynn Snodin were good mates. David Hirst was very funny. Ian Knight, Jon Newsome, Kevin Pressman and me were all a similar age and got on well.

Thanks for your time Tony.

No problem, good luck with the book. It's bringing back some great memories!

18.

Behind the Scenes

ANY LARGE and complex organisation needs good people behind the scenes for it to work effectively. Sheffield Wednesday in the mid-1980s was no exception. Club secretary Dick Chester praised the backroom staff in 1985 after a season back in Division One, saying, 'Everyone in all our departments has done an excellent job and they have adapted to the rigours and demands of First Division football.'

He gave special mentions to the ticket office staff, ground staff, commercial and development fund, the Inter City Owl and Young Owls, along with those working in marketing and sponsorship. 'The club wishes to express their sincere thanks to everyone concerned,' continued Chester. 'It has been a very good season for Yorkshire's only First Division club.'

Many of those behind the scenes had dedicated years of service to the club. Dorothy Pearson, for example, who worked with five other members of the cleaning and laundry staff, had been at Hillsborough for 23 years by 1985. 'The ladies in there were amazing,' Dylan Kerr told me. 'Everyone was so honest and hard-working.'

Norma Lane was another long-serving member of staff. Joining the club as a temp in 1966, she served every manager from Jack Marshall and was secretary to all those from Danny Williams onwards. Ron Ward joined the club as caretaker's assistant in 1950 before being promoted to the full position in 1958. By 1985 he was the club's longest-serving employee. In that year he was presented a Canon League loyalty award for his service – earning a Seiko watch and certificate for his efforts.

Lily Shelton followed closely behind him for long service. She racked up 31 years with the club, with jobs including sweeping the stand, working the laundry and in the 1980s taking responsibility for the boardroom areas.

One highlight of Lily's career came when chairman Bert McGee chose her to represent the club in a reception at Sheffield Town Hall with Prince Charles and Lady Diana. 'They were both very nice, and I hope I converted him into a Wednesdayite,' commented Lily afterwards!

In this chapter, I track down some of those who worked behind the scenes to gain the inside track on what life was like at that top Division One club. As Lily Shelton put it when interviewed for Keith Farnsworth's book *Wednesday Every Day of the Week,* 'There was always a friendly atmosphere about the place with some wonderful characters.' I wanted to see how much this held true in the mid-1980s.

First on my list was Mark Robinson. Mark, often nicknamed Robbo, was assistant groundsman during this period. He had a long career at Hillsborough, staying with the club until 1997 before moving on to work at Derby's Pride Park and elsewhere. We spoke in the summer of 2021.

Tell me how you started at Hillsborough, Mark?

I started on Mrs Thatcher's YTS scheme! 1984 it was. I originally worked at Middlewood Road on the training ground. I worked with Derek Blunkett, who was the brother of David – the politician. He'd been there since the 1960s and was a great bloke. David Barber started as head groundsman about the same time – he moved across from the university. It was a great job for me. I'd been following Wednesday since the mid-1970s, so I loved working for the club as well. It was hard, physical work, but I must have done OK as a few months in I was moved across to start working at the stadium itself.

Talk me through a typical day's work.

All our equipment was stored in a big blue shed at the back of the North Stand. So we'd move things around from there. The day started by clearing any dew off the grass. We'd then complete a single or a double cut. There'd usually be two double cuts a week. We'd mark out the pitch on a Friday if there was a game the next day. We very rarely cut the pitch on a matchday – that was more about making sure all the markings were spot on and the netting ready.

What was the condition of the pitch at the time?

We did some work in the summer of 1985 that caused a few problems. We wanted to improve the drainage, so we spoke to the people at the Sports Turf Research Institute, and they recommended something called sand-slitting. Basically, that involved cutting in a series of two-inch wide, eight-inch deep slits filled with sand across the pitch.

We got in a company from Leeds called Pullens to do the work. They'll be long gone now, but the STRI are still going. Anyhow, with all that sand it was difficult to grow the grass and keep it there. We used loads of fertiliser and tried to let the grass grow long. One time we borrowed a cricket roller to flatten the grass rather than cut it! I remember Watford's manager Graham Taylor having a go about the state of the pitch early the following season.

Hillsborough's not the easiest place to develop a good pitch. The drainage isn't great and there's not much sunlight in front of the North Stand. It's on a riverbed, and if you dig down too far there's too much stone, so it's difficult to improve things. The pitch did get pretty atrocious as that season went on. It improved the following summer, though. David Barber said at the time that it would take three years before everything was right. He got that spot on as the club won an award for the pitch a few years down the line. It was around the time that Rumbelows sponsored the League Cup and I remember David being presented with a TV from them as his prize!

How was your relationship with the management at the time?

The whole club was great. We were all in it together for the benefit of Sheffield Wednesday. That said, we had to play the game a bit with the management. Howard Wilkinson would sometimes say the grass was too long, for example. We'd brush the grass back up the other way and give it a quick trim and he'd be happy! Mick Hennigan would often ask for more water on the pitch on matchday. He'd come down the tunnel and have a quick scout around the pitch in front of the dugouts. We learned to add extra water round there and not so much over by the North Stand or in the corners!

Alan Smith was a great guy. He didn't like the St John's Ambulance people controlling the stretchers, though. So, on matchdays for a while me and others on the ground staff were on that duty. There was one game where John Fashanu got sent off while he was on the stretcher! We got him to the tunnel, and he jumped straight off – telling us that he was only trying to fool the referee!

Another time Howard had me helping in training as they were a player or two short. I could play a bit, but not at their standard. Anyhow, they were practising corners with the first team defending. Howard told me, stand on the 'D' at the edge of the area. The ball was headed out towards me, and Howard shouted, 'Play on!' I saw Meggo and Shelts coming towards me quick and before I knew it the ball was on me. I managed to catch it just right and attempted a chip over Martin Hodge in goal. He scrambled back and threw himself backwards to tip it over! The players were a joy by the way, great to work with and to see in action.

Great stories! Is there anything else I should include?

I said there wasn't much light on the pitch. Well, that could make it difficult in the winter, from November onwards. I remember us sitting on bales of straw to try and get one game on when the pitch was frozen. I tell you what though, we pulled a bit of a flanker for one game against Derby County in the cup. Lee Chapman was injured and Howard had suggested to us that it wouldn't be the worst thing in the world if the game were postponed!

This was before the undersoil heating, of course. We had the pitch covered with sheets but pulled some of them out of the way around the centre circle. We didn't know that Derby's manager was coming up for the pitch inspection, though. Luckily, we had the sheet back in time, so no one suspected what we'd done! The game was postponed and eventually Wednesday won on another rock-hard pitch at the Baseball Ground.

Thanks Mark.

No problem. It was great time with great people.

* * *

Next on my list was journalist Alan Biggs. Sometimes called the Godfather of Sheffield football journalism, Biggs has spent much of his 45-year-plus career focusing on the football teams of South Yorkshire. In the mid-1980s, Alan was a freelance journalist working for the national press and local radio, and writing for the club's programme. We spoke in summer 2021, chewing the fat for a while about the team's current chances, before discussing Alan's memories of the era.

Tell me about your work with the club programme.

The programmes improved with the team in a way. Back in Division One there was a push to project the club in a positive, forward-looking way. A lot of credit for that goes to the publisher J.W. Northend and the editor Roger Oldfield. I was involved in interviewing the players and staff. I'd get a lengthy piece in each programme.

I tell you what was different to nowadays – the honesty and frankness in the interviews. I was allowed a degree of objectivity that I don't think would be seen today. Also, a lot of it was done through personal contact. I'd have the phone numbers of many of the players and ring them directly to sort it. It was all done with the club's blessing and presumably Howard Wilkinson's – at least he never told me any differently!

'Coming up through the ranks': Tony Gregory (centre) makes his Northern Intermediate League debut for the Owls in a 3-2 defeat to Sunderland, 13 August 1983. Also in shot Dylan Kerr (left) and Simon Dwyer (right). Picture courtesy of Tony Gregory

Garry Thompson gets stuck in with Steve Terry of Watford in September 1985

Mike Lyons in typically determined pose during the Owls' 2-0 win at Anfield in September 1984

The classic yellow away shirt of the period complete with signatures from the 1986 FA Cup semi-final squad Picture courtesy of @ wednesdaywarehouse

Andy Blair in composed mode on the ball against Manchester United in November 1985

The 1980s were sometimes a dark time for the game. Crowd trouble during the English League Cup quarter-final second replay between Chelsea and the Owls at Stamford Bridge, 6 February 1985

Howard Wilkinson in pensive mood as the Owls take on Everton in May 1985

Imre Varadi runs at the Arsenal defence at Highbury in April 1985. Also in shot is future Owls defender, Viv Anderson.

Mel Sterland is consoled by supporters Andy Clayton and John Crooks after the Owls' defeat to Everton in the 1986 FA Cup semi-final. Courtesy of Steve Ellis, SWFC photographer

umbro

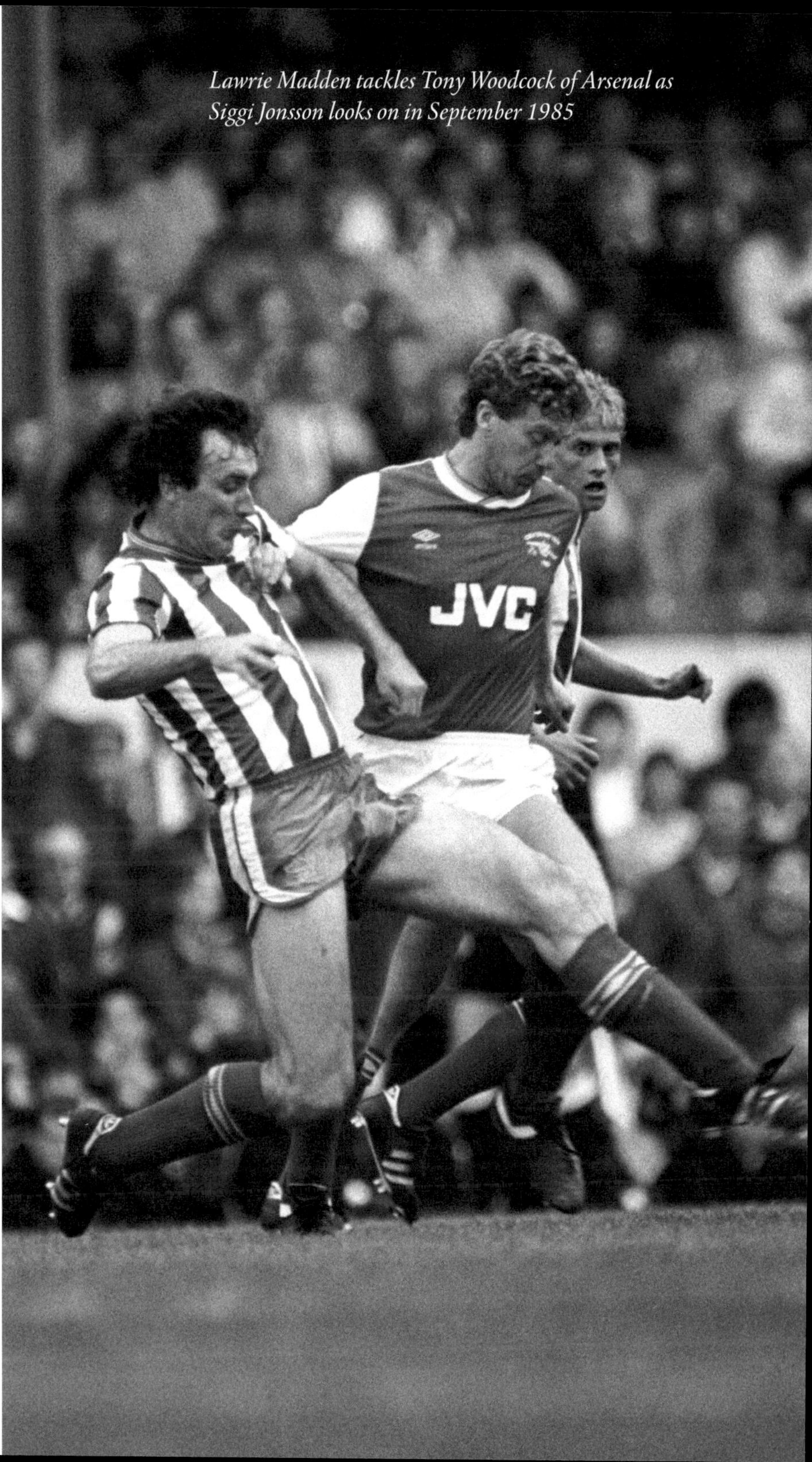

Lawrie Madden tackles Tony Woodcock of Arsenal as Siggi Jonsson looks on in September 1985

Mel Sterland is tackled by Coventry's Lloyd McGrath in October 1984

Michael Hennigan alongside members of the Owls youth team travelling on the ferry towards Bochum. (L-R are: Lee Oliver, Wayne Jacobs, Kevin Pressman, Paul Mullen and Michael Hennigan)
Photo courtesy of Sonia Hennigan

Gary Shelton with namesake
Photo courtesy of Shelton Whittaker

How was your relationship with Howard Wilkinson?

I'll start with the difficulties! He wasn't always easy to deal with. He could come across as condescending, which I doubt was his intention. I think that he believed that journalists lacked knowledge, having never been professional footballers. He also felt, I believe, that some journalism did not allow for sufficient study of the game to make valid points. He could be a bit 'headmasterly', if that makes sense.

I'd worked with him previously. He'd acted as a summariser for football commentary on Radio Hallam while he was working for the FA. Trouble is he wasn't the best summariser for the time constraints. He came across as very dour and his summaries were far too complex.

On reflection, I realised that he was a very deep thinker. He was intense to the point of being introverted. He couldn't understand why anyone at all would be interested in him. Problem being, 30,000 people at Hillsborough and many more who read the papers or listened to the radio were all interested! He also seemed very different to his predecessor Jack Charlton, who was actually very thoughtful and knowledgeable but portrayed himself in a more brash, 'man of the people' way.

Despite all that, Howard could be kindly, funny and friendly. He did offer me time – even if often he'd arrange his interviews at 7.45am with the noise of the coffee percolator soundtracking the tape! I remember one occasion where I'd interviewed him later in the day for the national press and when we'd finished he asked me whether I liked beaujolais. I answered positively and he produced a bottle with a couple of glasses, and we sat and talked for an hour or two.

Once I agreed to write a piece for the *Today* newspaper about Wednesday's notoriously tough training regime. The deal was that I'd spend a day training alongside the players. It was a roasting hot summer's day. Howard barked at me as we started, telling me that any time he asked I must stop and repeat this phrase, 'Success is only a matter of luck. Ask any failure.' I still remember it!

It got to lunchtime and Howard came in to where I was having a break and a coffee and asked me simply if I had what I needed. I suggested that there was an afternoon session as well and could I join that? He agreed, but when the session started I found that it involved running, running and more running! I kept up, just, but it was bloody hard work. I'd like to think that Howard gave me some grudging respect afterwards!

He had a sense of humour. On his unveiling as the Owls' manager, one of the press corps asked him what he had taught as a schoolteacher. 'Children,' came the simple, but very dry, reply. I used to help record interviews for the ClubCall phone line. The one where people could ring a premium rate number for all the news and gossip about the club. Anyhow, we'd arranged an interview after a defeat with Glynn Snodin. When the time for the interview came, Howard turned up. The guy at the other end of the line was still expecting Snodin. So when it came to it, Howard put on his best Glynn Snodin impression and told the interviewer how 'the gaffer had people up against the wall' and that 'we're all in for extra training'! A couple of minutes in he turned his voice back on a sixpence and said, 'It's Howard!"

I'll give you one last example. I was working for Radio Hallam doing a behind-the-scenes thing at Hillsborough. On my desk was a half-drunk pint of bitter and the best part of a pack of 20 cigarettes. Different times! I interviewed Howard and noticed afterwards that the glass and the cigs had gone. Only Howard could have taken them, so at the end of the day I went and knocked on his office door. I asked him if he'd seen them. He denied all knowledge but did say that he'd seen a massive cigar which he immediately produced and offered to me as if by way of compensation!

Thanks Alan, great stories!

No problem. Let me tell you this, though. No manager could have got more out his players and resources than Howard Wilkinson did at Hillsborough. He moulded a team of exceptional athletes who were also dependable, professional, honest and analytical.

Good people, in short. He has to be one of the best managers in Wednesday's history and probably didn't get as much credit as he deserved. Certainly the club should have fought harder to keep him when he left for Leeds, who were, after all, a division lower at that point.

* * *

Alan's comment about success helps link to my next contact. Steve Woodhead is the son of Dennis Woodhead. The senior of the two men helped transform the club's development fund in the 1970s, becoming a major factor in the club's return to financial good health. Steve helped me understand Dennis's role and contribution in the 1970s for my previous book *Our Lowest Ebb? A New History of Sheffield Wednesday's Darkest Times – 1973–76.* I knew that Steve had been involved with the club in various ways in the 1980s so I picked up the phone again to see what he could tell me.

Thanks for talking to me again Steve. Can you start me going with what your job title was at Hillsborough in the 1980s?

That's a tough one for starters! Lottery assistant I think! Let me think about it, I'll try and remember during our conversation.

Fair enough! I do know that you were in charge of the club transport for fans at this time. When did that start?

Yes, the Inter City Owl as we called it. We started it in 1979. So by your era it had been going for a few years and was pretty successful. I'll give you a good example from your years. In September 1984, we took two full trains to Liverpool. The 'we said we'd be back – we are we are' game, if you remember? Previously, if we'd been to Liverpool, we'd had problems with windows being smashed and the coaches being damaged. This time, we did a deal that got us the train to Edge Hill and then local buses on to the game. The thinking was that they wouldn't smash up their own! They didn't, so we ran a similar train to the game at Everton that season as well. Mind you, we had issues on the way back that time. British Rail had a rule that the staff could only work on lines that they were familiar with. We got halfway back and the driver pissed off as he was at the edge of his area. We had to wait ages for another crew!

What was the atmosphere like on the trains?

It was great. Sometimes for the real big games we'd have a couple of coppers on – but they didn't usually need to move from the guards' section. We'd have hot drinks and food laid on. [Club director] Geoff Hulley's two lads prepared and sold the sandwiches. It would be a great day out – especially if we won!

Sometimes the trains got delayed a bit. It was usually by a few minutes, but I do remember one game down at Portsmouth. It had chucked it down and it was an open terrace, so the fans were soaked. We seemed to get delayed at every stage on the way back. Must have been 2am before we got back in. I remember some fans hanging their trousers up on the luggage racks to get them dry and warm! We almost always got there on time – there was one time where snow held us up on the way to Southampton, but we still made it.

There was another time at Cardiff where we lost a couple. We were due to set off back at 9.40pm, I think. There used to be a pub right next to the station. Anyhow, a few minutes before we were due to go I felt the train moving. The guard just said, 'We're off'! A count-up of the fans showed two missing. I got on to British Rail as soon as I could, and they told me, 'We know!' I don't know to this day how or if they got home!

Sounds great fun. Why was it, then, that you stuck to coaches in later seasons?

Money. Cost. The price for train tickets goes up every January. The train companies would hold our prices though, until the following season in August. The prices on the coach could be very reasonable. I looked one up from your years. Brentford – £3.50 return. You wouldn't get a tram ticket for that nowadays!

Anyhow, in the summer of 1985 they called a meeting of football supporters in London to 'discuss' pricing on the trains.

I couldn't go as I was on holiday. Just as well, as they increased prices between 18 and 72 per cent! We couldn't justify charging that, so went with coaches from then on – using the Pride of the Road coach company. They were great with us.

Mind you, we went out on a high. The train companies would often allocate the oldest trains and rolling stock for the football specials. Our last one, though, was a trip to Arsenal on an Inter-City 125 – the most modern and fastest train of the time. We were back in Sheffield in less than two hours!

> This story was taken up in the *Green 'Un* in 1985. Steve was quoted as having organised a survey of fans – of which 55 per cent preferred travel by road than rail. 'The longer it goes on, the less I'm bothered and the more I'm satisfied with coaches,' said Steve at the time. Mr G. Anderson, 'Area Passenger Manager', replied by post the following week. 'It is only common business sense that an organisation like our own, under government pressure to make a profit, do so.'

We didn't allow alcohol anyhow, but we had to be really careful after 1986. The law changed and if one person on a football supporters' coach was found with a drink the whole coach was turned around. There was no chance of any beer!

I've remembered my job title by the way! Commercial assistant. I was running the transport part-time, but I knew that it was making a bit of money for the club. I was made redundant from my other job and luckily enough the club asked me to work for them full-time.

Is that when the Young Owls started?

Yes, 1981. The club wanted something to encourage youngsters to be involved with and support the club. It launched with a full-page article in the programme featuring Mike Pickering. We ran trips and events. We took kids to Chester Zoo and Gulliver's Kingdom. We organised open days and the kids all got something for being a member – card, scarf, that sort of thing.

I felt something was missing though, so in 1982/83 we launched football teams. We started with under-10s and over the next few years progressed upwards. We had some good players at one time or another. We were particularly strong in the early 1990s.

I think Wednesday were a bit nervous about offering our lads a trial if they weren't quite the finished article. Maybe they didn't want to let them down. Naming a few names though – Mark Platt, Steve Haslam and Nicky Weaver all played for us at a similar time.

Nicky played centre-forward more often than in goal! We also had Simon Weaver, who is Harrogate's manager now, and Lawrie Madden's daughter who was a great player. Richard Hinds a few years later also, and David Silverwood who went on to play professional tennis. Leroy Chambers, I think, was the only one from your years who went on to make the first team – he'd have been in the under-13s in the mid-1980s.

How did the ball boy/girl system work?

I think the kids just volunteered. We probably had them fill in a form or something. As time went on we got a bit more 'professional' about it though. I remember telling the kids to vary where they were standing depending on whether we were winning or losing! One time against Barnsley we were winning and one of their reserves raced to get the ball when it ran out of play. He managed to fall over the accidentally trailing leg of one of our ball boys. I was very proud at that moment, let me say!

Thanks Steve, some great memories there.

No problem. Let me tell you this – the job I had at Hillsborough was the best job I ever had. They were great times.

* * *

Some of Steve's role crossed over with the community aspect of the club's work. Joe Dunn worked with the club in the 1980s – completing some scouting assignments and also helping organise community activities such as the 'Sportacular' events which took place in school holidays. I met Joe alongside Michael Hennigan. Joe and Michael remain good friends to this day. After that meeting I rang Joe to further pick his brains about his role in the 1980s.

I know that you helped organise the 'Sportacular' events around Hillsborough. Tell me a little more about how they came about.

They were held over October and February half-terms. The inspiration for them came out of a study I did as part of my football education as to how other countries organised their clubs. Hamburger SV caught my attention as the SV stands for Sport Verein, or Sports Club. Many of the German clubs provided facilities for other sports. It would not be uncommon for a family to do most of their sporting activities, including classes, at the SV. This seemed a pretty smart way of expanding the fanbase and creating revenue – a win-win!

At the time the Sheffield Recreation Department had the 'Passport to Leisure' scheme which enabled young people to access the city's leisure facilities. We also had a thriving Young Owls community, so this was the ideal opportunity to combine the two for a week of activities. It would raise the profile of the club, whilst increasing the use of Passport to Leisure and boosting Young Owls membership.

Over time we saw increased demand and the number of activities and staff grew significantly. We utilised the facilities in Hillsborough Park, including the lake, tennis courts, grass surfaces and the then athletics stadium. Together with the SWFC facilities it proved an ideal set of venues for a multi-sport 'Sportacular', all within close proximity.

I didn't do it all myself! I would pay tribute to the coaches and sports clubs who provided equipment, including two former Olympic medal-winners in John and Sheila Sherwood, who coached the athletics. There are some photos in the club magazine or programme that show the canoe club and BMX, for example. It wasn't all about which kids were the best at sport.

We also used the idea of 'sports personalities'. These were young people who had impressed the coaching staff during the week and were presented with their certificates as guests of the club at a first-team game. There's a great photo pitchside at the following home game with the winners together with myself and Mark Smith.

Once the 'Sportacular' was established I wanted to expand it to the visually and hearing impaired and those with physical disabilities. There were two excellent schools in Sheffield at Tapton Mount and Oaks Park. I contacted them to see if their pupils would be interested. The response was overwhelming, as was the impression they made on everyone. Martin Hodge wrote a good piece in one of the papers I gave you detailing the effect the children had on the seasoned professionals of the first team.

> Joe had indeed lent me a series of newspaper articles and match programmes relating to the 'Sportacular' events. They made for fascinating and moving reading. In one picture, Owls defender Paul Hart is shown giving a youngster named Michael Weaver from the Tapton Mount school a lift in the dressing room. The *Star* interviewed some of the pupils, including the then 17-year-old Ian Troops who suffered from cerebral palsy: 'I live for Sheffield Wednesday, and it was a thrill for me to meet the players.' In a cutting from the *Weekly News*, Martin Hodge described how he and the Owls squad played a game against the blind children, using a ball with a barely perceptible bell inside. This was followed with a game against the children who were described in the language of the time as 'handicapped'. Hodge described how the Owls team played on their hands and knees and ran the risk of being 'bashed about and run over by wheelchairs!' He went on to say: 'You can win all sorts in this game, but the satisfaction we gained that day brought a lump to my throat.'

It sounds very forward-thinking, Joe.

It was. We're speaking during the Paralympics in Tokyo, and I can't help but think back to the pioneering work that was done at the football club during the Wilkinson era. The club was ahead of its time on the field of play but also behind the scenes. They were great days.

Were the 'Sportaculars' the only event you organised?

No, there was also the 'Bobby Robson Fun Week'. Bobby Robson was part of the FA's technical department and devised a programme. It was purely soccer coaching sessions and lots of competitive small-sided games. Steve Woodhead and I organised it as an incentive to Young Owls members. I was course director and did the coaching alongside, I think, two others. Keith Adams was one, but I can't remember the other. There was a really good turnout from the kids. One mum wrote to either the *Star* or *The Owl* saying how much her son had enjoyed it and that it was 'most excellent in every way'.

Following this, we organised courses that had girls groups. We asked them what they wanted, and they said they'd like to have separate groups from the boys. We brought in a coach from Doncaster Belles who had the FA preliminary coaching award – I can't remember her name. This was a great success and we saw a significant increase in the number of girls taking part – we were perhaps a little ahead of our time!

I know you did some scouting for the club at the time. Talk me through how that worked.

I'd started by doing a bit for Howard when he was at Notts County. I'd watch school and youth games and invite any promising youngsters down to Meadow Lane for trials. I remember bringing Marco Gabbiadini down when he was 14, for example. When Howard moved to Hillsborough, he'd ask me to watch teams that the Owls would be playing in the near future or occasionally players that he was interested in.

I think I was one of four or five people who would be doing similar work in advance of games. Howard had developed detailed documents for us to complete. There were ticks to be placed and tallies to be made in all sorts of areas – for example, how many crosses each side had and what happened to them.

I'd often be there alongside scouts from other clubs. They would sit there taking in the game, and perhaps making a few notes. I was busy all game scribbling away and keeping track of what was happening! It would then take another couple of hours later that evening or the following day to write it all up. It was hard work, but a clear example of how meticulous Howard was.

For the individuals it was more a matter of watching them and their contribution to the game. They would be players that Howard was already interested in, so it wasn't a matter of spotting some undiscovered gem. I watched the Snodin brothers, for example, and David Hirst. I'd look for some specifics, but it was less of a regimented routine than watching the Owls' next opponents.

Thanks Joe, that's very helpful.

No problem, they were great times. I remember being lucky enough to be in the changing room after the final game of the 1985/86 season having a drink with Howard and Michael. They were disappointed not to have reached the cup final but satisfied, with a sense of joy about what they had achieved. It's a forgotten story in a way but Howard built a team to be proud of.

* * *

Joe's articles about the 'Sportacular' events led me to thinking about how the Owls were reported in the press. Alan Biggs had given me some idea of the national papers and the development of the programme. I wanted to find out more about the local press. The Owls reporter for the *Sheffield Star* and *Green 'Un* at the time was Paul Thompson. I knew that Paul had retired a few years previously, but with some help from his modern-day equivalent and other journalists who knew him, I was able to track him down. Still living in Sheffield but happily retired, Paul chatted to me about his memories of the era on a windy February day in 2022.

When did you start reporting on the Owls?

I'd been a general sports reporter at the *Star* for a few years. At the end of the 1979/80 season, though, I was asked whether I'd take on the Owls reporting full-time. I was told that I'd be expected to do it for at least five years as they didn't like changing too often. Thirty-four years later, I retired!

How much access did you have to the club?

I basically had free access. The club relied on the local papers and to some extent the local radio stations. I rang Jack Charlton and later Howard Wilkinson every day. Under Jack I travelled on the team coach and had meals with the directors on away trips. I'd stay over in the same hotel. Howard wanted the coach as more of an extension of the dressing room, so I was no longer on board. I could talk to Howard whenever I needed, though. He was 100 per cent available. So much so that during the after-match press conference I'd often try and find the players I wanted to talk to – knowing that I'd be able to speak to Howard later. He even rang me at home on a Sunday from time to time to fill me in on anything he thought I needed.

How about the players, were there any you could rely on for a good quote or two?

They were all helpful. It was much different to today. I would get the home phone number of each player when he signed. No mobiles, remember. There were no press officers, so I would just ring up for a chat. They all accepted it, I think. I certainly don't remember any problems. I ghosted a column in the *Star* for a few players over the years – Terry Curran, Nigel Pearson and others. Never an issue.

Did all this access come at a price? Could you write about all you wanted to?

Ron Atkinson's assistant Richie Barker put it this way to me a few years later: 'You can't hunt with the hounds and run with the hare!' I always took it that I couldn't go too far. The national press were sometimes able to take something and really run with it. I felt that it was best to not go that far. It didn't mean that if something had gone wrong in a game or performance that I wouldn't write about it, more that I knew where the limit was. I remember one time when Howard asked me not to publish something. It was in advance of the FA Cup semi-final in 1986 and there was a risk that Martin Hodge would not be fit for the game. The news had already leaked out in Sheffield, and I said as much to Howard. He accepted it and we ran an interview with Iain Hesford saying that he'd be ready to deputise if needed.

How about at the *Star* itself – was there a rivalry between the reporters on each club?

(Laughs) No, there was no rivalry between us. We were actually big mates. Over the course of the season we'd cover for each other, so there were times where I'd be ringing up and reporting on goings on at Bramall Lane as well as at Hillsborough. Tony Pritchett [the *Star's* Sheffield United reporter] and I used to have a cup of tea together most days.

The choice of lead story in the paper was down to the sports editor. I know that Blades fans used to argue that the paper was biased towards the Owls and vice versa. I used to think that, if they both thought that, then we must be doing something right! Some of it, I think, dated from the *Star*'s 'Save Our Owls' campaign in the 1970s. We used to get United fans complaining that there had never been an equivalent for the Blades. That was true, but even that campaign was really to sell papers.

Thanks Paul.

No problem, give me a shout any time. Let me tell you this, though, in your years Howard Wilkinson transformed the club. He took Division One by storm, it was a great era.

* * *

Paul Thompson's thoughts about transforming the club had me thinking about how the matchday experience was also modernised in our period. I knew that 'Stevie Splash' was the club's official DJ in our years. I assumed that it was not his real name! He took a little bit of finding, but given some detective work by Steve Woodhead and help from the members of a popular online forum, I found him. He does, of course, go by a different name, but as our conversation began with the immortal words: 'Hi John, it's Stevie Splash', I'm not going to spoil the magic here by revealing his real name.

Thanks for speaking to me Stevie – can you tell me how came to work for the club?

It was easy. I went in to see Dennis Woodhead one day. I told him that the entertainment they had on matchdays was rubbish – and that I could do a better job! He told me that I could start straight away! That would be in Jack Charlton's time. I'd started as a DJ at the Gate and the Ball pubs in Hillsborough. We had the odd player in those places; they knew it would be friendly for them.

Later on, I ran clubs in Sheffield including Sinatras and Charlie Parkers. Sinatras had a bit of food – jacket potatoes, that kind of thing – but was mostly drink and dancing. Charlie Parkers was a bit more food-based, or the meals were higher quality. We had the players in both, they had a good time and no bother. So I guess the club knew they could trust me. Howard Wilkinson used to let me go where I liked around the place. 'He's a professional, he knows what he's doing,' he used to say!

Did you get on well with the management and players?

Yes, like I say the players came into the clubs often with their wives or girlfriends. We sometimes had both them and Sheffield United in, but there was no problem. Howard let me get on with things. One of my favourite memories is recording a single with the players, management and fans. We got two Americans in to help with it. The producer was a guy called Charlie Skarbek and the other fella was a bloke called Rick Blaskey, who for a short time was Whitney Houston's manager. So I introduced Howard Wilkinson to Whitney Houston's manager!

The song was called 'We are the Owls' and we recorded it at Radio Hallam's studios. It was a Thompson Twins song, and we did it with them, the players and the management. Howard sang on the record, no problem!

The B-side was recorded by us and the fans. It was actually based on a song that Kevin Keegan had recorded previously, but with different words and a new arrangement. I think the whole thing was credited to 'Stevie Splash Productions'. It didn't make any money – but it was great fun to do.

Sounds great! I've seen pictures of a charity event at Sheffield City Hall involving some of the stars of the time. What memories do you have of that?

Yes, that was an event raising money for the Ethiopian famine. It was at the time of the miners' strike though – so I think 1,000 tickets or so were given away for free to them. I was compere, though I only got 20 minutes' notice! I remember that Tony Capstick was the comedian for the evening, and that the Human League and Alvin Stardust were also on. There were plenty of Wednesday players there as well. A good event.

Tell me about what you did on a matchday.

I was responsible for all the music and entertainment. We had a new sound system in your period which improved things. One of the directors, Ernest Barron I think, wanted me to play marching band music, which they had done for years. I managed to move things on a bit and got some modern music played as well.

> That new sound system was described in Wednesday's regular magazine *The Owl*. The report said that the new system was installed by Sheffield-based D.P. Sound Systems with amplifiers totalling 1,320 watts of output and with 200 speaker units. 'We have been told by an impartial yet authoritative person that this system is one of the best he has ever heard.'

I had my bit in the programme each week. I'd run quizzes in some of the pubs. There used to be a rule that there could be no dancing in pubs, so quizzes encouraged people to come in. Anyhow, I thought that putting a quiz question or two in there for a small prize would be a good idea. I used to ask for entries to be sent to my home address – different times! One time I had a prize of a signed picture of Pelé from when he came to Hillsborough in the 1970s. There were over 7,000 entries – all sent to my house!

I loved working at the club. I didn't do it for any money. I did it because I enjoyed it and there were some great people on and off the pitch. I moved on as the club felt that I couldn't help out with things like wedding receptions or parties as I had my own clubs I was working at. Steve Claxton replaced me, who was a great guy – but he told me that he never got asked to do those things anyway! I suppose the conspiracy theory is that someone behind the scenes at Wednesday felt I was pushing my clubs at the expense of another one in Sheffield. I wasn't, but I have no hard feelings about it. As I say, they were great times.

Thanks Stevie

No worries, give me a call any time!

* * *

In conversation with these former employees, and others who surrounded the club, it seems clear to me that there was a positive atmosphere around Hillsborough at the time and that many people did thoroughly enjoy their jobs. Howard Wilkinson put it to me in 2021 that maybe this was because he and the club 'created a pathway for everybody, that there was a vision, objective and journey and that everyone needed to understand and believe that they were part of that – from the groundsman to the ladies who did the laundry'.

That certainly seems a reasonable conclusion to draw. Lily Shelton's memories of a friendly atmosphere and great characters are also clearly supported by those I have spoken to. Every person I interviewed who was employed by the club used some variation of 'great times' to describe those years. I can't put it better myself!

19.

An Interview with Ian Knight

IAN KNIGHT made his debut for the Owls towards the end of our period, playing the final four games of the 1985/86 season. Born in Hartlepool, he moved to the Owls from Barnsley before making a first-team appearance for the Oakwell club. He made a real success of his move to Hillsborough, seamlessly moving through the youth team, into the reserves and then into the first team during the 1985/86 campaign. Knight's success saw him called up for the England Under-21 team and he gained two caps in the autumn of 1986.

Knight kept his place in the Owls team in the early part of that campaign but suffered a horrendous leg injury in an FA Cup tie against Chester in 1987. The injury saw Knight's leg broken in seven places – it was 20 months before he played again for the reserves and nearly two years before he returned to the first team. In total Ian played 27 games for the club. He now lives in Canada, and it was from there that we spoke in the spring of 2021. We chatted a little about the book and football generally before turning to Ian's career.

Tell me about how you arrived at Hillsborough.

After school I'd signed a two-year apprenticeship with Barnsley. I was 18 in the October, and they agreed to keep me at the club until the end of the season and give me a decision then. There'd been a few changes at the club. Norman Hunter, who was manager, had left at Christmas. Bobby Collins, who'd taken over as manager, told me that I hadn't made enough progress and he was releasing me. Luckily for me, during a couple of close derby battles with Sheffield Wednesday in the Northern Intermediate youth league, Mick Hennigan had noticed me.

Mick reached out once my name was circulated on the PFA list of free players and he invited me to Hillsborough for a month to be evaluated, I guess. The big conversation was about my position. Mick thought that given my height I'd be suited at centre-back, rather than centre-midfield where I'd been playing at Barnsley. I'd filled in occasionally at the back before, but I hadn't been coached there. Funnily enough, Norman Hunter did once say that I'd make a good centre-half, but nothing really came of it there.

So you went straight into the youth team at Hillsborough in defence. How long was it before that one-month trial became more permanent?

It was rapid, a very exciting time for me personally. Within the month the club offered me a one-year professional contract. I played a few games for the youth team as I still qualified age-wise. Mick Hennigan soon approached me and offered me the captaincy as well. I played regularly that autumn, and as it got to Christmas the club offered me an extension to the contract. It was just a whirlwind!

I soon moved up into the reserves as well. I loved it; it was a great group, great camaraderie. The Central League, where the reserves played, was fantastic, great for kids' development. It was a man's league. I remember playing at Old Trafford once, up against Mark Hughes, and managing to score a goal past Chris Turner. It was great way of developing young players.

Did the reserves and youth team play in the 'Wednesday way' at the time, with three centre-backs for example?

Probably not so much in the youth team, but I remember the reserves playing in a similar way. It was direct like the first team also. It was pretty seamless moving between the teams as there were always kids being called up to get involved in practice games and training activities with the first team.

In terms of training with the first team, it never really happened until I'd made my debut! The first team were very thorough at practising things like set pieces. It was difficult to copy that precisely in the reserves as we weren't a team as such – we were a mixture of players who were coming back from injury, or out of the team or coming up from the youth squad. So some of the senior players would tend to lead on that and we'd copy what the first team were doing the best we could.

How about in terms of fitness?

The whole club basically did the same fitness training. Many trips out to Ewden dam and around the reservoirs. It was very demanding and very regimented. It was hard but fair. Howard Wilkinson had a level of expectation and, if you did the work for him, he'd look after you. It gave us a confidence. There was a period when I was playing for the reserves and the youth team where it seemed like we were playing every night! I remember once on the coach to the Baseball Ground, I was flat out asleep on the way to the game as I was shattered. A quick chocolate bar and I was playing, though! Without the level of base fitness that the club demanded, we wouldn't have been able to do it.

What are your memories of your first-team debut?

Well, the day before, on the Friday, there was a ritual of sticking up the team list on the dressing room wall after training. I'd never been on there before, but there was my name at the bottom of the list. There was a fitness test happening on the Saturday morning for Glynn Snodin, though, so it wasn't guaranteed that I was in.

I was at the stadium on Saturday morning, and I heard a couple of rumours that he'd failed his test. I went up to the hotel with the rest of the players and Howard popped his head round the door of the players room: 'Knighty, I want a word.' He sat me in another room and told me I was going to start. Everything became a blur! This was about 1.30pm in the hotel. We came back to the ground and about 2pm came out to warm up. I was brought back down to earth when a ball went off the side of the pitch and I went over to collect it and this kid shouted at me, 'Who are you?!'

Do you remember much of the game itself?

Well, I remember the first interaction with the ball I had. I got caught in two minds from a long ball out. Should I go for it, should I drop off? Well, of course, the ball bounced over my head! More positively, I was up against Simon Stainrod, who'd been at Hillsborough before moving to Villa. So that gave me a bit of confidence. I soon played a through ball for Garry Thompson into a channel and I was away. After the game, I got showered and changed and quickly got a taxi to the train station because my mum was getting married that day and I quickly travelled up to Hartlepool to help celebrate that. I'll never forget the date!

Who helped you in your transition to the first team?

Playing alongside Paul Hart, Lawrie Madden, Peter Shirtliff for a while and Mark Smith – they were all top, top guys. Mel Sterland on the right of me as well; you couldn't fail to enjoy being among those guys! They were terrific. I remember one game early the following season against Chelsea, who had Kerry Dixon and David Speedie as the partnership up front. Harty said to me before the game, 'Leave him to me,' meaning Speedie. As the game kicked off and the first ball came forward, Harty went straight through the back of him, wallop! It would be a straight red card these days. 'Welcome to the big league,' I thought at that point!

You stayed in the team for the remainder of the season?

Yes, I remember travelling to West Brom midweek and the last home game against Ipswich. We travelled to The Dell to play Southampton as well. That was an experience, I don't think they were happy, the Southampton supporters. It was the last game of the season for them at home, so they'd got people trying to get on to the pitch. There was a kind of police escort to get us off the pitch as we were spat at and fans were hurling abuse. It was not a good experience. We got back to the dressing room, though, and it was successful trip for us!

The team went undefeated for the last seven games of the season, following defeat in the FA Cup semi-final. What do you think drove the team on in those weeks?

I can't speak of the immediate aftermath as I wasn't in the team. It speaks about the character of the players we had, though. Nobody sulked after the FA Cup defeat. Obviously they were frustrated and disappointed, but they didn't let it overwhelm them and then we aimed to push on and try and do the best we could on the league front. I think it worked out quite well that season!

You were called up for the England Under-21 squad early in 1986/87 – how did that come about?

That blew me away to be honest! I remember playing at Tottenham and getting back on the coach after the game. Howard Wilkinson then asked me in passing what my date of birth was. I thought it was a bit of a strange question, but a week later I'm there in his office and he's telling me I've got a call-up. Mindblowing really. Dave Sexton was the coach, but without doubt it was Howard's recommendation that got me the call. The first game was away in Sweden and to be in the same team as Tony Adams and Des Walker was just unbelievable. I still get goosebumps now thinking about it. From being out of work, essentially, having been let go by Barnsley 12 months previously, to that was amazing.

You suffered a career-limiting injury later that season. Is that something you are at peace with?

My story disappeared as quick as it arrived! There's always that bit of a rankle – what could have been. You can't dwell on it, you know. One of the reasons I got into coaching, one of the motivations was to help kids have some of the opportunities that I had. That's my drive now every day, that's what keeps me going.

Moving on to the management then, how did the main people work together?

Howard Wilkinson was a very good motivator. He was a master at getting inside people's heads! He knew the character of each of his players. He knew which buttons to press, and he got the best out of us. Howard brought it all together, he got the individual characters to work together as a unit. It wasn't always love and peace and harmony, but he got us playing!

The staff that he had around him were terrific, magnificent people. Peter Eustace and Alan Smith were great. Even Mick Hennigan from the youth set-up would mix it with the first-team group and give out his banter as well. It helped make a fantastic, close-knit group. A good family environment, you might say. Everyone felt comfortable with each other; an awesome environment.

How about the tactics? Is it fair to describe them as 'kick and rush'?

That was people's interpretation. I would say that it was a direct style of play with purpose. We made use of the strengths of the team and the players that we had. Howard was the man leading that – it was his philosophy and tactics – and as players we carried it out as best we could.

Tell me more about Alan Smith.

Well, after my injury I almost became his adopted son! He'd come and pick me up from my house and drive me into Hillsborough. I was in a full-length cast for six months. My mum had also come down to stay for a period, as I was living on my own and pretty useless, couldn't do anything. Alan would call in every day, take me down to the club, do my daily workout and whatever I needed to do. I can't speak highly enough of him personally and professionally. Without him guiding me, cajoling me and putting his time in, I wouldn't have got back to even playing. He was very professional, very articulate and set the standards. I've still got a shirt that Alan Smith sorted out for me. After my injury I was due to go with England Under-21s to Spain, Alan brought me a shirt back signed by Glenn Hoddle and all the England team. [The shirt took pride of place on Ian's wall as we spoke via Zoom.]

After a short return to the Owls team you moved over to Grimsby?

Yes, I was very grateful to get back to any semblance of playing, even if not back to my previous standard. I enjoyed the environment there, but in all honesty it became two years of frustration, with one injury after another, all related back to the original one. So my playing days came to an end, and I admit I was stuck: what am I going to do?

I was lucky that Grimsby then asked me to do some coaching in summer camps they were running. I began my coaching qualifications and Grimsby kept giving me experience in schools and camps. Eventually a job came up and I was lucky to be able to run the community programme for a couple of years. I then moved back to Hillsborough for a season and did a similar role. In the meantime John Cockerill, who had helped me at Grimsby, had moved up to assistant manager there and approached me to take over as youth-team boss. I was fortunate to get it and moved back to Grimsby! I stayed at Grimsby until 2002, when I was let go after the ITV Digital fiasco meant that clubs lost lots of money and had to make cutbacks.

In my time with Grimsby I'd made links with some teams in Canada. It was through that relationship that I got an offer in early 2003 to move out to Ontario. That didn't work out, but I was lucky enough that another role came up in British Columbia. I moved there in 2005, as a technical director of a club in Chilliwack. In 2010 I moved to a club in the next town along, Abbotsford, and I've been there ever since! Football, or soccer as it is over here, is the number-one sport for participation. The organisation and structure over here for grassroots football is excellent.

Thanks for your time Ian.

Thanks John, appreciate it!

20.

Management and Tactics

'Howard Wilkinson knew how to win football matches' – Michael Hennigan, 2021

'The real villains were Sheffield Wednesday who bear the same relation to the beautiful game as Rambo to the Sisters of Mercy. As you watch the average Wednesday player – over-developed torso, under-developed between the ears – interminably pumping the ball into the air like a mortar launcher, you feel overwhelmed by a prehistoric nightmare that can only get worse' – The Guardian, *September 1985*

THE OWLS' success in our period was driven by the management of Howard Wilkinson. That much was made clear to me in the process of researching this book. Press coverage of the team at the time was often much less favourable, with disparaging comments about the style of play featuring regularly. In this chapter I speak to Wilkinson and explore how he went about trying to win games and discuss those infamous tactics.

Wilkinson took over the reins at the Owls prior to the 1983/84 season. Born in Netherthorpe, Sheffield, Wilkinson began his playing career at Hillsborough. He appeared 22 times and scored three goals as a useful winger between 1962 and 1966. Frustrated at a lack of first-team opportunities, Wilkinson decided to drop to Division Three and ply his trade at Brighton & Hove Albion.

After five years and well over a hundred appearances, Wilkinson decided to move again – this time to Boston United, who played in the Northern Premier League. In 1972, Wilkinson's managerial career began when he was appointed player-manager at Boston, succeeding Jim Smith, who moved into league football with Colchester United.

In the meantime, Wilkinson had also graduated and qualified as a PE teacher. After a successful two years with the Pilgrims, winning the league title in both campaigns, Wilkinson was again on the move – joining Mossley as player-coach and leading them away from the lower reaches of the NPL with a 19-match unbeaten run. Wilkinson took a break from management at this stage, being appointed as the FA's regional director of coaching for the North East.

Wilkinson was well suited for this position. His degree had covered sports science, sports medicine, psychology and sociology. He followed his teacher training with two years teaching PE at his former school Abbeydale in Sheffield. Combined with his managerial and playing experience, the role at the FA provided the opportunity for Wilkinson to work with some of the most forward-thinking people in the game and spread his ideas and methods among the coaches of South Yorkshire.

He learned from the FA's top coaches and spent time at their Lilleshall training centre. He was given further opportunity to spread his ideas and methods when the FA asked Wilkinson to manage their semi-professional team in 1979. It was a position he held on a part-time basis until 1982. Under his tutelage, the FA team won the Four Nations title in 1979.

In December 1979, Wilkinson was appointed as a coach at Notts County under the management of Jimmy Sirrell. He soon moved up to the assistant manager's position at Meadow Lane and, at a similar time, took over as England Under-21 boss. In Wilkinson's first full season at the club they were promoted to Division One. In 1982, Sirrell proverbially moved upstairs at Meadow Lane and Wilkinson was appointed as head coach. He led the team to a respectable 15th-place finish in the top flight in his only season in overall control. In the summer of 1983 the Owls came calling. Wilkinson accepted the job at Hillsborough and, as we know, secured promotion to the top flight at the first time of asking.

Wilkinson immediately went about assembling his backroom team when he arrived at Hillsborough. First up was the recruitment of Peter Eustace as assistant manager. Eustace, like Wilkinson, was a former Owls player, who made nearly 250 appearances for the club in two spells and appeared in the 1966 FA Cup Final. In 1983 he was chief scout at Sunderland but was delighted to be asked to move to Hillsborough. Quoted at the time, he said, 'Only those people who knew me when I was here can have any conception of how I feel about walking through these doors again.'

Completing Wilkinson's original team was physio Alan Smith. The two men had worked together with the England semi-professional team. Smith is quoted in Daniel Gordon's *A Quarter of Wednesday* as saying, 'My initial attraction had been to work with Howard but then … you form a love for the club which is a very strong feeling and one I will always have.' Smith went on to say, 'Our success was based on organisation, fitness, superb tactics and the overall strength of feeling for the club.'

Those tactics provoked great discussion during the 1980s. It does not require much of a search of the newspaper archives to find references such as my favourite from the *Hammersmith Gazette* in 1985, describing the Owls' style of play as 'bruising, Northern, long-ball kick and rush'.

Imre Varadi felt moved to defend the Owls' tactics from those 'kick and rush' accusations in the *Liverpool Echo* in 1984 – soon after the team's victory at Anfield in September that year. 'The criticisms we have faced have been unfair,' said Varadi. 'We give our supporters value for money, we prefer to play our football in the last third of the field and therefore we try and get the ball into that area as quickly as possible.'

Supporter Paul Walshaw, in a 1985 letter to the *Green 'Un*, agreed that fans got value for money from the 'all action, non-stop running and attacking strategy which is the hallmark of

Wednesday's style'. Chris Malle, writing in the same paper in October 1985, felt that it was a 'grave injustice' to describe the Owls' style as 'kick and rush' and that the team 'play fast and skilful attacking football that is also, dare I say it, entertaining'.

The *Sheffield Star*'s Owls correspondent Paul Thompson was in no doubt that, by the end of 1984/85, any accusation of Wednesday being a 'hard-running, long-ball side with no finesse were a gross over-simplification'. Thompson went on to explain how the Owls' tactics and style of play had changed dramatically over the season, with recent weeks seeing 'thoughtful, accurate approach work, much of it on the ground, with passes played to feet'. These comments reminded me of a conversation I had with Joe Dunn, who remembered how opponents would be surprised when facing the Owls for a second time that season and coming up against a very different approach.

Wednesday's style did not please everyone, of course. The ever-controversial W.M. Lee won the £5 letter prize in the *Green 'Un* early in the 1984/85 season for a missive that suggested Wilkinson had made mistakes with a team that had 'hard-working character but was lacking in skill and confidence'. More recently, a lifelong Owl supporter told me how he and several others had boycotted games in the mid-1980s due to their frustration with the tactics and perceived lack of entertainment. Thompson's comments at the end of the 1985/86 campaign suggested that Owls supporters 'salute a fine season' with a team that were 'getting better all the time'.

* * *

I wanted to explore some of these areas with Wilkinson himself. Initially, finding him proved tricky as my enquiries via ex-players, other authors and journalists drew a resounding blank. Neither did initial enquiries via the League Managers' Association. A spot of digital stalking eventually did the job though, with a hunt for Howard's email address bearing fruit. An hour or two after I sent my initial email asking to chat, Howard replied positively. A bit of to and froing later in terms of setting up a time and place occurred before we spoke via Zoom in the late summer of 2021.

Prior to meeting with Howard, I'd asked the advice of several of those who knew him or had worked with him. Their descriptions of his meticulous nature and focused approach made me a little nervous that my discussions with him might prove difficult. They were nothing of the sort, as Howard proved a generous interviewee both with his time and his responses.

Michael Hennigan had already told me that 'Howard Wilkinson knew how to win football matches'. I began, therefore, by asking Howard how important winning games was to him. 'I'd recognised the game within the game,' he told me, 'and that related to the increasing frailty of a manager's position.' I nodded as Howard expanded on the more recent stats produced for the League Managers' Association showing how first-time managers in modern football rarely make 75 games with their first club and are usually out of the game within five years. 'So, you've got to win football matches.'

He went on to lay out the philosophy he'd adopted to do just that back from his days at Boston. 'What you find as a manager is a group of players; they are there because they are talented. The manager's job is to take those talents, bring them together so that those individuals combine together to make it as a team.'

Football teams can play in many different ways, of course, and I wondered if Howard's methods catered for that. 'You've got to try to come up with a suit that almost fits everyone as if made to measure,' was his metaphor. Meaning that he was prepared to adopt a 'horses for courses' approach. 'I used to ask the players at my clubs a question on the day before a game,' he went on. 'Do you want to come off the pitch having played well and enjoyed it, or do you want to come off the pitch having won the game?'

I bet the answer was 'both', I replied. 'Yes, but which do you want most?' was Howard's reply. 'And brutal as it sounds, as time went on, most of the players would reply that they wanted to win.'

With that priority established among his players, Howard went on to discuss how he would decide on tactics. 'We worked backwards to find a way that you, and him, and him and the rest of the team could combine every week and produce a way of playing that was the best for us to win.'

I wondered how far those methods varied between his clubs and teams. 'At Notts County, I had to wait six months before I could start because I had to complete my contract with the FA,' he explained, 'so I was able to watch the players and plan and prepare what I was going to do with the team when I started.'

I knew that team were known for a passing game. 'Yes, it was pass, pass, pass, pass, pass. I got them in seven weeks early for pre-season and we worked on ways in which that team could get the ball from the defensive third to the attacking third. We played with full-backs who acted as wingers, with a sweeper, with one forward. We passed our way out of the Second Division!' I knew that Howard had changed systems the following season. 'By Christmas we were bottom of the league and going to pass our way back into Division Two! Fortunately for us it snowed, and I told the team that I had a proposition for them – to change from pass, pass, pass to the opposite in order to have a chance of staying up.'

Notts County did stay up that season, and the following year when they mixed the two approaches. I asked Howard what this said about his philosophy of football. 'My philosophy is nowt to do with how we played,' he explained. 'It's about who you are and how you get others to buy into your ability to take them through the jungle and out the other side.'

In a way, therefore, Howard had already explained why his tactics were much different at Hillsborough to the passing approach at Notts County, but I pressed for a little more detail. 'It was a drop back from Division One to Division Two and I didn't make my mind up about the job until late June. When I got there, not having a lot of chance to see them, the squad was unbalanced. There was an abundance of centre-halves, all of whom were good enough to be in the team. So I looked at them all, and I think we were the first in the country to play three at the back. Two in midfield. Two full-backs who were wingers. Three strikers as I hadn't really got any wide players.' Horses for courses again. 'We walked out of that league! We were promoted too early, or we'd have won the league. Chelsea sneaked up on the outside.'

Lawrie Madden had told me previously about his work on statistics relating to the Owls' promotion season. I knew that this was an area that Howard was interested in. I asked how it had come about. 'I was quite interested in the stats side of things even as a player. When I went to Brighton, I had a bit of time on my hands after training and I discovered the library.' Libraries even then, of course, having a sports section. 'I discovered books by and about athletics coaches in Australia, American football and basketball coaches in the States and all intelligent enough to write bloody books un' all!'

This wasn't directly related to football, I wondered. 'No, but then I heard that Wolverhampton Wanderers were using stats and Graham Taylor made great use of Charles Reep's work. It gets laughed at a little now, but I remember the POMO idea – position of maximum opportunity – and it's not wrong!'

I recalled Joe Dunn and Michael Hennigan talking about that with me. 'It helped me sign Chappy [Lee Chapman],' Howard recalled with a smile. 'He came to see me and sat in my office, and I said to him, "If I can guarantee you four chances a game in the area in front of goal how would you feel?"'

I bet he'd be delighted! 'Yes, but then I asked him whether he knew how he scored his goals, and with how many touches, and he wasn't quite sure. I pushed it and asked how many goals he scored with eight touches – not many – and said that we could guarantee four chances in the zone in front of the goal with time for one or two touches. I knew that at that time 85 per cent of all goals were scored that way.'

This brought the conversation back to tactics. 'It wouldn't matter to Lee how we got the ball there, we could do it like Pep Guardiola's team, like Stan Cullis's team, or do we finish by getting it in there by playing like our team? What can we do with this group of players to give us the best opportunity of creating those chances which I knew are where goals came from?'

This meticulous attention to detail fascinated and impressed me. I saw how Howard linked his knowledge of players, statistics and tactics to help develop a winning team.

Howard knew that I'd previously talked to Lawrie Madden so told me a little about how Lawrie fitted into his plans at Hillsborough. 'He wasn't one of those who delighted in the training, and the need for phrases like load and intensity and oxygen debt, but put him on a football field and he came to life. I remember being at Watford once and their bench shouted at Luther Blissett, I think, to "run him – he's as slow as arseholes!" I looked over and just shook my head!'

I wondered whether the fitness regime that Howard introduced was more demanding than that of other clubs. 'I think it was, but then I'd been interested in coaching from very early on. I'd listened to Jack Marshall and Alan Brown when I was a player at Wednesday, who were looking at logical ways of improving what we did. I'd read into Vince Lombardi in American football. I'd been at Lilleshall and learned about physiology and sports science. So I'm thinking "bloody hell!" Oxygen debt – nobody had ever talked to me about that, or how football is an endurance activity but one that puts more focus on more physical activity than any other game. So the basis of it all was keeping your body ready for all that and your brain clear.'

At this point, I understood much more clearly what the purpose of the infamous training regime was. 'It was about improving our ability to avoid oxygen debt and more than that, when we are dealing with it, to recover quicker than other people. We were looking for any competitive advantage we could get.'

Did it work, I wondered? 'I remember playing Charlton early on, and Lennie Lawrence, their manager, saying to me afterwards that they just couldn't cope with us.' Did the fitness factor into the style of play, I asked. 'If I could wake up one morning with a football team playing just the way I liked it, they'd play like [Pep Guardiola's] Manchester City, and I'd have their players! It's not disrespectful of anyone I had as I knew I also needed to improve. There were coaches winning European championships in my time for example.' Fitness, it became clear to me then, was a means to an end. The end being winning football matches.

I asked every player I interviewed for the book about the fitness regime. There are further interesting memories among the autobiographies of others. Brian Marwood discussed the training in his book, *The Life of Brian*. 'Oh, that training! Never, never have I experienced anything like it. Amazingly it didn't stop with pre-season. We trained even harder in the winter.'

Mel Sterland's autobiography discussed how, 'when Howard came to Wednesday, he worked us a lot harder than Jack [Charlton] had done, running the balls off us!' Lee Chapman, in his book *More than a Match,* outlines how the runs 'became a test of endurance' whose 'severity eventually became a barrier to the club's attempts to sign new players'.

Mark Chamberlain described his time at Hillsborough in less than glowing terms in the 2012 book *Match of My Life – Stoke City*. In his interview, Chamberlain describes how he 'actually knew that Wednesday weren't the club for me because of Howard's reputation'. Chamberlain goes on to say that 'Howard's football was horrible and it's almost dead now thankfully'. Some corroboration to Chapman's theory, therefore. I have no further support for this, and several players who told me directly how excellent they felt both the tactics and Wilkinson's management were. Not every player, though, loved the running. Chapman's story of some players hitching a ride on tractors to avoid completing the full distance is corroborated by Sterland – so maybe there is more truth in that tale!

How about recovery between games and those coming back from injury – what was Alan Smith's role? 'Smudger was great. I tried to take him to Leeds with me later on as well. A player's physical talents he's born with, but they can be improved and, a bit like a motor car, they need an engine. Alan helped keep those engines running and fixed them when they broke down!'

I attempted to build on that metaphor by asking whether diet and sports drinks were used to oil the engines of the players. 'I'd spent time listening to people in the athletics world, right back from my time at Boston, who were beginning to really tune into the idea of diet. At one point there was the unpopular notion that the best time for players to take on nutrition was in the hour after the game. So we'd have them on the coach back from London or wherever chewing on a Mars bar! So yes, diet was important, back to the analogy of the engine – by all means have the best mechanic, but make sure you use the best fuel.'

I had heard of Howard's use of sports drinks, so asked about their use. 'At Leeds I extended it so far that we did urine tests on the players and provided individual drinks based on the nutrients they needed – it hadn't got that far at Hillsborough, but we were among the first to use Gatorade drinks to help with rehydration.' I could hear Michael Hennigan's voice at this moment. 'Howard left no stone unturned,' he told me. I was gaining a more detailed understanding of what he meant.

Scouting and preparation was the next topic. I wondered how Howard had the opposition scouted in advance of games. 'I had a guy called George Wilkinson, who was a PE lecturer up in the North East. He would watch our upcoming opposition and also watch films of our games. He'd use that to provide me a breakdown of areas we could focus on.'

We returned to an earlier topic around statistics. 'You'll need to check this, but I believe that top-level managers – over 250 games at the top level – will not win more than about 45 per cent of the games the stats say they should have won.' I wondered why that might be, just luck? 'It relates to the open and closed skills continuum.' I had to admit an ignorance of what that is. 'Closed skill is, say, world championship snooker – same cue, same balls, same conditions, the opponent can't interfere, and the influence of the referee is minimal. Football is at the other end – you play in 360 degrees, you can run, tackle, the weather, grass, pitch size and much else can be different. All sorts of factors influence the result.'

My knowledge duly expanded, I wondered how Howard had used this knowledge to help his teams. 'Do you tell the players everything? No. It's all part of an information package that you help the players assimilate so that on the pitch they are hopefully able to make better decisions. A manager from Pep downwards needs to accept that stat I gave you. If you're unlucky it'll happen to you in a Champions League Final or in a Euro 2020 final that goes to a penalty shoot-out!'

Brian Marwood discussed how Howard shared information – 'Every detail was accounted for, how many times you touched the ball, passes made, tackles won. You couldn't argue with him because it was all on video and on his graphs. He must have spent hours on Sunday working it out.' I began to understand from all this how Howard knew both the limitations and usefulness of statistical analysis. The knowledge of both his own team and that of the opposition was used to better prepare his players with the understanding that much, much else may affect the final result.

We moved on to discuss Howard's attempts at the time to encourage good behaviour among the fanbase and to discourage his team from picking up bookings and sendings off. I wondered if the two things were related – as an attempt to show the club and city in its best light. 'At that time, and to some extent, I'd like to think now, that as the manager you are in a position where you can influence about things other than what was directly happening on the pitch. I remember talking to the press alongside Ron Atkinson for Manchester United and saying that although we were rivals on the pitch we expected the best of behaviour from the fans.'

Was the behaviour of the players as important to you? 'That was just common sense really. I can't pick you if you've been suspended as you've been booked too often or sent off and that affects all the other stuff about tactics and fitness and whatever else. Most importantly, it would affect our ability to win football matches.'

Understanding Howard's overarching philosophy of the importance of winning matches, and his meticulous and detailed approach to doing so, I wondered how confident he was going into Division One with a broadly similar team to the one that earned promotion from the second tier. 'My bar was not as high as what we did finish, but even back then I'd worked out how many points we needed to survive, which was always the first target. We discussed where we'd like to finish, but the first line in the sand was having enough to stay up. Cold, hard facts really. From there I broke it down into six-game chunks. It was an adjustment from what I'd done in Division Two. It was based on history and how many points were needed in each circumstance.'

Wilkinson's winning team in our era was one on the up. By the later 1980s, it had maybe peaked. 'I'd still be at Sheffield Wednesday now if after my fifth season I hadn't sat down with the directors and told them that we were in a position where if we were to continue to improve we needed to invest in the team.'

Howard reminded me how then chairman Bert McGee had taken control of the club in the dark days of the mid-1970s. 'We had a long, long discussion. There were two directors of the eight or so who were in favour of my view, but the spectre of where the club had been loomed over the rest.'

What was the focus of the discussion, I wondered? 'We had players who had given it their best shot, but I felt that if we were to progress we needed to spend big, as it were – which in those days meant fees of three, four or five hundred thousand plus the wages.'

Howard continued describing the discussions. 'Although we'd improved the youth development set-up there wasn't yet the conveyor belt of players through to the first team.' I wondered if the development of the stadium and the money spent on the Kop roof may have influenced the board's reticence to also spend on the team. 'Yes, it came into the equation. I can see that for them it was important. They were all successful businessmen and could see the need for it to be right on the shop floor, but I can see that they also needed to move the club with the times – the Kop was open and the fans there had the right to be covered.

'I'm not looking back and saying it was wrong or a disaster. In business you sit around a table and make decisions and you might not always agree with them. Those decisions were made genuinely by people who thought they were in the best interests of everybody.'

I admired Howard's thoughtful and magnanimous responses to my questions around this area – it was clearly a frustration to him that he left in those circumstances, and I sensed a feeling of 'what might have been' in my conversations with him. His subsequent achievements elsewhere amplify that feeling among many Owls supporters.

In my research for this book, I often crowd-sourced a few questions for my interviewees using social media. A common question for Howard revolved around why he left S6 for Leeds United. I explored that with him further. 'I remember in my last season, a home game where we'd either drawn or lost, and I was walking through the changing room a long time after the game to go for a drink with the other coaches. Nigel Worthington was still there, and I don't know if he remembers this, but looked up at me and said, "Gaffer, I think you need to leave." I can't remember his exact words after that, but it was something like "you can only squeeze so much juice from an orange".'

I wondered if Howard had decided to leave at that stage. 'Well, what happened quite soon after that was that I was contacted in a roundabout way by Leeds United. I went from, "Are you interested in Leeds? Shut up, you've got to be joking, they're second bottom of Division Two!" to having over four or five long meetings with their chairman, who was so persistent and who agreed to bankroll my plans for the club from a blank sheet of paper upwards. He agreed to all that, with the plan that in ten years they'd be one of the best clubs in Europe. Can you imagine that?!'

Howard took the opportunity to move to West Yorkshire, soon returning Leeds United to the top flight before winning the final Division One championship before playing in Europe. His players at Leeds included many of those who had worked with him at Hillsborough, including Lee Chapman, Mel Sterland, Imre Varadi and Carl Shutt. The latter famously scored at the Camp Nou to complete his ascent from non-league football. As Michael Hennigan correctly told me, 'That lad would score anywhere!'

In conclusion, it is clear that Howard Wilkinson was successful in squeezing the juice from that proverbial orange in our two seasons. His teams were athletic, fit, well-organised and hard-working. To describe them as a 'kick and rush' team seems to me to be an over-simplified view. More than one former player described the tactics as 'direct with a purpose'. Ball-playing midfielders such as Andy Blair and Gary Shelton discuss elsewhere in the book how much they enjoyed playing in Wilkinson's team – not the sign of a team where the midfield watched the ball fly over them on its way to the strike force!

Wilkinson was adept at changing formations and tactics across his clubs and to suit the players available to him. He adapted his tactics at Sheffield Wednesday. By 1985/86, Owls fans were watching skilful but slight players such as Glynn Snodin and Mark Chamberlain. A step away from the 'bruisers' that some in the press suggested were the bedrock of the team. Many fans thoroughly enjoyed watching a successful team and the tactics they employed. Of course, some did not, and it is not possible to please all the people all of the time. Howard Wilkinson's focus on winning bore fruit whether the tactics impressed all or not.

Fitness was an integral part of the regime. My conversations with Howard showed me how it was not fitness for its own sake. The routines could be brutal and, although many players enjoyed the lengthy runs and focus on fitness, there were others who did not. Tales of players working so hard that they vomited, getting lost on training runs or sneaking away to take a bus back or go to the pub are amusing to recount, but also show how difficult some found the regime.

Again, though, results count. Wilkinson's team were known for their fitness and would often score late goals as the opposition tired. The team were drilled and organised. Lengthy training sessions driven by Wilkinson's desire to drill his team along with his data-driven understanding of their strengths and weaknesses ensured that the team were well prepared for each game. The strength of the defence at set pieces and in playing the offside trap countered with the number of goals scored as a result of free kicks and corners is clear evidence of this.

Wilkinson worked effectively as part of a management team. There were clear roles for Wilkinson, Peter Eustace, Alan Smith and Michael Hennigan. All helped ensure the success of the first team. Finally, Wilkinson was an excellent man-manager. Not every player always saw eye to eye with him, of course. Wilkinson was able to bring players down the proverbial peg or two when needed but also bolster confidence of individuals and the team.

Howard Wilkinson certainly did know how to win football matches and consistently did just that.

21.

An Interview with Garry Thompson

GARRY THOMPSON is a Birmingham-born striker who began his career in the West Midlands with Coventry City. After a six-year spell with the Sky Blues, Thompson moved to West Bromwich Albion. It was from the Baggies that Howard Wilkinson smashed the Owls' transfer record spending £450,000 to bring in Thompson during the summer of 1985/86. Thompson stayed at Hillsborough for one season, playing 42(+2) games and scoring eight goals.

At the end of the 1985/86 season the Owls were approached by Thompson's boyhood club Aston Villa and accepted a £450,000 offer for his services. The Owls made a small profit on the deal. Thompson's playing career continued until 1999 and he scored an impressive 154 goals in total for his nine clubs. Still living in his native West Midlands, we spoke in the summer of 2021.

Tell me about how you came to sign for Sheffield Wednesday.

I knew a couple of people up there. Andy Blair was there, who I knew from Coventry, and Gary Bannister had been there who I knew well, so I'd made a couple of calls about it. At that stage I'd been top scorer for West Brom for a couple of years and I knew there were other teams in for me – Arsenal and QPR, for example. The plan, to be honest, was for me to go to Villa – as I'm a fan! I sat down with Villa manager Graham Turner and the West Brom chairman and I soon realised that there was no chance of that happening! So it looked like I was staying at Albion. Then, one day the guy who did my finances called me up and said that another club were interested – and they play in a similar kit to the Albion! It took me a while, but I figured out who it was.

I knew Howard Wilkinson from the England Under-21s, and he rang me a couple of times and persuaded me to come up for a chat. So I drove up with my missus and the nipper. We came off the motorway and saw all the factories and chimneys and I was prepared to stop and come right back! My missus persuaded me to carry on and speak to Wednesday. Howard's wife took my wife into Sheffield to do some shopping and then on to look at some houses. I stayed at Hillsborough with my lad. There were discussions with agents and about money and the next thing I realise is that I couldn't see my lad. So I looked around and there he was out on the pitch with Howard Wilkinson practising scoring goals and celebrating in front of the Kop!

I thought then, 'If this fella's prepared to spend time with a three-year-old kid – I'm happy with that.' My missus came back, and she loved Sheffield. She'd been shown some lovely houses and liked the place. Albion needed to sell as they'd already bought my replacements in – so it all fell into place really. Chelsea came in at a similar time but neither me nor the missus liked Ken Bates so that was it – I signed for Wednesday.

How did you find it on arrival at Hillsborough?

It was only a week or two after signing that I was into the team for the first game. That was against Chelsea, funnily enough. I hadn't done anywhere near enough fitness work – just one pre-season game, I think. I might as well have not played! I got 70 minutes or so under my belt, but for the next game on the Tuesday I was on the bench. From there onwards Howard moulded me into the Sheffield way – where you pick up the jockstraps and he runs you into the ground!

I knew what to expect in a way as I'd played against Wednesday the year before and scored both goals in a 2-2 draw. Wednesday were just a force, a whirlwind that day. They were relentless and

I remember thinking that if I played for them I would get plenty of chances to score goals.

How did you find the training?

To be so relentless, the team needed to be fit. I remember when I arrived, though, not being impressed by the regime as it consisted of an awful lot of running. Now, I can run. At Albion I'd train hard on a Monday and Tuesday and then calm down later in the week to be ready for Saturday. At Wednesday it was relentless, so by Thursday I'd be knackered!

Howard was ahead of the game – he broke the training down, so we'd work on elements of the game. Defence, midfield, corners, whatever. I just wanted a game of five-a-side sometimes but looking back he knew what he was doing. Me and Mark Chamberlain both complained to Howard early on about the training, but once we realised we'd get no joy we both knuckled down and stuck with it.

How about the tactics?

We had a good season. My only gripe about Sheffield Wednesday is me. I went there as a centre-forward. I'd played with centre-forwards all my career – Cyrille Regis being a great example. I was the record signing at Hillsborough, and I wanted to be the guy who scored goals. I played with Lee Chapman, though, who I got on great with, but he was nowhere near as mobile as me. So he stayed central, and I got pushed out wide or behind. I worked hard, but I never felt I did myself justice in terms of scoring the goals. I remember Peter Eustace telling me that the fans up there loved a centre-forward and that, after a season, when I knew how it all worked, I'd be able to kick on and really shine.

I hadn't really talked about the tactics when I signed. We talked a lot about the club and where Howard wanted it to go. He talked about playing a bit more football but not about where he wanted me to fit in. That was different from any other club I signed for. I remember signing for Palace for example and knowing that I was there to replace Ian Wright, who'd broken his leg and was out for a couple of months. I never really got that at Hillsborough, but

I do remember thinking that I'd get chances. Shelton and Blair in midfield, Zico up and down the wing, I thought I was going to score goals!

How was your relationship with Howard Wilkinson?

We had a bust up in the October time. It happened in a Sheffield Senior Cup game against Rotherham in front of a small crowd. After about 70 minutes, a cross came over and their keeper caught it. He threw it out to the full-back and I thought, 'F*** this, I'm not chasing back.' Howard went mental on the touchline! I said, very politely, 'Go away Mr Manager!' At full time he ripped into me – 'We're all in this together, or we're not in it at all,' kind of thing.

I actually asked to leave the next day. Howard screwed up the letter and threw it in the bin. We had a heart-to-heart chat later. Howard's chats like that were basically, 'You can do it my way, or you can f*** off!' I agreed to do it his way! I knuckled down in training and there was a spell over Christmas where I began to score goals.

I've talked before about how Howard called me a 'big black dozy'. He was a blunt Yorkshireman but there was nothing racial in it. I know when I'm talking to a racist, believe me! He called me that after a few days when we were running round Ewden Valley. He was trying to gee me up, and as the record signing bring me into the group. Meggo and Shelly took it on and called it me as well just to try and piss me off I think! It was the language of the time, and not acceptable today, but I was called far worse elsewhere.

Howard Wilkinson rang me after the season had ended and told me that the club had received an offer from Aston Villa. And that was the extent of the conversation – I could stay, or I could go. Now, years later, I realise that Howard was basically a blunt f*****, and that was just his way. If Peter Eustace had made the call, he'd probably have talked through how the season had gone and what I could do to improve and make me feel more wanted. As it was, I decided to speak to Villa as a bit of a f*** you to Howard.

Now I'm older, I realise that I acted as a bit of spoilt brat. I should just have knuckled down, stayed the second year and regrouped.

Where would you put Howard Wilkinson in and among other managers you worked with?

That's a difficult question! When I was there I don't think I appreciated how good a manager he was. He was clued in and forward thinking. I probably took it for granted. I remember moaning at Villa about how they weren't doing things as well as at Sheffield Wednesday, so he must have done something right! If I were to put them in order, Gordon Milne would be my number one for introducing me to professional football and teaching me the game. Steve Coppell next for helping me find my love for the game again. Howard third.

How were the fans with you?

The fans treated me like a prince! They gave me so much love. I didn't deserve it. There was no racism from the terraces that I heard, and neither did my wife, who came to all the games with our son – who was mixed race. I used to feel guilty that I didn't deserve the support as I hadn't scored enough goals. I had a great time away from the football. Chappy took me to a bar called Hanrahans and we met Heaven 17 and the Human League. It was up a level from what I'd been used to in the Midlands! There are some people in Sheffield who are very tough – and they'd let you know. I remember being asked by a few hard-looking fellas to 'feel my muscles'! There was nothing aggressive about it though, just the way they were. I found the people extremely friendly.

Who did you most like playing alongside?

I know I moaned about playing off him, but Chappy was brilliant. Shutty was different class for a while: young kid, full of energy and no fear. Brian Marwood and Mark Chamberlain were two top-drawer wingers. Zico, though, was the man. To watch him in full flight, he'd deliver the ball and I'd be thinking, 'That's top class.' A hell of a player! Megson was the manager of the team on the pitch. He ran the show along with Paul Hart. They organised us on the pitch. As players and men they were top class.

Tell me finally about shin pads!

Early in my career I broke my leg playing for Coventry. When I got back from the injury I just found wearing pads really constricting. I just couldn't have anything on my shins. You've got to be able to concentrate playing football and wearing shin pads meant I couldn't. I couldn't physically function with shin pads, so I took them off and played with two pairs of socks to cushion any blows. People used to say I was hard, but it wasn't that. I couldn't function with pads. Graham Taylor tried to make me play with them on when I went to Villa, but it only lasted a couple of months and I was back to wearing socks!

Thanks Garry

No worries, give me a shout any time about it all!

22.

The Fans' Perspective

MANY YEARS ago, the legendary Scottish manager Jock Stein was quoted as saying, 'Without fans who pay at the turnstile, football is nothing.' His words are engraved on the base of his statue outside Celtic Park. To misquote someone else, I agree with Jock. This chapter is, in many ways, the most important in the book. Fans flocked to Hillsborough in our years and also followed the team in huge numbers away from home. This chapter is my attempt to reflect the experiences of some of those supporters.

It cannot represent every individual experience as there as many of those as there were fans. I aim instead to consider a number of different perspectives and give a flavour of how supporters experienced those times.

Supporters' Club

The Sheffield Wednesday Supporters' Club could trace its roots back as far as 1929. In the 1960s and 1970s it boasted several thousand members. It organised coach travel, produced an annual handbook, sold merchandise, voted for a player of the season and held an annual dinner-dance. The club charged an annual subscription and there were auxiliary branches around South Yorkshire and further afield.

The club was managed by a committee, the chairman having his name added to a chain of office. It was always a man as chair, but women did serve on the committee. By the 1980s, it still featured in the club's *Owl* magazine and its committee members would be contacted for opinions on the events of the day by the local press. On promotion in 1984, secretary Rita Nettleship described in *The Owl* how the supporters' club had 24 branches and over 3,000 members. Overseas branches extended as far as Malta, Ireland, South Africa and Australia.

My research for this book found only limited memories from fans about the supporters' club. I wanted to know why, given its large influence in previous decades. Fortunately, I was put in contact with Mick Green. Now into his seventies, Mick was the final chair of the supporters' club and was able to fill me in about its activities in the 1980s.

We met in a Hillsborough coffee shop on a freezing January day in 2022. Mick had brought with him examples of the supporters' club's membership card and merchandise. 'We used to make a fair bit of money from the things we sold – badges, key rings, pennants,' he told me. 'We also helped out selling programmes and took a share from that.'

I knew that travel to away games was a large part of the supporters' club experience. 'Yes, we ran coaches everywhere! We didn't run them for profit, but as a service. We had such a good laugh on them over the years. There was no booze, no hooliganism but we had a great time.'

Mick continued to tell me about one trip to Watford. 'We had two coaches, but one broke down on the way. There was no way of getting it fixed so all the passengers piled on to one coach. They were sat three to a seat, down the aisles. Everywhere!' I laughed at the thought. 'Yes, it was funny,' continued Mick, 'until we got close to Watford and the police waved us down. We stopped and they told us that we had to get off where we were and walk to the ground.'

I wondered if Mick was panicking at this stage. 'Well all the fans got off, and kept coming and coming, and of course the policeman asks how many are on the coach. To this day, I don't know where it came from, but I told him that they were walking round the back and coming through twice as a joke!'

I asked Mick when the coaches stopped. 'We carried on as long as we could,' he told me, 'but it became difficult to get hold of coaches. We used to use Sheffield United Tours – or "Sooties" as we preferred to call them! We also struggled when the club started the Inter City Owl. They'd said it was only going to be trains, but as time went on they added coaches as well. They could guarantee a ticket for the match also, so we were stuck.'

How did this affect the membership, I asked? 'Well, it dropped off, we were down to a few hundred by your time. We still had some great times. We ran an annual dinner-dance. Bert McGee would come every year and donate a bottle of something for the raffle. He was a great guy – he used to call me Richard Stilgoe as he thought I looked like the musician!'

How long did the club continue, I wondered? 'Well, we were still going into the 1990s. I presented a pennant on the pitch at Kaiserslautern in 1993 for example. Mind you, I couldn't understand a word that was said to me as it was all in German! People moved on from the committee over time. Some gave up, others moved away, the local branches stopped. There's still a bank account with a few quid in which I'm going to donate to charity I think, and a few badges and bits of merchandise.'

Mick left me with a supporters' club subscription card, keyring and badge. More importantly, though, I was left with a slightly melancholic feeling. The supporters' club had been a large part of many fans' experiences in previous years. By the 1980s, it was fading to a shadow of its former self. Times move on, and the club took on many of the roles that the supporters' club had fulfilled. Mick holds no hard feelings, but I could not help feeling a little sorry at the decline.

Young Owls

The supporters' club's decline was countered by a growth in the activities that Sheffield Wednesday organised directly. The Young Owls club began in 1981 and was very popular among the younger Owls followers of the time. Managed by Steve Woodhead, the club had its headquarters in a terraced house on Penistone Road (later knocked down during works to build the Kop roof). Membership of the club was priced at an initial £3, with a further £1 payable for an annual renewal. The club would also take the passport-style photographs needed for the membership card at a cost of 30p each. At its peak in the mid-1980s, Steve remembered that the club had a membership of between 1,500–1,700.

The club provided its members with an identification card, autograph book, team poster and silk scarf upon joining, along with opportunities to play football, to act as ball boy/girl and to meet the players at the Christmas party. The party was held for two or three years in the mid-1980s at the Ballroom in Sheffield City Hall.

Anne Stokes-Moorhouse remembers the process of joining the Young Owls with affection. 'My sister sorted tickets for the Liverpool game in March 1986, for my birthday – it was my very first game,' she says. 'Before the match my dad took me to the Young Owls office behind the South Stand and registered me. I had my photo taken and was told to go after the match to pick my photo card up.

'After the game we went back round to the Young Owls office and he said it was the first time in all his career that someone had closed their eyes while having their photo taken, so I would have to have it taken again and my photo card should be ready by the next home game!'

Members could also claim a ten per cent discount in the club shop and free admission to Central League fixtures. The club is fondly remembered by many who took part in its activities. Jon Darling put to me simply that joining the club and 'getting the team photo, autograph book and I think a pennant, just felt so special'.

Derren Francis took me through the process of becoming a ball boy. 'It was some kind of lottery to decide who got it,' he told me. 'We lived in Banbury at the time, and had been on holiday, so when we received the letter we had to rush straight up!' He went on to explain how it worked on the day. 'We had to meet in the sports hall at a certain time to be trained up. I got a new tracksuit to borrow, and brief instructions to get the ball back ASAP to our players and to collect the corner flag at full time.'

I asked Derren which game it was. 'It was the Forest match, the first one back. I was by the corner flag in the north-west corner. I was in prime position to see myself on TV, and for Mel Sterland's penalty! I didn't have too much to do during the game, but I did forget the flag at the end and had to go back for it! A great experience though.'

One supporter didn't have such a good time at the Leppings Lane End, telling me that during one game in the promotion season of 1983/84 'those nice Swansea fans were spitting on me all match and hurling insults. I think we won something like 6-1. Mick Lyons scored a header at the Leppings Lane End, came straight over to me, gave me a high-five and gave the Swans the RODS!'

Another supporter told me the tale of how he was ball boy against Wolves again in the promotion season. 'My main memory was Gary Megson screaming, "Give me the f****** ball," at me, and Gary Bannister smiling and winking at my mate when getting the ball off him. Another kid did a spectacular arse-over-tit trip over the advertising hoardings, too, which got the biggest cheer from a dour game which I think ended 0-0!'

Some ball boys were also invited to assist at reserve games with one such supporter telling me how much he'd enjoyed sharing the empty Kop between him and another lad. Great memories, clearly, for those who were lucky enough to be invited or win the lottery for a place.

Becoming a mascot was not arranged through the Young Owls club. As we see elsewhere, the club's marketing manager Bob Gorrill organised the sale and subsequent arrangements. Derren Francis takes up the tale of what it was like. 'I knew nothing about it! Normally me, my dad and his mate went to the games, but this time Mum came also. We got up early and hung about the players' entrance.'

I wondered what game it was. 'It was the Luton game in the League Cup – where Andy Blair scored the hat-trick of penalties. All of sudden from the players' entrance we were called inside, and I was given a kit in one of the lounges. I realised then what was going on! Imre Varadi was my favourite player at the time, so I went out with him. I actually met him before the game, and he was completely starkers in the bath! We were given specific instructions in the tunnel to follow the team out, so as not to be trampled by Mike Lyons and all!

'I found Imre on the pitch, had a few passes with him. We then had a photo taken with me on Imre's knee and then we were off again. It was bit of a blur really. I kept the kit and had my photo in the programme. A little later, a black-and-white photo arrived in the post. We caught Imre at another game, and he signed it. And that was my five minutes of fame!'

The Young Owls club also organised football sessions for its members in the club's sports hall behind the North Stand. These sessions were for players of all abilities. The club did, though, take the sessions seriously and regularly sent youth coach Clive Baker to help organise the youngsters.

One such youngster, Alistair Dean, remembered someone else supporting the group. 'Mick Lyons would often come to the sports hall when we played in there on Monday nights,' he said. 'I've never been the most gifted player but could usually stop others playing, so used to stay back, but one night I scored and just turned away. Mick Lyons came across screaming at me, "Us defenders don't score many, get yourself round the pitch!", and he ran with me around the sports hall with my arms aloft. Great memories of some great times, and Mick Lyons to this day is one of the very few footballers that really mean something to me. He gave a lot of his time up to Young Owls.'

The Young Owls did organise teams in our era, as Steve Woodhead details elsewhere in the book. These teams were competitive at a good standard. Steve followed up our original conversation by sending me a picture of a very young Liam Palmer representing the Young Owls in the early 2000s as an example.

The club also organised Saturday morning sessions and 'fun weeks' at half-term, and helped support the 'Sportacular' sessions, which organiser Joe Dunn talks through elsewhere. Perhaps the height of excitement for Young Owls, though, was the publication of two photographs in the matchday programme (remember those passport pictures?). The members featured could claim two tickets for the next home game. As a Young Owl myself back in the mid-1980s I never succeeded in seeing my photo – making do instead with my name featuring in the programme and *The Owl* magazine in celebration of my birthday and others who fell in the same month!

Away Days and Travel

Travel to away games with the club's official Inter City Owl scheme was well-organised and efficient. Steve Woodhead, the man in charge, discusses his experiences elsewhere in the book. Travel to games was also organised by the supporters' club. Again, this was generally a sensible affair. Other methods of getting to the games could be a little more laissez-faire, though. Methods of travel varied from coaches organised by local pubs and clubs to minibuses booked by friends and even a converted ambulance. Other supporters ignored the trains chartered by the club and made their own way on British Rail.

One local pub that organised coaches to away games was the now defunct Rose, on Penistone Road. Gavin Henderson was a regular on these trips and talked me through how he particularly enjoyed away days in the promotion season of 1983/84.

'The Rose opened early,' he told me, before detailing how 'they sold beer and bacon sandwiches from six or seven o'clock in the morning!' The trips themselves were often memorable. Comedian and actor Ted Beyer was a regular on the coaches and would keep the fans entertained. Gavin remembered how many of the supporters were what he called the 'Josephine's crowd', after the Sheffield night spot.

These were men in their thirties who would dress in the smart-looking 'casual' way common among certain supporters at the time. Gavin recalled a trip to Southampton in 1984, where the Rose booked a double-decker coach. The casuals took the lower deck and, as the coach approached Southampton, they were spotted by the police. The smart look of the supporters fooled the officers into believing it was the club coach and the group was waved through to the city nice and early!

There was no legal restriction on alcohol on supporters' coaches at the start of our period. Gavin told me how his entrepreneurial cousin made a killing on the Rose coaches by using his cash-and-carry card to buy beer in bulk and then sell it on to fans.

The police were at a loss to do anything about this. An example was when the Rose coach took a wrong turning approaching Newcastle United's St James' Park. Parking up outside a notorious Tyneside boozer at 2.50pm, the Owls fans found chaotic scenes as Newcastle supporters attempted to attack the coach and the people on board. The police boarded the coach to find huge amounts of alcohol and 'blind drunk' Wednesday supporters but had no legal leg to stand on.

Another anonymous tale of a supporter on the Rose coaches not exactly obeying the law was relayed to me via social media. The unnamed fan told me, 'Our coach stopped for a toilet break on the way to Stoke in 1984/85. In a small village, everyone piled off and one lad decided to go to a house nearby. He jumped back on the coach a minute or two later with some salmon he had nicked out of a freezer in the kitchen of the house!'

The law around alcohol on coaches changed in 1986. Coaches became much more strictly regulated after that, which is no doubt for the greater good, but perhaps at the expense of a story or two as relayed here.

However fans travelled to the games, the journeys provoked memories from many. Matt Summerhill remembers 'as a kid being taught card games on the Inter City Owl! Dad used to buy some R Whites shandy, so that I could "booze" with him, my uncle and the other lads. Happy days!'

The less glamorous side to travel was relayed to me by Anthony Bullivant, whose transport was a small van. 'We went to Man City in the 1980s – the year we got promoted to Division One,' he told me. 'On the way back, stuck in traffic near Mottram, a furniture van pulled in front of us. Suddenly their tarpaulin rolls up and some lads hang a body out of the van. He throws up, they drag him back in and the tarpaulin comes back down!'

Gavin Henderson told me how he graduated from travelling by coach to car-sharing with a group of friends. One of them had a Nissan Bluebird, which, as he put it, went 'like shit off a shovel!' So quick was said motor that, after leaving a game down in Southampton at 4.45pm on the final whistle, they arrived back in Sheffield and had their first pints of the evening just after 8pm. 'We must have gone at 110mph all the way,' he told me, 'and no one in the pub believed we'd been to the match!'

The London Owls supporters group thoroughly enjoyed travelling to fixtures during this period. Colin Grant, a lifelong Owls supporter who had followed the club from the dark days of the 1970s, told me that the 'London Owls were in dreamland off the pitch as well, with the British Rail buffet car often replaced by an executive coach – complete with on-board catering, bar and toilet'.

He went on, 'The government ban on alcohol on coaches going to sporting events in 1985/86 put a dampener on the bar activities but not on the rest of this little slice of luxury! It led to some memorable trips, like the day we got mistaken for the team coach … at Old Trafford of all places.'

I laughed at this and asked Colin to explain. 'We used to have a 'Sheffield Wednesday' sign in the front of the coach,' he told me, 'and when we pulled up outside the ground, the stewards waved the posh-looking coach straight through the traffic to the main entrance. However, as the door of the coach opened and this group of largely overweight and ageing chaps began to step down, we were politely asked to get back on board while the driver was instructed to reverse back out to the nearby cricket ground car park!'

Some supporters travelled a distance to attend games. There were regular coaches arranged by supporters as far afield as Worksop, Lincoln, as well as London for example. One fan possibly holds the record for the distance travelled as a regular supporter. Terry Evans contacted me via his Twitter account of @

islandowl to ask if I'd be interested in a few stories from the time. I replied, and soon learned that the 'island' was in fact the Isles of Scilly, which are over four miles off the southernmost point of the British Isles and a mere 413 miles from Hillsborough.

Terry told me how his trips to Sheffield would begin on a Wednesday or Thursday for a Saturday game, when he would fly to Land's End airport. From there it was a five-mile drive to Penzance. A lengthy train journey then took Terry to London. He would stay with his wife's sister in London and then join the London Owls on their coach up to the game before repeating the journey in reverse to return home.

Nowadays, at the age of 65, he still gets just as excited for the games, but will often treat each visit as a mini-holiday, staying in Sheffield or the surrounding countryside. What Terry's story, and many of the others, reminded me of was the dedication to their team shown by many supporters. The players also appreciated it, with Brian Marwood quoted in the club programme when asked about Terry's exploits as saying that they were 'phenomenal … it defines the word fanatical. There are so many others similarly dedicated it makes you realise how lucky you are to be associated with Sheffield Wednesday.'

Memorable Stories

Supporters remember these times for all sorts of reasons. This section includes some of the wackier tales I have heard. The stories that have been regaled in pubs over a pint or two or on the coach to another away day. The kind of stories that gain mythical or legendary status! I have left some stories anonymous to protect the innocent, as they say.

The first tale is from Andy Clayton, talking about John Crooks, who we last met on the pitch at Villa Park after the 1986 FA Cup semi-final. 'We went to a game in London in a transit van with about ten of us,' Andy told me. 'Gary Bannister was playing for QPR, so it would have been 1985 I think. It was the first time we had seen the plastic pitch and John wanted to touch it! So he goes up to a policeman and asked if he could have a feel.

The policeman said, "No you can't effin touch the pitch." All you could hear was John saying, "Bleedin' hell, tha'd think ad asked to touch their lasses' tits, he f***** me off. I only wanted to stroke it!"'

Back to Villa Park, one supporter told me how he and four friends, who were all of school age at the time, travelled to the game together. One of those friends would later become a Premier League footballer. On that day, though, they were cramped on to the Holte End along with thousands of other Owls followers. At half-time, the future footballer 'announced he was going to the bogs, to which everyone around just laughed and said you've no chance. His response? "Don't laugh cus I'm gonna do it here then," and erm, he did!'

Tim Evans remembered getting close to the players. 'I was stood on the Kop with my cousin and before the game went down to the front to get players' autographs,' he says. 'I remember saying to Lee Chapman, "You need to score a couple of goals today." He did just that and when he scored his second he looked towards where we were stood on the Kop and stuck his thumb up!'

Chris Lee remembers his younger brother writing to the club in the 1980s, inviting Imre Varadi to his birthday party. The Owls striker did not attend the celebrations, but the club did send a signed postcard! Chris's father was the iconoclastic W.M. Lee – who supporters might remember from his contributions to fanzines in the 1990s and letters to the local press. He often held opinions which were contrary to the majority. He did rate Howard Wilkinson and was grateful for him putting together the team that returned the Owls to the big time. On one occasion, though, he was so displeased with Wilkinson that he decided to tell him!

Chris continues the story. 'Towards the end of a game my brother and I were told to get up, and we proceeded to follow my dad on his way down the South Stand towards the dugout,' he says. 'We weren't really too sure what was going on, but I remember being a little shocked when my dad started banging on the side of the Perspex dugout telling Wilko exactly what he thought of him! To his credit Wilkinson didn't respond, and Peter Eustace came over and urged my dad to go and sit back down! Eventually, and thankfully, my dad sat down a few rows back.'

Terry Evans, who we met above on the Isles of Scilly, told me a rather different story of Howard Wilkinson and Peter Eustace. Terry had heard that both men were keen gardeners. So on their appointments at Hillsborough, and as his father was a daffodil farmer, he sent a box of bulbs to Sheffield with a good luck message. A few days later, Terry's phone rang – with Howard Wilkinson on the other end expressing his thanks. Howard invited Terry to come and see him at Hillsborough next time he was up. Terry did just that, having a detailed chat about all things Owls in Howard Wilkinson's 'broom cupboard' of an office. Peter Eustace then took Terry into the dressing room to meet the players as they were in the middle of a game of head tennis!

Terry's tale did not end there. He ran a shop on the island at the time. One summer, an unfamiliar face came in and asked Terry if he was a Wednesday fan. It turned out to be Charlie Wain, the Owls scout. Terry took him fishing each year for the next three years and Charlie regaled him with stories of his discoveries such as Charlie Williamson, the Shirtliff brothers and Mel Sterland.

Shortly after his final visit, a box turned up on Terry's doorstep. It was from Sheffield, courtesy of Charlie and groundsman Dave Barber. In there was grass seed as used on the Hillsborough pitch. Terry likes to think that his lawn still has the same grass growing on it as that played on by his heroes!

One tale is from just before our era – but it made me smile so it's staying in! Owls supporter Ian Taylor, often nicknamed the Wasp, travelled to away games in a transit van with a group of friends. On the cup run of 1983, before a match against Burnley, 'we stopped at Todmorden for a drink, went in one pub which had a carvery, and when we got back in the van a leg of pork had appeared!' Ian recalled another tale of standing on the corner of the Kop and that his mate 'had a box of matches in his pocket but caught them on a wall and set himself alight!'

Mick Green relayed the tale of travelling to Portsmouth with the supporters' club and staying overnight. On the Sunday morning a group of fans jumped on the hovercraft which took passengers to the Isle of Wight. On arrival on the island, they discovered that everything was closed, as was common on a Sunday morning in the 1980s! Travelling back on the next hovercraft, they entertained themselves and no doubt the other passengers with a rousing chorus of the song: 'Stop the bus I want a wee-wee'!

A longer story comes from Gavin Henderson. Gavin has been a dedicated Owls supporter since 1960s, starting to attend away matches on a regular basis in the mid-1970s. He only missed six competitive games throughout the 1980s and liked to take in pre-season and friendly fixtures as well. In 1986, the Owls announced a short pre-season tour to Finland. This gave Gavin the opportunity to follow the Owls abroad for the first time. It was, though, a long way, and for a young man in his mid-twenties without lots of spare cash, it took some planning.

'I sold my van to pay for that trip!' Gavin told me. 'I'd worked out that with an interrail card, and by staying in youth hostels and taking ferries, I could just about afford it.' The trip was a marathon effort. Starting in Sheffield on a Friday evening, Gavin and his two friends, Craig Ward and Alan Wheen, travelled to Harwich for a ferry to the Netherlands, before taking the train up to Copenhagen. Arriving in Denmark on the Saturday evening, they stayed until the Monday morning and managed to fit in watching three games of football on the Sunday!

The group set off on the Monday morning by taking another ferry ride to Sweden. This was followed by a seven-hour train journey to Stockholm and a further ferry journey to Helsinki, where the Owls were based. Craig confirmed with me the details of the trip, and that the group were away for around eight days. He also told me that one fan took only a change of clothes in a Tesco carrier bag. So despite turning their underwear inside and out and doing their best to handwash things, it was a bit stinky on the way home!

The three supporters were joined by one further fan in Finland, making a contingent of four following the team. They were rewarded by the opportunity of watching three matches in consecutive days, with the Owls losing to HJK Helsinki (3-2) before beating a Finnish select XI in a very friendly encounter (5-3) and finally defeating FC Kuusysi by two goals to one. The Kuusysi team had reached the quarter-finals of the European Cup in 1986, so this was a much more competitive fixture.

The small group of Owls fans also had the opportunity to mix with the team. As Gavin told me, 'We managed to get into an after-match bar and charge a few pints to the club's tab!' The bar had reserved an area for the Owls team along with the Finland national women's team, who were preparing for an upcoming game against Czechoslovakia. 'We blagged about ten pints each at £3.50 a drink,' Gavin told me before adding how they chatted with Mel Sterland, Carl Shutt and Nigel Worthington, who were all 'a good laugh'.

Howard Wilkinson remained more aloof – 'he basically ignored us' – but did not stop Gavin and his friends hitching a lift on the team coach to the final of the three fixtures. In advance of that game, the squad were told to rest in their rooms for the afternoon in preparation. The fans found somewhere to buy a beer or two and sat outside for the afternoon. Before long, they heard a loud banging from one of the windows. Looking up they saw Owls reserve goalkeeper Iain Hesford, who shouted out to them asking where the beers came from.

On their reply, Hesford shouted back that he'd be down in a minute to join them. He never made it down, either thinking better of it or being diverted by the Owls staff. Hesford did sit next to the group at that evening's game. He was still to make his Owls professional debut at this stage and told Gavin and his friends that he'd been trying to persuade Howard Wilkinson to give him a few minutes up front as he was unable to dislodge Martin Hodge in goal! Gavin and his two friends made their way back to Sheffield by the same route as which they had arrived. The fourth fan, Andy Henderson, had only a train pass – and, as Gavin put it to me, 'took the railway all across the Arctic Circle' to get home!

Gavin and other supporters talked about how they found meeting the players. Our next story is from Chris Carver, who met Howard Wilkinson and Martin Hodge in somewhat unusual circumstances. 'In the early 1980s, my RAF career had taken me to a flight-testing role in Wiltshire,' Chris began, 'meaning that I had weekends free.' Chris had other commitments in his life. 'My two boys were seven and five and I was beginning to make my way in non-league football as a referee. Therefore travel to Sheffield was limited to about once every six weeks or so.'

One such weekend match was against Arsenal. 'Having travelled on Friday evening, I decided that it would be best to get tickets in advance, but in those days you actually paid a booking fee to order them over the phone. So on the Saturday morning the boys and I walked down to the ground to buy them from the old ticket office behind the South Stand.'

It was still early in the day and Chris was surprised to see the manager enter the car park so far from kick-off. 'Howard Wilkinson climbed out of his car and came over and said hello. He was interested in where we came from and after a while asked if we would like to see the ground and dressing rooms. After a quick look at the tunnel area and the pitch, he took us into the home dressing room. Martin Hodge was already there and changed before noon. Howard explained that it was part of his normal pre-match ritual!' Wilkinson and Hodge spent time chatting with Chris and his boys and signed their Young Owls autograph book. Chris still has the book and the autographs and sent me pictures to prove it!

Hooliganism

Nationally, football hooliganism was seen by some as a huge problem in the mid-1980s. At a meeting with the Football League and the FA in April 1985, Prime Minister Margaret Thatcher recommended a list of measures aimed at reducing hooliganism. These included the installation of CCTV, a ban on the sale of alcohol at grounds, searching of fans, better segregation and more use of police intelligence.

Thatcher's Conservative government went as far as investigating the possibility of a national identity card scheme for football supporters. This measure was included in the 1989 Football Spectators Act but never implemented. The Taylor report into the Hillsborough disaster of 1989 argued powerfully that such a scheme would not be a success and it was therefore dropped.

The idea followed a similar project at Luton Town, who – after a riot at their Kenilworth Road stadium during a game against Millwall in March 1985 in which more than 30 police officers were injured – banned away supporters and introduced an ID scheme restricting entry to the ground to those who could prove they had a local address.

Chelsea's maverick owner Ken Bates went one step further by proposing the introduction of electric fences to discourage pitch invaders. Bates was intent on fitting such devices on top of the existing 11-foot-high fences and barbed wire at Stamford Bridge. Only the intervention of the then Greater London Council prevented his plans coming to fruition. The council, who had the responsibility of issuing safety certificates, threatened legal action before the 12-volt charge was turned on. Bates backed down and the devices were dismantled shortly afterwards.

Sheffield Wednesday had faced problems with hooliganism in the years prior to our period. Owls supporters were banned from following the team to a series of away games and the standing areas at Hillsborough were closed for a period after ugly-looking scenes on the away terrace at Oldham Athletic in 1980, for example. Jack Charlton came on to the pitch at that game and appealed for calm. Charlton worked hard at improving the club's reputation, to the extent that in his autobiography he was able to claim that 'Wednesday's supporters enjoy the reputation of being some of the best behaved in the country'.

Howard Wilkinson continued the efforts to ensure that Hillsborough was a safe and friendly place for fans. He used his programme notes to condemn poor behaviour and encourage positive support. His efforts were rewarded in 1986 as Wednesday's supporters received the *Daily Star*'s Top of the Kops award in recognition of their good behaviour and support of the team.

This does not, of course, mean that hooliganism was not a problem at Sheffield Wednesday games. Paul Allen's book *Flying with the Owls Crime Squad* details the actions of one crew. Allen comments, though, how 'there was a real sense of optimism throughout the whole organisation' in 1984/85, meaning Sheffield Wednesday overall, and that 'on the hooligan front I was not active in any real sense'.

He does describe a vicious clash with West Ham supporters, along with an attack on a coach full of Nottingham Forest supporters at Hillsborough Corner. Indeed, in much of Allen's book any violence tends to be at away games or outside the ground. John Firth's fan's memoir *I Hate Football* supports that perspective. 'I cannot say that I have seen any trouble between rival fans at Hillsborough for a very long time,' he said, 'but there was still an air of uncertainty about going to away games.'

My research provided further evidence to support this view. Hooliganism was by no means dead but happened more commonly at away games or away from the stadium. Owls supporter Ian Taylor recounted the story of how, having travelled to London for the Milk Cup second replay vs Chelsea in 1985 but failed to get a ticket, he 'got back on the minibus, got bricked and someone got glass in their eye, so we had to go to Balham hospital'. A depressing evening ended at 5am the next morning with Ian going straight into work.

Derren Francis remembers that game vividly. 'Chelsea's fans were terrifying,' he says. 'We got in early and were put in one of the pens and then shut in. Chelsea's fans gave us all sorts of abuse and chucked coins at us. It took ages to clear the ground afterwards as we were kept back.'

The *Sheffield Star* reported on a 16-year-old Owls supporter who was knifed in the face following the 4-4 draw with Chelsea that led to the second replay at Stamford Bridge. James Church remembers being on the receiving end of coin throwing at Maine Road where his 'brother filled his pockets with coins thrown from City fans'. Some away trips remained notorious, therefore, for trouble.

Other fans remember heavy-handed policing. Kevin Rowles recalls being trapped between police horses and the metal railings of Stanley Park when being escorted to a game against Everton at Goodison Park, for example. A letter to the *Green 'Un* by S. Turton in December 1984 detailed a trip to Newcastle where Owls supporters were 'pushed and jostled by some young constables using unprintable language'.

Gavin Henderson felt that the police in some areas were notorious for treating fans poorly. He often took the risk of sitting in the home end in order that he could get a decent view of the game rather than being placed in one of the pens that were often the lot of the away fan. Sitting in the home end also meant that he could leave the game on time rather than being held back as often happened in the away end. It did run the risk of trouble with the home supporters, however, especially as Gavin and his friends were not shy of celebrating an Owls goal.

Gavin remembers trouble at Arsenal and at Newcastle, where after celebrating a late Carl Shutt winning goal early in the 1986/87 season, he and his friends were 'set upon by a large number of Newcastle fans wearing suits, presumably out of the executive boxes somewhere'.

Other supporters such as Dave Reid feel that 'hooliganism was not really an issue, I just kept myself to myself and was interested in watching the football'. Derren Francis recalled one occasion where hooliganism did reach Hillsborough, when Chelsea supporters 'ripped down the Howarth Timber advert from the Leppings Lane stand'. Derren also remembered the Owls' attempts to encourage good behaviour, with the slogan 'Wednesdayism is not Hooliganism' being a regular feature on the scoreboard and the names of fans who had been involved in some trouble at an away game in Leicester being widely publicised and even broadcast at the next home game. The seven fans were barred for life from entering Hillsborough.

The harshness of the response from the club provoked some debate on the letters page of the following week's *Green 'Un*. One respondent felt that the lads involved 'had not had the chance to tell their side of the story'. A separate letter writer said that 'I heartily support chairman Bert McGee's decision'.

In conclusion, hooliganism was by no means dead in the mid-1980s. Nationally it remained a huge issue and one that Wednesday were not immune to. It was a hot political potato and high-profile instances of the so-called 'English disease' kept it in the media and public eye. The Owls did their level best to control the issue and encourage good behaviour. In some ways they were successful in this, with the award of the Top of the Kops prize demonstrating how Owls fans supported the team in a positive manner.

This is not to say that there was no trouble. There is enough evidence of issues at away games, in the pubs and clubs of Sheffield, in the areas surrounding the stadium and occasionally at Hillsborough itself, to prove that football hooliganism was not yet dead.

Memorabilia

Football fans have a treasure trove of material displayed in their man (or woman) caves and offices, on their bedroom walls or hidden away in dusty boxes in the attic or shed. This section is my homage to the memorabilia that Owls supporters have shared with me from our period.

My own collection was in a cardboard box in my mum's loft before I began this project. I found copies of almost every programme, *The Owl* magazine and posters from 1980s magazines such as *Shoot* and *Match*. The posters came complete with original 1980s Blu Tack from where they were stuck to my bedroom wall when I was a child!

Tucked between the programmes and posters was an original seven-inch vinyl copy of 'We are the Owls'. Unfortunately, when I attempted to play it on my now retro record player, it had warped over the years, and I could only hear a garbled version!

Sticker albums were hugely popular in the 1980s. Playgrounds across the country echoed with children excitably telling their friends that they had 'got' or 'needed' the stickers that their pals were offering to swap. The producer of those albums was a company called Panini. The Owls had featured from as early as 1981. The album called 'Football 85' was the first time, though, that the club had a full, two-page spread. The return to Division One brought exciting times for the sticker-swapping youth of South Yorkshire!

Despite my best efforts looking through my mum's loft and hunting in my brother's shed, it seems that the Dyson family copy has gone forever. A message or two on social media soon identified several supporters who had surviving copies of the albums.

Those albums had survived the years in differing ways. Matt Summerhill's copy was kept by his mum. Another supporter told me he kept them safely in a cupboard after some other memorabilia got water damaged in a house move. He was able to send me pictorial proof only a few minutes after me posting online.

Paul Weatherstone was able to immediately put his hands on his copy. The Owls page was signed by many of the players and Paul also had the 'stars of the past' (as they were described) George Best and Denis Law sign their stickers. Other supporters have gone even further with one fan keeping his copy in a safe at home along with his family heirlooms! Andrew Jones has framed the Owls stickers from several years' albums and keeps them on display at home.

Many of the stories I heard referred to fond family memories. A common theme was having the final stickers posted to the home address of various family members or receiving large numbers of packs of stickers as Christmas or birthday presents. The memories provoked were clearly fond ones, partly explained by the Owls stickers but more importantly as nostalgia for childhood.

* * *

I used social media to help with my research and to help spread the word about this project. A post asking what memorabilia people owned and kept prompted a response from the Twitter account known as 'Wednesday Warehouse' (@wedwarehouse1). The owner of the account also runs a similar Instagram feed. He prefers to remain anonymous but shared some of his fantastic collection with me, including a player-issue jacket and signed shirt from the 1986 FA Cup semi-final.

I contacted the owner to find out more about the collection. He told me it is his personal collection that he has spent the last 35 years building. He collects purely for the joy of it, not for profit. He finds his items online, at car boot sales and charity shops and loves simply adding more and more to the collection. The material is literally kept in a warehouse (hence the account name) and the Instagram and Twitter feeds are well worth a follow by Owls fans of any era. For my period, I was grateful for the chance to see some items that are very rare and unavailable anywhere else. I was also reminded of the dedication that supporters show, in this case over decades.

The surname 'Mellor' may be a familiar one to Owls supporters. Ian 'Spider' Mellor scored in the Boxing Day Massacre of city rivals United in 1979. His son Neil scored 20 goals for the Owls in 2010/11, including a famous hat-trick of headers at MK Dons. Ian's son, and Neil's brother, Simon contacted me via social media to ask if I'd be interested in his story of following the team. He began by telling me about a collection of scrapbooks that he had kept since the 1980s.

'I probably started my scrapbooks because I was always geeky about recording scorers, collecting programmes and memorabilia, etc.,' he says. 'I remember being desperate to watch Wednesday, but I could only go four or five times a season at best because my dad was still playing, first in Hong Kong and then at the likes of Worksop Town. I had nobody to take me, so the scrapbooks were my way of getting my fix of Sheffield Wednesday!'

Simon went on to tell me a little about his love for the club. 'I started supporting Wednesday in August 1979 when my dad signed for them from Chester. I don`t remember much about supporting the Owls until around the 1980/81 season, when I was six or seven and can recall actually being at games. My dad left Wednesday in 1982 and went to Bradford, so I became a Bradford fan for a while because it was who my dad played for. When he left Valley Parade, a year before the fire, I returned to being a Wednesday fan again! I remember my primary school in Chapeltown being about 80 per cent Wednesday and only a small number of Blades in the early 1980s when we were two divisions apart. It`s probably very different now!'

Simon went on to tell me that he continues to support the team decades later, attending games as often as he can from his home in the North West and between a busy life bringing up three children and teaching. Back to the scrapbooks, he told me how 'I would meticulously cut out headlines, photos and reports from the *Green 'Un* on a Saturday night, the Sunday papers and the *Star* on a Monday. It was rare that Wednesday would appear in *Match* or *Shoot* magazine, and that was a real bonus!'

Great memories of a great time to be a fan, from someone who almost literally grew up with the team.

Conclusions

Jock Stein was right. Without fans the game is nothing. As I write this, the 2021/22 season is approaching its conclusion. Covid-19 and its various lockdowns and restrictions is slowly becoming a memory (touch wood). That period of the game without fans at the stadiums brought Stein's point into sharp focus. Sheffield Wednesday supporters of the mid-1980s have interesting stories to tell and fantastic memories of a positive period for the club. It is not feasible to tell every story, but it is possible to provide a flavour.

The period had a dark undercurrent in the national game of violence, hooliganism and disaster. It would not be fair or correct to suggest that Sheffield Wednesday was immune from that. There are supporters who remember the difficulties of the period and who had direct experience of them. I do not aim to downplay those memories. However, after a concerted effort from the club, the fans were named as Top of the Kops.

There are also many supporters who remember the period fondly – with tales of away days, Panini stickers, the Young Owls club, interactions with players and management and much more. There are examples of supporters who were dedicated to the cause beyond the call of duty, and those who attended matches in a more prosaic way.

However the fans' stories are told, it is clear to me that their experience is an important part of the club's history. I hope that this chapter offers a taste of the varied experiences of supporters. Without them, this book would be incomplete.

23.

Snippets

THE RESEARCH for this book threw up some interesting extras. As they do not fit anywhere else directly, here they are!

- The Owls released an LP titled *Alive and Well* at the end of 1984/85 to commemorate a successful season back in the top flight. It also aimed to offer a positive note after some of the difficulties football had faced nationally at that time. Alongside snippets of commentary and interviews with key people, local singer Lynn Carter sang the title track. The lyrics included the chorus, 'Football's alive and well at Hillsborough, at Wednesday the game's still going strong'. The record appears to be somewhat of a rarity nowadays, with copies selling online for around £20.
- In a sign that things were different in the 1980s from today, the Owls ran an annual Miss Sheffield Wednesday competition. In 1985 the judges were Ernest Barron (director), Martin Hodge and Mr and Mrs Howard Wilkinson (as described in *The Owl* magazine). The winner was Jacquie Stocks, aged 22, of Norfolk Park. Second was Heather Jones and third, Claire Wooley.

  The event was held in the club's Riverside Suite in July 1985 and was described by Bob Gorrill as 'not a beauty contest'. The prize the previous season was £150. Jacquie was to represent the club on matchdays during the 1985/86 season.
- The Owls finished fourth in the Fiat 'Club of the Year' awards in 1984. The first prize was won by Oxford United, with Everton second and Liverpool third. England manager Bobby Robson announced the award in London at an event attended by Dick Chester and Bert McGee. The club won a £500 prize which was donated to a local boys' club.

- One Owls-supporting family were so taken with the success of the team that they named their son after two of the players. Shelton Lee Whittaker takes his names from Gary Shelton and Lee Chapman.
- The club programme was placed seventh in a national competition to find the top programmes in the country in 1984/85. Judged by the Football League Executive Staffs' Association, the Owls dropped one place from 1983/84. Everton won the award.
- The Owls helped raise money towards supporting those affected by famine in Ethiopia in a number of ways. The team sang the song 'We are the Owls' at an event at Sheffield City Hall, for example. Director Ernest Barron auctioned a Liverpool-branded bottle of whisky, signed by the two scorers in the Owls' 2-0 win in 1984, for over £500 to add to the support. Players raised a further £1,000 and fans another £3,340. *The Owl* magazine reported in 1985 that the money was spent on a vaccination programme in Eritrea, helping prevent the spread of meningitis and tuberculosis and saving many lives.
- The club put on a pantomime at Sheffield City Hall in January 1986. Titled 'Cinder Owl and the Seven Dwarfs', Mark Smith described it at the time as 'a traditional panto but with ad-libbing with reference to the club and players'. The pantomime was initially planned in aid of Smith's testimonial fund.
- The Owls won the Radio Hallam team quiz trophy for 1985/86. Chris Morris, Peter Shirtliff and Paul Hart represented the club and wrested the trophy back from Sheffield United.
- Owls supporter Stephen Linley finished third in the Football Fan of the Year awards of 1986, sponsored by Braun and *Shoot* magazine. From 1975 to 1986, Stephen had missed only two games and watched the Owls on 87 grounds.

24.

Conclusions

WITH MY historian's hat on (or a tweed jacket with elbow patches), I began this project with the aim of investigating whether some of the received wisdom about Howard Wilkinson's team was accurate. It did not take much research to find examples from the national press criticising the Owls' style of play. *The Guardian*'s likening of the team's style to that of 1980s action anti-hero Rambo attempted to damn Wilkinson's tactics outright. Other articles also went directly for the jugular – 'bruising, Northern, long-ball kick and rush' anyone? Further reports were snider, with comments about craned necks, missing the ball in low cloud and regular reference to the offside trap.

My research has shown me that these comments were exaggerated at best. Yes, the Owls often played direct football, but to quote more than one player, it was direct with a purpose. It was also exciting and successful. Wilkinson was prepared to change his methods. Several teams were surprised to find the Owls approach a second game of the season in a different way to the first.

Wilkinson's meticulous attention to detail meant that he was able to identify the weaknesses of the opposition and attack them head on. His focus on set pieces paid dividends time after time. It was, though, only one tool in an armoury that was designed to ensure that his team had the greatest chance of success. The Owls scored goals from all angles and were solid in defence. The regular use of three central defenders allowed for Mel Sterland and others to join the attack. A modern-looking system to these 21st-century eyes. Just as importantly, a successful one.

Wilkinson's understanding of what nowadays would be known as sports science put him years ahead of his time. In diet, fitness, psychology and tactics he got everything he could from his teams. Which brings me to my second piece of received wisdom. Were Wilkinson's men committed discards? Players who made up for what they lacked in talent with effort and dedication? In a word, partly.

Wilkinson certainly recruited players who were committed to the cause. Several of those players had seen their careers go adrift elsewhere. Martin Hodge, Lee Chapman and others can be grateful to the Owls for reinvigorating their careers. That is not the full story, though. Wilkinson inherited a group of players who had come through the youth system at Hillsborough and formed their own band of brothers during the club's rise from Division Three to Division One. Sterland, Mark Smith, Peter Shirtliff and others were excellent players who knew exactly what the club was about.

The manager was also able to recruit talented players who were in demand from elsewhere. Imre Varadi and Garry Thompson were both top-quality strikers with a proven success rate in Division One. Brian Marwood stepped up the leagues but was coveted by other clubs and went on to gain international recognition. Hardly discards.

A trickier question is whether Wilkinson would have gained greater success if the purse strings had been loosened further. His later success with Leeds United certainly gives some credence to this view. There are enough questions about what did happen in history to fully focus on the 'what ifs'. It is a tempting thought to wonder 'what if' Wilkinson had enough money to recruit Gary Lineker rather than Garry Thompson, say. Would those players have fitted in with the Wilkinson way? Questions for Owls fans to debate over a drink or two after the next game!

My final aim in researching and authoring this book was to bring to life some of the lesser heard stories of the time. A football club is more than the players and management. It is the backroom staff, the local press and, perhaps most importantly, the supporters. My research made clear that those people in the most part remember this period with great fondness.

This was a difficult period for English football with hooliganism and disasters staining the image of the sport. Sheffield Wednesday bucked the trend of declining attendances. The fans supported the team in considerable numbers and have some fantastic stories to tell. Behind the scenes the club was moving into the modern era, with developments at the stadium and a more innovative commercial approach. All of those I spoke to who worked for and with the club remember the period with positivity. It is of major credit to the club that in such changing times this remained so.

So, direct tactics? Yes, sometimes, but with a purpose. Committed discards? Only partly. Lesser told stories? Hopefully plenty, with a common theme of nostalgia for a great period.

By the summer of 1986 the club was on a high. Great players. Great management. Great support. Moving forward on and off the pitch. The club was back from its lowest ebb of the 1970s and was more than holding its own in the big league. History tells us what happened next, and that is material for another story. The success of the first two years back in the top league deserves recognition. I have aimed to do just that. These were great times. The Owls were back. *Back in the Big Time.*

Acknowledgements

I COULD not complete a project such as this without the support of many people. I am hugely grateful to everyone who has helped me. Firstly, to my wife Shelana. Without her good humour and wisdom, I could not have written this book. For putting up with me spending massive amounts of time researching and writing. And, even when not typing away at the PC, having my head somewhere in the 1980s! To my two children, Joe and Sam, who are now the fourth generation of Owls supporters in the Dyson family. To Mum and Dad who took me to Hillsborough in these years. Rest in peace, Dad, I think you would have enjoyed this book.

A substantial number of supporters have helped me. Many are quoted in the text. I am thankful to you all for sparing your time and thoughts. Social media has been a huge help and I am indebted to those who have communicated with me via my Twitter account, on various Facebook groups or on forums such as Owlstalk. Many fans took the time to fill in an online survey for me. Thank you to all who did. Various people have gone above and beyond, so individual thanks are due to:

Adrian Biggs – for material around the Kop roof fun run and Queen's visit

Anne Stokes-Moorhouse – for material around the Kop roof fun run

Andy Clayton – for material identifying the fans who consoled Mel Sterland

Derren Francis – for memories of being a ball boy and mascot

Gavin Henderson – for great memories and information about travel to games far and wide

Adrian Hurst and Mick Green – for information about and memories of the supporters' club

I could not have completed a book such as this without reference to previous histories of the club. Thanks are due, therefore, to Jason Dickinson, Jason Brodie, Tom Whitworth, Dan Gordon and Keith Farnsworth for their combined efforts in the past. I do my best to clamber on the shoulders of giants.

Thank you to everyone I have interviewed or who provided thoughts. Including: Howard Wilkinson, Michael and Sonia Hennigan, Dick Chester, Alan Smith, Mike Lyons, Ian Knight, Lawrie Madden, Andy Blair, Garry Thompson, John Pearson, Gary Shelton, Peter Shirtliff, Mark Smith, Tony Gregory, Jay Maybury, Peter Rinkcavage, Dylan Kerr, Joe Dunn, Steve Woodhead, Mark Robinson, Alan Biggs, Paul Thompson and 'Stevie Splash'.

Thank you to those who have supported me in my research. Lee Hicklin, for his encyclopedic knowledge of reserve- and youth-team matters. To David Instone, Dave Simpson, Alex Miller, Nigel Dean, Shawn Shelton and Paul Smith for helping me contact various people. To Richard Crooks for support and regularly pointing me in the direction of interesting material. To the staff at Sheffield City Archives and Local Studies Library for helping me find archive materials, and for their patience with my regular enquiries. To all those who provided me with photographs, including SWFC club photographer, Steve Ellis.

To Pitch Publishing, Jane Camillin, for believing in the project and her help and support in getting it off the ground. To Duncan Olner for the outstanding cover design. To Rob Smyth for diligently editing the text, adding some magic dust to my words, and politely and accurately pointing out where it could be improved.

Any mistakes after all that assistance remain my own.

Bibliography

Sheffield Wednesday and Sheffield Football

Allen, Paul (with Douglas Naylor), *Flying with the Owls Crime Squad*, John Blake (2008)

Cooper, Andrew, *Eric Taylor: A Biography*, A. Cooper Publications (2011)

Cronshaw, Anthony, *Tales from the East Bank*, ALD Design and Print (2002)

Crooks, Richard, *Wednesday vs United: The Sheffield Derby*, Pitch Publishing (2018)

Dickinson, Jason, *One Hundred Years at Hillsborough*, Hallamshire Press (1999)

Dickinson, Jason, *Sheffield Wednesday: A Pictorial History*, Amberley Publishing (2014)

Dickinson, Jason, *Sheffield Wednesday Miscellany*, Pitch Publishing (2010)

Dickinson, Jason, *Sheffield Wednesday On This Day*, Pitch Publishing (2009)

Dickinson, Jason, *Sheffield Wednesday: The Official History*, Amberley Publishing (2017)

Dickinson, Jason, *WAWAW Fans' Memories Through the Generations*, Amberley Publishing (2017)

Dickinson, Jason (with John Brodie), *Sheffield Wednesday: The Complete Record*, DB Publishing (2011)

Dickinson, Jason (with John Brodie), *The Wednesday Boys: A Definitive Who's Who of Sheffield Wednesday Football Club 1880–2005*, Pickard Communication (2005)

Ellis, Steve, *Hillsborough: A 21-Year Photographic History*, Hallamshire Press (1997)

Farnsworth, Keith, *Sheffield Football: A History Volume II, 1961–95*, Hallamshire Press (1995)

Farnsworth, Keith, *The Blades & The Owls: A Pictorial History of the Sheffield Derby Matches*, Breedon Books (1995)

Farnsworth, Keith, *Wednesday!*, Sheffield City Libraries (1982)

Farnsworth, Keith (ed.), *Wednesday Every Day of the Week*, Breedon Books (1998)

Firth, John, *I Hate Football: A Fan's Memoir*, Peak Publishing (2009)

Gordon, Daniel, *A Quarter of Wednesday: A New History of Sheffield Wednesday 1970–95*, Wednesday Publishing (1995)

Hayes, Dean, *The Hillsborough Encyclopedia: An A-Z of Sheffield Wednesday FC*, Mainstream Publishing (1997)

Liversidge, Michael (with Gary Mackender), *Sheffield Wednesday: Illustrating the Greats,* Pickard Communication (2004)
Matthews, Tony, *The Men Who Made Sheffield Wednesday Football Club,* Tempus Publishing (2007)
Miller, Alex, *91: The Inside Story of Sheffield Wednesday's 1990/91 Season,* Vertical Editions (2021)
Platt, Gareth, *When a Giant Stirred: Sheffield Wednesday 1976–1993,* DB Publishing (2021)
Waring, Peter, *Sheffield Wednesday Head-to-Head,* Breedon Books (2004)
Whitworth, Tom, *Owls: Sheffield Wednesday Through the Modern Era,* Pitch Publishing (2016)
Whitworth, Tom (with Chris Olewicz), *Sheffield Wednesday 20 Legends,* Vertical Editions (2012)
Young, Percy M., *Football in Sheffield,* Dark Peak Publishing (1981) third edition

Auto/Biographies

Biggs, Alan, *Confessions of a Football Reporter,* Vertical Editions (2011)
Canoville, Paul, *Black and Blue,* Headline (2008)
Chapman, Lee, *More than a Match,* Random House (1992)
Charlton, Jack, *The Autobiography,* Partridge Press (1996)
Marwood, Brian (with Brian Woolnough), *The Life of Brian,* Mainstream Publishing (1990)
Palmer, Carlton (with Steven Jacobi), *It Is What It Is,* Vertical Editions (2017)
Regis, Cyrille, *My Story,* Carlton Publishing (2010)
Sterland, Mel (with Nick Johnson), *Boozing, Betting & Brawling: A Footballer's Life,* Green Umbrella Publishing (2008)
Thompson, Garry, *Don't Believe a Word,* Curtis Sport (2020)
Wilkinson, Howard (with David Walker), *Managing to Succeed,* Mainstream Publishing (1992)

Football and Related Matters

Crooks, Richard, *What was Football Like in the 1980s?,* Pitch Publishing (2020)
Hern, Bill (and David Gleave), *Football's Black Pioneers,* Conker Editions (2020)
Inglis, Simon, *The Football Grounds of England and Wales,* Willow Books (1983)
Lansdowne, Greg, *Panini Football Stickers: The Official Celebration,* Bloomsbury (2021)
Lowe, Simon, *Match of My Life: Stoke City,* Pitch Publishing (2012)
Simpson, Dave, *The Last Champions,* Bantam Press (2012)
Smith, Alan, *Soccer Injuries: Prevention and First Aid,* The Crowood Press (1989)
Whittle, Paul, *Before the Premier League: A History of the Football League's Last Decades,* Wibble Publishing (2021)

General Histories

Cooper, Tim, *The Story of Sheffield,* The History Press (2021)

McSmith, Andy, *No Such Thing as Society,* Constable (2011)
Turner, Alwyn W., *Rejoice! Rejoice! Britain in the 1980s,* Aurum Press (2013)
Stewart, Graham, *Bang! A History of Britain in the 1980s,* Atlantic Books (2014)

Magazines and Newspapers
Daily Mirror
Daily Star
FourFourTwo
Green 'Un
Guardian
People
Sheffield Morning Telegraph
Sheffield Star
Sheffield Telegraph
Sunday People
Sunday Times
Times
When Saturday Comes

Fanzines
Just Another Wednesday
War of the Monster Trucks

Websites
www.owlstalk.co.uk
www.swfc.co.uk
www.youtube.com

Other
All home programmes 1984/85 and 1985/86. A large number of programmes from away games and those played at neutral venues.
Personal records and scrapbooks
Sheffield Wednesday company accounts
The Owl magazine

Appendix One

Player Statistics 1984/85 and 1985/86

Surname	*Forename*	*Games 1984/85*	*Goals 1984/85*	*Games 1985/86*	*Goals 1985/86*	*Total Games*	*Total Goals*
Blair	Andy	51	6	24	1	75	7
Chamberlain	Mark			3(+24)	3	3(+24)	3
Chapman	Lee	49	19	38(+3)	15	87(+3)	34
Gregory	Tony			6(+1)	0	6(+1)	0
Hart	Paul			39	2	39	2
Heard	Pat	2	0			2	0
Hodge	Martin	52	0	52	0	104	0
Jonsson	Siggi	2(+1)	0	9(+1)	2	11(+2)	2
Knight	Ian			4	0	4	0
Lyons	Mike	47	6	13	1	60	7
Madden	Lawrie	23(+1)	1	30	0	53(+1)	1
Marwood	Brian	51	12	45	15	96	27
Megson	Gary			25	3	25	3
Mills	Simon	0(+2)	0			0(+2)	0
Morris	Chris	11(+7)	0	35(+1)	0	46(+8)	0
Oliver	Gavin	12(+4)	0			12(+4)	0
Pearson	John	5(+7)	2			5(+7)	2
Ryan	John	6(+3)	1			6(+3)	1

Shelton	Gary	49	5	35(+2)	1	84(+2)	6
Shirtliff	Peter	42(+1)	0	28	0	70(+1)	0
Shutt	Carl			23(+2)	13	23(+2)	13
Smith	Mark	42	2	21	1	63	3
Snodin	Glynn			34(+2)	1	34(+2)	1
Stainrod	Simon	5(+4)	1	3(+3)	1	8(+7)	2
Sterland	Mel	31(+3)	6	47(+1)	11	78(+4)	17
Thompson	Garry			42(+2)	8	42(+2)	8
Varadi	Imre	44(+1)	21			44(+1)	21
Worthington	Nigel	46(+1)	1	16	1	62(+1)	2

Appendix Two: League Tables

Canon League Division One: 1984/85

Pos	*Team*	*Pld*	*W*	*D*	*L*	*F*	*A*	*GD*	*Pts*
1	Everton (C)	42	28	6	8	88	43	45	90
2	Liverpool	42	22	11	9	68	35	33	77
3	Tottenham Hotspur	42	23	8	11	78	51	27	77
4	Manchester United	42	22	10	10	77	47	30	76
5	Southampton	42	19	11	12	56	47	9	68
6	Chelsea	42	18	12	12	63	48	15	66
7	Arsenal	42	19	9	14	61	49	12	66
8	**Sheffield Wednesday**	**42**	**17**	**14**	**11**	**58**	**45**	**13**	**65**
9	Nottingham Forest	42	19	7	16	56	48	8	64
10	Aston Villa	42	15	11	16	60	60	0	56
11	Watford	42	14	13	15	81	71	10	55
12	West Bromwich Albion	42	16	7	19	58	62	-4	55
13	Luton Town	42	15	9	18	57	61	-4	54
14	Newcastle United	42	13	13	16	55	70	-15	52
15	Leicester City	42	15	6	21	65	73	-8	51
16	West Ham United	42	13	12	17	51	68	-17	51
17	Ipswich Town	42	13	11	18	46	57	-11	50
18	Coventry City	42	15	5	22	47	64	-17	50
19	Queens Park Rangers	42	13	11	18	53	72	-19	50
20	Norwich City (R)	42	13	10	19	46	64	-18	49
21	Sunderland (R)	42	10	10	22	40	62	-22	40
22	Stoke City (R)	42	3	8	31	24	91	-67	17

Canon League Division One: 1985/86

Pos	Team	Pld	W	D	L	F	A	GD	Pts
1	Liverpool (C)	42	26	10	6	89	37	52	88
2	Everton	42	26	8	8	87	41	46	86
3	West Ham United	42	26	6	10	74	40	34	84
4	Manchester United	42	22	10	10	70	36	34	76
5	**Sheffield Wednesday**	**42**	**21**	**10**	**11**	**63**	**54**	**9**	**73**
6	Chelsea	42	20	11	11	57	56	1	71
7	Arsenal	42	20	9	13	49	47	2	69
8	Nottingham Forest	42	19	11	12	69	53	16	68
9	Luton Town	42	18	12	12	61	44	17	66
10	Tottenham Hotspur	42	19	8	15	74	52	22	65
11	Newcastle United	42	17	12	13	67	72	-5	63
12	Watford	42	16	11	15	69	62	7	59
13	Queens Park Rangers	42	15	7	20	53	64	-11	52
14	Southampton	42	12	10	20	51	62	-11	46
15	Manchester City	42	11	12	19	43	57	-14	45
16	Aston Villa	42	10	14	18	51	67	-16	44
17	Coventry City	42	11	10	21	48	71	-23	43
18	Oxford United	42	10	12	20	62	80	-18	42
19	Leicester City	42	10	12	20	54	76	-22	42
20	Ipswich Town (R)	42	11	8	23	32	55	-23	41
21	Birmingham City (R)	42	8	5	29	30	73	-43	29
22	West Bromwich Albion (R)	42	4	12	26	35	89	-54	24